The Tyndale New Testament Commentaries

General Editor: Professor R. V. G. Tasker, M.A., D.D.

THE EPISTLE OF PAUL
TO THE ROMANS

THE EPISTLE OF PAUL

TO THE

ROMANS

AN INTRODUCTION AND COMMENTARY

by

F. F. BRUCE, M.A., D.D.

*Rylands Professor of Biblical Criticism and Exegesis,
University of Manchester*

**Inter-Varsity Press,
Leicester, England**

**William B. Eerdmans Publishing Company
Grand Rapids, Michigan**

Inter-Varsity Press
38 De Montfort Street, Leicester LE1 7GP, England
Wm. B. Eerdmans Publishing Company
255 Jefferson S.E., Grand Rapids, MI 49503

© The Tyndale Press

First Edition 1963
Reprinted, November 1983

Published and sold only in the USA and Canada by
Wm. B. Eerdmans Publishing Co.

IVP PAPERBACK EDITION 0 85111 855 0
EERDMANS EDITION 0-8028-1405-0

Printed in the United States of America

Inter-Varsity Press is the publishing division of the Universities and Colleges Christian Fellowship (formerly the Inter-Varsity Fellowship), a student movement linking Christian Unions in universities and colleges throughout the British Isles, and a member movement of the International Fellowship of Evangelical Students. For information about local and national activities in Britain write to UCCF, 38 De Montfort Street, Leicester LE1 7GP.

GENERAL PREFACE

ALL who are interested in the teaching and study of the New Testament today cannot fail to be concerned with the lack of commentaries which avoid the extremes of being unduly technical or unhelpfully brief. It is the hope of the editor and publishers that this present series will do something towards the supply of this deficiency. Their aim is to place in the hands of students and serious readers of the New Testament, at a moderate cost, commentaries by a number of scholars who, while they are free to make their own individual contributions, are united in a common desire to promote a truly biblical theology.

The commentaries are primarily exegetical and only secondarily homiletic, though it is hoped that both student and preacher will find them informative and suggestive. Critical questions are fully considered in introductory sections, and also, at the author's discretion, in additional notes.

The commentaries are based on the Authorized (King James) Version, partly because this is the version which most Bible readers possess, and partly because it is easier for commentators, working on this foundation, to show why, on textual and linguistic grounds, the later versions are so often to be preferred. No one translation is regarded as infallible, and no single Greek manuscript or group of manuscripts is regarded as always right! Greek words are transliterated to help those unfamiliar with the language, and to save those who do know Greek the trouble of discovering what word is being discussed.

There are many signs today of a renewed interest in what the Bible has to say and of a more general desire to understand its meaning as fully and clearly as possible. It is the hope of all those concerned with this series that God will graciously use what they have written to further this end.

R. V. G. TASKER.

5

TO
ATHOL AND
ELLA FORBES

CONTENTS

The sustained argument of this Epistle makes it impossible to bring out its meaning adequately on a verse-by-verse basis. The procedure adopted, accordingly, is to present an exposition of the successive divisions of the argument, each section of the exposition being followed by more detailed verse-by-verse comments on the division just expounded. The student who wishes to consult the commentary for help on a particular verse should therefore read the exposition of the passage within which that verse falls as well as any comment that may be provided expressly on the verse itself.

CHIEF ABBREVIATIONS

AV	English Authorized Version, 1611.
RV	English Revised Version, 1881–85.
RSV	American Revised Standard Version, 1946–52.
NEB	New English Bible: New Testament, 1961.
LXX	Septuagint (pre-Christian Greek version of the Old Testament).
Arndt-Gingrich	*A Greek-English Lexicon of the New Testament,* edited by W. F. Arndt and F. W. Gingrich, 1957.
BJRL	*Bulletin of the John Rylands Library,* Manchester.
EQ	*Evangelical Quarterly.*
E.T.	English translation.
ExT	*Expository Times.*
JBL	*Journal of Biblical Literature.*
JTS	*Journal of Theological Studies.*
mg.	Margin.
MT	Massoretic Text (of the Hebrew Bible).
NTS	*New Testament Studies.*
TB	Babylonian Talmud.
ZNW	*Zeitschrift für die neutestamentliche Wissenschaft.*

AUTHOR'S PREFACE

NO more suitable preface could be supplied to the Tyndale Commentary on Romans than William Tyndale's own prologue to this Epistle which appears in the 1534 edition of his English New Testament. There is only one good reason against reproducing it here in full; and that is its length. It is a treatise in itself, about as long as the Epistle which it introduces. It begins thus:[1]

'Forasmuch as this epistle is the principal and most excellent part of the New Testament, and most pure Euangelion, that is to say glad tidings and that we call gospel, and also a light and a way in unto the whole scripture, I think it meet that every Christian man not only know it by rote and without the book, but also exercise himself therein evermore continually, as with the daily bread of the soul. No man verily can read it too oft or study it too well: for the more it is studied the easier it is, the more it is chewed the pleasanter it is, and the more groundly it is searched the preciouser things are found in it, so great treasure of spiritual things lieth hid therein.'

And towards the end of the prologue Tyndale says:

'Wherefore it appeareth evidently, that Paul's mind was to comprehend briefly in this epistle all the whole learning of Christ's gospel, and to prepare an introduction unto all the Old Testament. For without doubt whosoever hath this epistle perfectly in his heart, the same hath the light and the effect of the Old Testament with him. Wherefore let every man without exception exercise himself therein diligently, and record it night and day continually, until he be full acquainted therewith.'

It is noteworthy that Tyndale commends this Epistle as an introduction, not to the New Testament but to the Old; that is to say, he finds it an indispensable guide to the Christian

---

[1] The spelling is modernized. This prologue had been printed as a separate work at Worms in 1526. It presents many points of resemblance to Luther's preface to Romans, but Tyndale is no mere echo of Luther.

understanding of the books of the old covenant. In this he is in agreement with Paul's own mind; for Paul claims that the gospel which this Epistle sets forth was announced beforehand in the prophetic writings and that the way of righteousness which is opened up in the gospel was attested by the Law and the Prophets. The Old Testament was the Bible which the apostles and other Christians of the first generations used in their propagation of the gospel; it was the arsenal from which they drew their proofs that Jesus was indeed the Christ, the Saviour of the world; and the Epistle to the Romans provides an outstanding example of the way in which it served their purpose.

In the study of Romans, as of any of Paul's writings, it is necessary to be on one's guard against a temptation analogous to what has been called 'the peril of modernizing Jesus'.[1] There is an equal peril of modernizing Paul. The reader or interpreter of Paul's Epistles, especially when he finds himself strongly attracted by Paul's personality and reasoning power, is frequently tempted to tone down those features in Paul which are felt to be uncongenial, not to say scandalous, by modern standards. It is possible to go along with Paul so far, and then try to go farther, not by accepting more of his teaching, but by subtly and very often unconsciously modifying his concepts so as to bring them into closer conformity with current thought. But a man of Paul's calibre must be allowed to be himself and speak his own language. Our well-meant attempts to make him prophesy a little more smoothly than in fact he does can but diminish his stature, not enhance it. We of the twentieth century shall grasp his abiding message all the more intelligently if we permit him to deliver it in his own uncompromising first-century terms.

I am very grateful to Miss June S. Hogg, B.A., for help with the typing of my manuscript, and to my daughter Sheila for help with the proof-reading.

F.F.B.

[1] Cf. H. J. Cadbury, *The Peril of Modernizing Jesus* (New York, 1937).

INTRODUCTION

I. THE OCCASION OF THE EPISTLE

PAUL spent the ten years from AD 47 to 57 in intensive evangelization of the territories bordering on the Aegean Sea. During those years he concentrated in succession on the Roman provinces of Galatia, Macedonia, Achaia and Asia. Along the main roads of these provinces and in their principal cities the gospel had been preached and churches had been planted. Paul took with proper seriousness his commission as Christ's apostle among the Gentiles, and he might well contemplate with grateful praise not (he would have said) what he had done but what Christ had done with him. His first great plan of campaign was now concluded. The churches he had planted in Iconium, Philippi, Thessalonica, Corinth, Ephesus and many another city in those four provinces could be left to the care of their spiritual leaders or elders, under the overruling direction of the Holy Spirit.

But Paul's task was by no means finished. During the winter of AD 56–57, which he spent at Corinth in the home of his friend and convert Gaius, he looked forward (with some misgivings) to a visit which had to be paid to Jerusalem in the immediate future—for he had to see to the handing over to the elders of the church there of a gift of money which he had been organizing for some years past among his Gentile converts, a gift which he hoped would strengthen the bonds between the mother church in Judaea and the churches of the Gentiles.[1]

But when that business had been transacted, Paul looked forward to the launching of a plan which had been taking shape in his mind over the past few years. With the conclusion of his apostolic mission in the Aegean lands, he must find fresh

[1] See notes on Rom. xv. 25 ff. (pp. 258–265).

fields to conquer for Christ. In making choice of a new sphere of activity, he determined to go on being a pioneer; he would not settle down as an apostle in any place to which the gospel had already been brought; he would not 'build upon another man's foundation' (Rom. xv. 20). His choice fell upon Spain, the oldest Roman colony in the west and the chief bastion of Roman civilization in those parts.

But a journey to Spain would afford him the opportunity of gratifying a long-standing ambition—the ambition to see Rome. Although he was a Roman citizen by birth,[1] he had never seen the city whose freeman he was. How wonderful it would be to visit Rome, and spend some time there! All the more wonderful because there was a flourishing church in Rome, and many Christians whom Paul had met elsewhere in his travels were now resident in Rome and members of that church. The very fact that the gospel had reached Rome long before Paul himself, ruled out Rome as a place where he could settle for pioneer evangelism, but he knew that he would continue his journey to Spain with all the more zest if he could first of all refresh his spirit by some weeks of fellowship with the Christians in Rome.

During the early days of AD 57, therefore, he dictated to his friend Tertius—a Christian secretary perhaps placed at his disposal by his host Gaius—a letter destined for the Roman Christians. This letter was to prepare them for his visit to their city and to explain the purpose of his visit; and he judged it wise while writing it to set before them a full statement of the gospel as he understood and proclaimed it.

II. CHRISTIANITY AT ROME

It is plain from the terms in which Paul addresses the Christians in Rome that the church of that city was no recent development. But when we try to ascertain something about the origin and early history of Roman Christianity, we find very

[1] Acts xxii. 28: 'I was free born.'

little direct evidence to go upon, and have to reconstruct the situation as far as possible from various literary and archaeological references.

According to Acts ii. 10 the crowd of pilgrims who were present in Jerusalem for the Pentecost festival of AD 30, and heard Peter preach the gospel, included 'visitors from Rome, both Jews and proselytes' (RSV). We are not told whether any of these were among the three thousand who believed Peter's message and were baptized. It may be significant that these Roman visitors are the only European contingent to receive express mention among the pilgrims.

In any case, all roads led to Rome, and once Christianity had been securely established in Palestine and the neighbouring territories, it was inevitable that it should be carried to Rome. Within a year or two, if not, as Foakes-Jackson thought, 'by the autumn following the Crucifixion, it is quite as possible that Jesus was honoured in the Jewish community at Rome as that He was at Damascus'.[1] The fourth-century Latin Father whom we call Ambrosiaster says in the preface to his commentary on this Epistle that the Romans 'had embraced the faith of Christ, albeit according to the Jewish rite, without seeing any sign of mighty works or any of the apostles'. It was evidently members of the Christian rank and file who first carried the gospel to Rome and planted it there—probably in the Jewish community of the capital.

There was a Jewish community in Rome as early as the second century BC. It was considerably augmented in consequence of Pompey's conquest of Judaea in 63 BC and his 'triumph' in Rome two years later, when many Jewish prisoners-of-war graced his procession, and were later given their freedom. In 59 BC Cicero makes reference to the size and influence of the Jewish colony in Rome.[2] In AD 19 the Jews of Rome were expelled from the city by decree of the Emperor Tiberius (see p. 93), but in a few years they were back in as

[1] F. J. Foakes-Jackson, *Peter, Prince of Apostles* (1927), p. 195.
[2] *Pro Flacco* 66.

great numbers as ever. Not long after this we have the record of another mass-expulsion of Jews from Rome, this time by the Emperor Claudius (AD 41–54). This expulsion is briefly referred to in Acts xviii. 2, where Paul, on his arrival in Corinth (probably in the late summer of AD 50), is said to have met 'a Jew named Aquila . . ., lately come from Italy with his wife Priscilla, because Claudius had commanded all the Jews to leave Rome' (RSV). The date of the edict of expulsion is uncertain, although Orosius may well be right in placing it in AD 49.[1] Other references to it appear in ancient literature, the most interesting of which is a remark in Suetonius's *Life of Claudius* (xxv. 2), that the emperor 'expelled the Jews from Rome because they were constantly rioting at the instigation of Chrestus (*impulsore Chresto*)'. This Chrestus may conceivably have been a Jewish agitator in Rome at the time; but the way in which Suetonius introduces his name makes it much more likely that the rioting was a sequel to the introduction of Christianity into the Jewish community of the capital. Suetonius, writing about seventy years later, may have known some contemporary record of the expulsion order which mentioned Chrestus as the leader of one of the parties concerned, and inferred that he was actually in Rome at the time. He would know that Chrestus (a variant Gentile spelling of *Christus*) was the founder of the Christians, whom he elsewhere describes as 'a pernicious and baneful class of people', and it would seem quite a reasonable inference to him that Chrestus had taken an active part in stirring up these riots.

Aquila and Priscilla appear to have been Christians before they met Paul, and were probably members of the original group of believers in Jesus resident in Rome. We do not know

[1] According to Dio Cassius (*History* lx. 6) Claudius had imposed restrictions on the Roman Jews at the beginning of his reign: 'As the Jews had again increased in numbers, but could with difficulty be expelled from the city because there were so many of them, he did not actually drive them out, but forbade them to meet in accordance with their ancestral customs.' See F. F. Bruce, 'Christianity under Claudius', *BJRL*, XLIV, 1961–62, pp. 309 ff.

where or when they first heard the gospel; Paul himself never suggests that they were his children in the faith. But we may be sure that the original group of believers in Rome consisted entirely of Jewish Christians, and that Claudius's expulsion order involved its departure and dispersal.

The effects of the expulsion order, however, were short-lived. Before long the Jewish community was flourishing in Rome once more, and so was the Christian community. Less than three years after the death of Claudius Paul can write to the Christians of Rome and speak of their faith as a matter of universal knowledge. The expulsion edict may well have lapsed with Claudius's death (AD 54), if not before.[1] But in AD 57 the Christians in Rome included Gentiles as well as Jews, although Paul reminds the Gentile Christians that the base of the community is Jewish, and that they must not despise it even if they outnumber it (Rom. xi. 18).

Indeed, the Jewish background of Roman Christianity was not quickly forgotten. As late as the time of Hippolytus (died AD 235) some features of Christian religious practice at Rome still proclaim their Jewish origin—and an origin which should be sought in sectarian or nonconformist Judaism rather than in the main streams.[2]

If the greetings in Romans xvi. 3–16 were addressed to Rome and not to Ephesus (see pp. 266–277), then we may find in them some very interesting information about members of the Roman church in AD 57. These were presumably Christians whom Paul had met in other places during his apostolic career and who were at this time resident in Rome. They included some very early Christians, such as Andronicus and Junia (or Junias), who, as Paul says, were 'in Christ' before himself and

---

[1] Cf. T. W. Manson, *Studies in the Gospels and Epistles* (1962), pp. 37 ff.
[2] Cf. M. Black, *The Scrolls and Christian Origins* (1961), pp. 114 f. On the Jewish origin of the Roman church see also E. Meyer, *Ursprung und Anfänge des Christentums*, III (Stuttgart and Berlin, 1923), pp. 465 ff.; W. Manson, *The Epistle to the Hebrews* (1951), pp. 172 ff., 'Notes on the Argument of Romans (Chapters 1–8)', *New Testament Essays in Memory of T. W. Manson* (1959), pp. 150 ff.

were well known in apostolic circles, if indeed they were not actually recognized as 'apostles' (Rom. xvi. 7). The Rufus mentioned in verse 13 can very reasonably be identified with the son of Simon of Cyrene mentioned in Mark xv. 21; Paul may have known him and his mother at Antioch. Aquila and Priscilla, who had been compelled to leave Rome some eight or more years previously, were now back in the capital, and their house was one of the meeting-places for church members there. (The fact that the basilica, the regular style of early church edifice, preserves the outline of a private Roman house, reminds us that the house-church was the regular Christian meeting in primitive times.)

Indeed, Christianity may already have begun to make some impact in the higher reaches of Roman society. In AD 57, the year in which Paul wrote his Epistle to the Romans, Pomponia Graecina, the wife of Aulus Plautius (who added the province of Britain to the Roman Empire in AD 43), was tried and acquitted by a domestic court on a charge of embracing a 'foreign superstition', which could have been Christianity. But in the eyes of the majority of Romans who knew anything about it, Christianity was simply another disgusting Oriental superstition, the sort of thing that the satirist Juvenal had in mind sixty years later when he complained of the way in which the sewage of the Orontes was discharging itself into the Tiber. (Since Antioch on the Orontes was the home of Gentile Christianity, Juvenal probably thought of Gentile Christianity as one of the ingredients in that sewage.)

When, seven years after the writing of this Epistle, Rome was devastated by a great fire, and the Emperor Nero looked around for scapegoats against which he could divert the popular suspicion which (quite unjustly, it may be) was directed against himself, he found them ready to hand. The Christians of Rome were unpopular—reputed to be 'enemies of the human race' and credited with such vices as incest and cannibalism. In large numbers, then, they became the victims of the imperial malevolence—and it is this persecution under

Nero that traditionally forms the setting for Paul's martyrdom, and Peter's.

Three years after he wrote this letter, Paul at last realized his hope of visiting Rome. He realized it in a way which he had not expected when he wrote. The misgivings which he expressed about his reception at Jerusalem in Romans xv. 31 proved to be well founded; a few days after his arrival there he was charged before the Roman authorities in Judaea with a serious offence against the sanctity of the temple. His trial dragged on inconclusively until Paul at last exercised his right as a Roman citizen and appealed to have his case transferred to the jurisdiction of the emperor in Rome. To Rome, then, he was sent, and after shipwreck and wintering in Malta, reached the capital early in AD 60. As he was conducted northwards along the Via Appia by the courier-force in whose custody he was, Christians in Rome who heard of his approach walked out to meet him at points thirty or forty miles south of the city and gave him something like a triumphal escort for the remainder of his journey. The sight of these friends proved a source of great encouragement to him. For the next two years he remained in Rome, kept under guard in his private lodgings, with permission to receive visitors and to propagate the gospel in the heart of the empire.

What happened at the end of these two years is a matter of conjecture. It is not at all certain if he ever fulfilled his plan of visiting Spain and preaching the gospel there. What is reasonably certain is that, not many years later, having been sentenced to death at Rome as a leader of the Christians, he was led out of the city along the road to the seaport of Ostia and beheaded at the spot marked to this day by the Church of *San Paolo fuori le Mura* ('St. Paul Outside the Walls').

The blood of the Christians, however, in Tertullian's words, proved to be seed.[1] Persecution and martyrdom did not

[1] *Apology* 50.

extinguish Christianity in Rome; the church there continued to flourish in increasing vigour and to enjoy the esteem of Christians throughout the world as a church 'worthy of God, worthy of honour, worthy of congratulation, worthy of praise, worthy of success, worthy in purity, pre-eminent in love, walking in the law of Christ and bearing the Father's name'.[1]

III. ROMANS AND THE PAULINE CORPUS

'St. Paul's letter to the Romans—and others' is the title suggested for this Epistle by T. W. Manson.[2] For there are sound reasons to believe that, in addition to the copy of the letter which was taken to Rome, further copies were made, and sent to other churches. One pointer to this is the textual evidence at the end of chapter xv (see p. 28) which indicates that there was in circulation in antiquity an edition of the letter which lacked chapter xvi—which, with its personal greetings, would have been relevant only to one church. Paul himself may well have been responsible for the despatch of copies to various churches—not only because the contents of the greater part of the letter were of general Christian interest and relevance, but also (it may be) because his misgivings about what awaited him at Jerusalem (cf. Romans xv. 31) moved him to deposit this statement of the gospel with the Gentile churches as a kind of 'testament'.[3]

The copy which was taken to Rome was certainly treasured in the church of that city, and survived the persecution of AD 64. About AD 96 Clement, 'foreign secretary' of the Roman church, shows himself well acquainted with the Epistle to the

---

[1] This description comes from the preface of Ignatius's *Epistle to the Romans*, c. AD 115. I have given some account of the progress of Christianity at Rome in the years following AD 64 in *The Spreading Flame* (1958), pp. 162 ff.

[2] *Studies in the Gospels and Epistles*, pp. 225 ff.

[3] An alternative, but much less probable, view is that the Epistle to the Romans as we know it was expanded from an earlier general Epistle 'written by St. Paul, at the same time as Galatians, to the mixed Churches which had sprung up round Antioch and further on in Asia Minor' (K. Lake, *Earlier Epistles of St. Paul*, 1914, p. 363; cf. F. C. Burkitt, *Christian Beginnings*, 1924, pp. 126 ff.).

Romans; he echoes its language time and again in the letter which he sent in that year on behalf of the Roman church to the church in Corinth. The way in which he echoes its language suggests that he knew it by heart; it could well be that the Epistle was read regularly at meetings of the Roman church from the time of its reception onwards. It must be added that, while Clement is familiar enough with the language of the Epistle, he does not seem to have grasped its meaning as fully as might have been expected—but Clement is by no means alone in that respect among readers of this Epistle!

It is clear from Clement's letter that by AD 96 some of Paul's letters had begun to circulate in other quarters than those to which they were sent in the first instance;[1] Clement, for example, knows and quotes from 1 Corinthians. And not many years after, an unknown benefactor of all succeeding ages copied at least ten Pauline letters into a codex from which copies were made for use in many parts of the Christian world.[2] From the beginning of the second century Paul's letters circulated as a collection—the *corpus Paulinum*—and not singly.[3] The second-century writers, both orthodox and hetero-

[1] Paul himself took some initial steps to ensure this; cf. his directions in Col. iv. 16 that the Colossians and Laodiceans should exchange letters received from him. His letter to the Galatians was sent to several churches (Gal. vi. 11 implies that originally the one MS passed from church to church, rather than that one was sent to each church; but some of the churches would make copies for themselves before passing it on). The Epistle to the 'Ephesians' was designed as a circular letter and was probably despatched in a number of copies at the outset.

[2] Cf. G. Zuntz, *The Text of the Epistles* (1954), pp. 14 ff., 276 ff. Dr. Zuntz gives reasons for thinking that the corpus was compiled and published at Alexandria, since it gives signs of 'dependence upon the scholarly Alexandrian methods of editorship' (*op. cit.*, p. 278). A widely prevalent view is that it was compiled in Ephesus (cf. E. J. Goodspeed, *Introduction to the New Testament*, Chicago, 1937, pp. 217 ff.; C. L. Mitton, *The Formation of the Pauline Corpus of Letters*, 1955, pp. 44 ff.); a romantic embellishment of this view is J. Knox's thesis that the prime mover in the work of compiling the corpus was Onesimus, Philemon's former slave and now (c. AD 100) bishop of Ephesus (*Philemon among the Letters of Paul*, Chicago, 1935).

[3] There were probably earlier 'regional' collections, such as a collection of letters sent to the province of Asia (Ephesians, Colossians, Philemon) or of those sent to Macedonia (1 and 2 Thessalonians and Philippians).

dox, who refer to the Pauline letters, knew them in the form of a corpus.

One of these writers—of the heterodox variety—was Marcion, a native of Pontus in Asia Minor who came to Rome about AD 140 and a few years later published a Canon of Holy Scripture. Marcion rejected the authority of the Old Testament and held that Paul was the only faithful apostle of Jesus, the others having corrupted His teaching with Judaizing admixtures. His Canon reflected his distinctive views. It consisted of two parts—the *Euangelion,* an edition of the Gospel of Luke which began with the words, 'In the fifteenth year of Tiberius Caesar Jesus came down to Capernaum' (cf. Lk. iii. 1, iv. 31); and the *Apostolikon,* comprising ten Pauline Epistles (excluding those to Timothy and Titus).

Galatians, for which Marcion had a natural predilection because of its anti-Judaizing emphasis, stood first in Marcion's *Apostolikon.* The other Epistles followed in descending order of length, the 'double' Epistles (i.e. the two to the Corinthians and the two to the Thessalonians) being reckoned for this purpose as one each. Romans thus came after 'Corinthians'. To each of the Epistles a preface was attached. That to Romans runs thus: 'The Romans are in the region of Italy. These had been visited already by false apostles and seduced into recognizing the authority of the law and the prophets, under pretext of the name of our Lord Jesus Christ. The apostle calls them back to the true faith of the gospel, writing to them from Athens.'

This is not the natural inference which one would draw from Paul's argument, but Marcion approached the Epistles with strongly-held presuppositions. Where he found statements in the Epistles running counter to these presuppositions, he concluded that the apostolic text had been tampered with by Judaizing scribes, and amended it accordingly (see pp. 27 ff.). But such was the influence of Marcion's Canon, even beyond the limits of his own following, that many 'orthodox' MSS of the Pauline Epistles contain the Marcionite prefaces.

Our oldest surviving MS of the Pauline Epistles, dating from the end of the second century, contains the shorter *corpus Paulinum* of ten Epistles together with the Epistle to the Hebrews. This MS (papyrus 46, one of the Chester Beatty biblical papyri) comes from Egypt, and in Egypt (unlike Rome) Hebrews was regarded as a Pauline Epistle as early as AD 180. In P[46] (as we shall henceforth call it), Romans comes first.

Romans comes last among the Pauline Epistles sent to churches in another document from the later years of the second century, the 'Muratorian Canon' or list of New Testament books recognized at Rome. This list recognizes the longer *corpus Paulinum* of thirteen letters, for after the letters to churches it adds those addressed to individuals—not only Philemon but also Timothy and Titus.

In the order which ultimately became established Romans takes pride of place among the Pauline Epistles. Historically, this is apparently because it is the longest Epistle; but there is an innate fitness in the according of this position of primacy to the Epistle which, above all the others, deserves to be called 'The Gospel according to Paul'.

IV. THE TEXT OF ROMANS

a. English versions

This commentary is designed as a companion to the study of the Epistle to the Romans; it cannot be used without constant reference to the text which it endeavours to expound and annotate.

The Tyndale New Testament Commentaries are based on the Authorized (King James) Version of the English Bible. This version, while published so long ago as 1611, is still widely used throughout the English-speaking world. It was formally a revision of the 1602 edition of the 'Bishops' Bible' (first published in 1568) and more generally a revision of several earlier English versions (including the 'Geneva Bible' of 1560 and the 'Great Bible' of 1539), going back ultimately to William Tyndale's version of the New Testament (first edition, 1525) and of about half the Old Testament (1530 and following years). Even in 1611, then, the language of the Authorized Version had a somewhat archaic flavour, being more Elizabethan than Jacobean. It is naturally much more archaic today.

Quite a number of English words, for instance, have changed their meanings in the course of the last three and a half centuries and do not now have the same force as they had when the Authorized Version appeared. A good example in this Epistle is the word 'atonement' (Rom. v. 11), which no longer means reconciliation ('at-one-ment'), as it once did. Again, the word 'meat' is used repeatedly in Romans xiv (as in many other places in the Authorized Version) in the general sense of food; it did not in 1611 have the more restricted sense of flesh or butcher-meat which it now has.

For detailed study, the Authorized Version labours under another disadvantage. The men who produced it deliberately adopted the policy of using a variety of English synonyms to render the same Greek word, even when it appeared several times with the same meaning in one circumscribed context. This was done for stylistic effect, and from this point of view their policy cannot be condemned. But the result is that we may miss something of the strength of Paul's argument in places where the argument depends on the repetition of the same word. Thus, Romans v. 1–11 owes a good deal of its effect to the threefold occurrence of the Greek verb *kauchaomai* ('exult'). In the Authorized Version of the paragraph this verb is variously rendered 'rejoice' (verse 2), 'glory' (verse 3) and 'joy' (verse 11).[1]

An even greater defect in the Authorized Version arises from circumstances over which the translators had but little

---

[1] The practice of rendering one Greek word by a variety of English synonyms is followed in the New English Bible; but in Rom. v. 2, 3, 11, it very properly translates *kauchaomai* uniformly by 'exult'.

control; they based their translation on a printed edition of the Greek New Testament which reproduced the text of late and inferior MSS.[1] Thanks to the great advances in New Testament textual studies of more recent times, we can now operate with a Greek text much nearer to that of the first century AD than that which was available to the translators of 1611. The later English versions—in particular the Revised Version of 1881 (with its American counterpart, the American Standard Version of 1901), the Revised Standard Version of 1946–52, and the New English Bible of 1961—represent a much more accurate Greek text than did the Authorized Version.

For these and similar reasons it will be helpful to have some other version or versions at hand for consultation when studying the Epistle to the Romans—for verbal precision, the Revised Version or American Standard Version; for smoother reading and more contemporary idiom, the Revised Standard Version or the New English Bible, or one of the numerous private translations into modern English which have appeared this century. Time and again in the course of the following commentary, the simplest way to explain some rather archaic expression in the Authorized Version has been to set alongside it the rendering of the Revised Standard Version or the New English Bible.

b. *The early Pauline text*

How many copies of the Epistle to the Romans were in circulation between AD 57 and the end of the first century we have no means of knowing. But from the time that the *corpus Paulinum* was compiled about AD 100 Romans, like each of the

[1] The printed Greek text which became standard in England was that issued in 1550 by the Paris printer Robert Estienne (Stephanus). This was Estienne's third edition; he issued a fourth from Geneva in 1557—the first to contain modern verse divisions. In some respects the translators of the Geneva Bible of 1560 showed greater acumen in textual matters than did those of the Authorized Version. The expression 'Received Text', as used occasionally in this commentary, denotes the text of the early printed editions of the Greek New Testament; more precisely, it was the publisher's designation of the 1633 edition printed by the house of Elzevir in Leiden.

other Pauline Epistles, no longer circulated separately but as a component part of the corpus.

The question naturally arises whether some evidence may not have survived in the textual tradition of the Epistles which goes back to a time before the corpus. The quotations in 1 *Clement* (*c.* AD 96) probably represent the pre-corpus text; but nearly all the other elements in the extant textual tradition are derived from the text of the corpus. Sir Frederic Kenyon's statistics showing the measure of agreement and disagreement between P[46] and other principal MSS reveal significant variations in this regard from one Epistle to another; Romans, in particular, stands apart from the others—a state of affairs which Kenyon thought could best be explained if the textual tradition goes back to a time when the individual Epistles circulated separately.[1] Dr. G. Zuntz mentions a few examples of 'primitive corruption' and marginal annotation (whether by Paul or by someone else) which the compiler of the corpus probably found already present in one or another of the manuscripts which he used, and copied into his edition. But Dr. Zuntz rightly regards the *corpus Paulinum* of *c.* AD 100 as the archetype which textual criticism of the Epistle must strive to recover, the archetype from which the common text of the second century and the main text-types of following centuries are all derived. He shows good reason, too, for believing that the corpus was at first a critical edition which noted variant readings, according to the technique characteristic of Alexandrian scholarship.[2]

From the end of the second century onwards we can distinguish two main text-types for the Pauline Epistles—an eastern type and a western. In addition to P[46], our earliest witness, early witnesses to the eastern text-type are B (the fourth-century *Codex Vaticanus*); *Aleph* (the fourth-century *Codex Sinaiticus*); 1739 (a tenth-century Athos minuscule), or

[1] F. G. Kenyon (ed.), *The Chester Beatty Biblical Papyri*, Fasc. iii, Supplement (1936), pp. xv ff. If copies were sent to various churches at the outset (see p. 18), the possibility of textual variation goes back to AD 57.

[2] G. Zuntz, *The Text of the Epistles*, pp. 14 ff., 276 ff.

rather the very ancient and excellent MS (no longer extant) from which its text of the thirteen Pauline Epistles and Hebrews was copied;[1] citations in Clement of Alexandria (*c.* AD 180) and Origen (d. AD 254); and the two main Coptic versions (Sahidic and Bohairic).[2] The western text of the Pauline Epistles is attested chiefly by citations in Tertullian (*fl.* AD 180), by the other authorities for the Old Latin version (other patristic citations and the text of *d*),[3] and by the common ancestor of the codices D, F and G.[4] This western text goes back to the popular and rather corrupt text of the second century; the relative purity of the eastern text is probably due to the constant application to it of the editorial techniques of Alexandrian textual scholarship.[5]

c. Early recensions of Romans

There are a number of indications in the textual history of Romans that it circulated not only in the form in which we know it but in one or even two shorter editions. These indications appear mainly towards the end of the Epistle, but there are two pieces of possibly significant evidence at the beginning.

1. *The beginning of the Epistle.* (i) Romans i. 7. In this verse the words 'in Rome' were absent from the text on which Origen's commentary on Romans was based, and also, probably, from the text on which Ambrosiaster's commentary was based (although in the MS tradition of both commentaries the basic text has been conformed to that in common use). The margins

---

[1] The text of this ancient MS (the ancestor of 1739) agrees with the text known to Origen; the MS may well have belonged to the great library of Pamphilus in Palestinian Caesarea.

[2] It is noteworthy that nearly all these witnesses (including P^{46}) are of Egyptian provenience.

[3] The Latin text of the bilingual codex D (see next note), which is independent of the accompanying Greek text.

[4] D is the sixth-century *Codex Claromontanus*; F and G, bilingual codices of the ninth century (*Augiensis* and *Boernerianus* respectively), are probably copies of the same original (their Latin texts, *f* and *g*, unlike *d*, have no independent value).

[5] Zuntz, *op. cit.*, pp. 269 ff.

of 1739 and 1908[1] attest the omission of the words from Origen's text and commentary.

The Graeco-Latin codex G, one of the western witnesses to the text of Paul, also omits the reference to Rome in this verse, presenting the reading 'to all who are in the love of God' where the common text has 'to all who are in Rome, beloved of God'. Other western witnesses, all of them Latin, exhibit the shorter reading of G adapted to the common text by the addition of the words 'in Rome', thus: 'to all who are in Rome in the love of God' (so *d*; the Vulgate codices Amiatinus, Ardmachanus and two others; Pelagius, and the MSS of Ambrosiaster).

(ii) Romans i. 15. The words 'that are at Rome' are omitted by G, while some of the companions of this codex show attempts to adapt this abridged form to the common text.

It looks as if the ancestor of the codices D and FG[2] (called 'Z' by P. Corssen[3]) omitted 'in Rome' in i. 7 and i. 15 alike. That the omission was not exclusively western is indicated by the fact that Origen's text also lacked 'in Rome' in i. 7.

2. *The end of the Epistle.* Some phenomena towards the end of the Epistle suggest that various recensions of it came to an end at different points. A suitable conclusion might have been provided by any one of the benedictions or quasi-benedictions of xv. 5 f., xv. 13, xv. 33, xvi. 20b (which AV repeats in xvi. 24). But the most interesting textual phenomenon at the end of the Epistle concerns the position of the final doxology (which in our versions appears as xvi. 25–27).

(i) In the Vulgate codex Amiatinus and a few other codices the Pauline Epistles are supplied with 'chapter-summaries' (Lat. *breues*) taken over from a pre-Vulgate Latin version. In them Romans is divided into fifty-one 'chapters' or sections. For the last two of these the summaries are as follows:

---

[1] An eleventh-century MS in the Bodleian (Oxford), related to 1739.

[2] G's sister-codex F lacks Rom. i. 1–iii. 19, so its evidence is not available for i. 7, 15.

[3] 'Zur Überlieferung des Römerbriefes', *ZNW*, X (1909), pp. 1 ff., 97 ff.

'50. Concerning the danger of grieving one's brother with one's food, and showing that the Kingdom of God is not food and drink but righteousness and peace and joy in the Holy Spirit.

'51. Concerning the mystery of God, which was kept in silence before the passion but has been revealed after his passion.'

The summary of section 50 corresponds to the substance of Romans xiv. 1–23; that of section 51 corresponds to the doxology in Romans xvi. 25–27. This suggests that a shorter edition of the Epistle existed in which the concluding doxology followed immediately after xiv. 23. There are some other indications that such a shorter edition was known and used.[1]

(ii) The *Book of Testimonies* ascribed to Cyprian (*c.* AD 250) includes a collection of biblical passages which enjoin withdrawal from heretics; this collection does not include Romans xvi. 17, which might have been thought an apt passage for his purpose. This argument from silence, which would have little weight if it stood alone, must be taken along with other pieces of evidence.

(iii) Although Romans xv and xvi are so full of potential anti Marcionite ammunition,[2] Tertullian nowhere quotes from these chapters in his five books *Against Marcion*. In the fifth book of that treatise, however (chapter 13), he does quote Romans xiv. 10, and says that it comes in the concluding section (Lat. *clausula*) of the Epistle.

(iv) Rufinus (*c.* AD 400), in his Latin translation of Origen's commentary on Romans, says on Romans xvi. 25–27: 'Marcion, who introduced interpolations into the evangelic and apostolic scriptures, removed this section completely from this Epistle, and not only so, but he cut out everything from that place where it is written "whatsoever is not of faith, is sin" (xiv. 23) right to the end.' There is no reason to doubt that here Rufinus has given a straightforward translation of Origen's own words.

---

[1] In the Vulgate MSS 1648, 1792 and 2089 the Epistle ends at xiv. 23, followed by a benediction and the doxology.

[2] For Marcion's point of view see p. 20.

(v) In the Byzantine textual tradition the doxology of xvi. 25–27 comes after xiv. 23 and before xv. 1. Origen knew of MSS which put the doxology in this position, but he also knew of others which put it after xvi. 24, and believed (not unnaturally) that the latter was the proper place for it. But those MSS which place the doxology between chapters xiv and xv are probably witnesses to an edition of the Epistle which came to an end with xiv. 23, followed by the doxology.

(vi) G (with some codices known to Jerome) does not have the doxology at all. It is probable, indeed, that the ancestor of D and FG (Corssen's 'Z') did not have the doxology. Moreover, since this ancestor appears to have had a western text in chapters i–xiv but a text with several peculiar readings in chapters xv and xvi, Corssen inferred[1] that behind it lay a text which came to an end with xiv. 23 (omitting the doxology). It is more than a coincidence that this is how Marcion is said to have ended the Epistle.

(vii) A few witnesses (A P 5 33, and some Armenian codices) have the doxology both after xiv. 23 and again after xvi. 24.

(viii) In P[46] the doxology comes between chapters xv and xvi. This has been regarded as evidence for an edition of Romans which came to an end with xv. 33, followed by the doxology.

We thus appear to have evidence for two shorter editions of the Epistle—one ending at xv. 33 and the other ending at xiv. 23 (with or without an added doxology). We also have evidence for an edition which lacked the words 'in Rome' in i. 7, 15; this edition may have been identical with one or other of the two shorter editions just mentioned.

There is no difficulty in understanding why an edition should have circulated without chapter xvi. If copies of the Epistle were sent to a number of churches, because of the general interest and relevance of its contents, all but one of these copies would very naturally have lacked chapter xvi,

[1] *ZNW*, X (1909), p. 9.

which with its many personal messages could have been applicable to one church only. Whether this church was Rome or Ephesus is discussed later (pp. 266 ff.).

But why should an edition have circulated without chapter xv? The argument which begins in xiv. 1 continues into chapter xv and leads on naturally to Paul's personal statement in xv. 15 ff.[1] We have, however, Origen's statement that Marcion cut off from the Epistle everything after xiv. 23, and brought it to an end at that point. Why Marcion should have done so will be apparent to anyone who looks at the series of Old Testament quotations in xv. 3–12, or at the statement in xv. 4 that 'whatsoever things were written aforetime were written for our learning', or at the description of Christ in xv. 8 as 'a minister of the circumcision for the truth of God, to confirm the promises made unto the fathers'. Such a concentration of material offensive to Marcion can scarcely be paralleled in the Pauline corpus.

To Marcion, then, we may assign the edition which ended at xiv. 23.[2] But such was the influence of Marcion's edition that his text, like his prefaces, was reproduced in greater or lesser degree in many orthodox lines of transmission, especially in western and, more particularly, Latin copies.

What now can be said of the omission of the references to Rome in i. 7, 15? One view is that this omission might naturally belong to the more generalized edition of the Epistle which lacked chapter xv. One may think of Ephesians as a parallel case. As is well known, there is strong early evidence for a text of Ephesians which lacked 'in Ephesus' in Ephesians i. 1 (P46, *Aleph*, B, etc.). Ephesians was evidently designed from the first as a circular letter, and a blank was left in the opening

---

[1] I cannot agree with F. C. Burkitt, who held that 'Rom. xiv. 23 indeed is a real conclusion: nothing but a Doxology is really in place after it', and supposed that xv. 1–13 was 'a weld, a join, an adaptation', by means of which Paul attached the following personal details when he expanded his earlier circular epistle (see p. 18, n. 3) and sent the expanded form to Rome (*Christian Beginnings*, p. 127).

[2] For the view that the doxology was first composed by Marcionites to be appended to this edition see pp. 281f.

salutation which could be filled in with any appropriate place-name. (Marcion appears to have known it in an edition which read 'in Laodicea' where we read 'in Ephesus'.) *Some* place-name (preceded by the preposition 'in') was necessary, as the construction is not Greek otherwise.

On further reflection, however, this explanation of the omission of the place-name in Romans i. 7, 15, is unsatisfactory. The cases of Romans and Ephesians are not really parallel. Any other place-name within the territory of Paul's Gentile mission could stand in place of 'Ephesus' in Ephesians i. 1 and would be equally suitable in the context. But no other place-name could stand in place of 'Rome' in Romans i. 7, 15, because the context (Rom. i. 8–15) refers to Rome and Rome only. And even if 'Rome' were struck out of i. 7, 15, without being replaced by the name of any other city, that would have left the local references in verses 8–15 (and in xv. 22–32) unintelligible, or at best requiring to be elucidated by intelligent inference.[1]

What can be said, then, about the possibility of relating the edition which omitted 'in Rome' from i. 7, 15, to the edition which came to an end at xiv. 23—Marcion's edition, in all probability? Here we can but speculate, since we have no such evidence for Marcion's text of i. 7, 15, as we have for his omission of chapters xv and xvi. Why, in any case, should Marcion have struck out the explicit references to Rome from his text of the Epistle? When the Roman church repudiated Marcion and his teaching, he might have judged it unworthy to be mentioned in the text of his *Apostolikon*. 'This is no more than a conjecture',[2] and against it must be set the fact (as it

---

[1] The context 'imperatively demands a particular reference to a well-known community not founded by Paul or hitherto visited by him' (T. W. Manson, *Studies in the Gospels and Epistles*, p. 229).

[2] So T. W. Manson (*op. cit.*, p. 230), whose conjecture it is. He would explain the omission of 'in Ephesus' from Eph. i. 1 in the same way, since it was 'at Rome and Ephesus that Marcion received two great and humiliating rebuffs'; but this explanation is much less probable for Eph. i. 1 than for Rom. i. 7, 15. As has been said above, the two situations are not parallel.

seems to be) that in his Canon the Epistle retained the title 'To the Romans'.

V. ROMANS AND THE PAULINE GOSPEL

Romans was the last Epistle written by Paul before his prolonged period of detention, first at Caesarea and then in Rome. It is thus later than his letters to the Thessalonians, Corinthians and Galatians (and probably to the Philippians); earlier than those to the Colossians and Ephesians (not to speak of the Pastoral Epistles). This is a conclusion which can be reached not only by external evidence and incidental chronological indications in the Epistles, but also by a study of their subject-matter.

Some of the themes of Paul's Corinthian correspondence recur in Romans: we may compare what is said about the food question in 1 Corinthians viii, x, with what is said in Romans xiv. 1 ff.; we may compare what is said about the members of the body and their respective functions in 1 Corinthians xii with what is said in Romans xii. 3 ff.; we may compare the antithesis between Adam and Christ in 1 Corinthians xv. 21 f., 45 ff., with Romans v. 12 ff.; we may compare the references to the collection for Jerusalem in 1 Corinthians xvi. 1 ff. and 2 Corinthians viii, ix with Romans xv. 25 ff. In some of these instances the Romans passage is self-evidently later than the parallel in 1 or 2 Corinthians. More particularly, Romans viii reproduces much of the argument of 2 Corinthians iii. 17–v. 10—combined with part of the argument of Galatians iv, v—in a manner which has been described as 'the free creation, on two separate occasions, of verbal clothing for familiar logical outlines'.[1]

Of all the Pauline Epistles, however, the one which has the closest affinity with Romans is Galatians. A comparison of the two leaves no doubt that Galatians is the earlier; the arguments

---

[1] C. H. Buck Jr., *JBL*, LXX (1951), p. 116, in the course of an important article on 'The Date of Galatians' (pp. 113 ff.).

which are pressed on the churches of Galatia in an urgent and
ad hoc fashion are expounded more systematically in Romans,
Galatians being related to Romans 'as the rough model to the
finished statue'.[1]

The Epistle to the Galatians was written to churches in the
Roman province of Galatia (in all probability to those in South
Galatia which were founded by Paul and Barnabas about
AD 47, as related in Acts xiii. 14–xiv. 23), to warn them against
relapsing from the gospel of free grace at the instigation of
those who taught them that their salvation depended on their
being circumcised and observing certain other requirements
of the Jewish law.[2] Those teachers no doubt represented these
requirements as being additional to the one requirement of
faith in Jesus as Lord on which Paul's gospel insisted; but in
Paul's eyes these requirements were not so much an addition
to the gospel as a perversion of it. This teaching nullified the
principle that salvation is bestowed by grace and received by
faith; it gave men a share in that saving glory which, according
to the gospel, belongs to God alone. The whole scheme proposed by those teachers was a different gospel from that which
Paul and his fellow-apostles preached;[3] it was, in fact, no
gospel at all.[4] In his endeavour to show his Galatian friends
where the truth of the matter lies, Paul raises the fundamental
question of man's justification in the sight of God. That God
was the supreme Judge of the world was common Jewish
doctrine, as was also the belief that a day would come when He
would pronounce final judgment on all mankind. Paul, however, taught that, thanks to the work of Christ, the verdict of

[1] J. B. Lightfoot, *St. Paul's Epistle to the Galatians* (1890), p. 49.
[2] According to J. H. Ropes, *The Singular Problem of the Epistle to the
Galatians* (Cambridge, Mass., 1929), Galatians deals also with an antinomian group that denied Paul's apostolic authority; but even if this is so,
this phase of the argument does not have much to do with the Epistle's
relation to Romans.
[3] Cf. 1 Cor. xv. 11 for Paul's witness that he and the twelve apostles
preached the same basic message.
[4] Cf. F. F. Bruce, 'When is a Gospel not a Gospel?', *BJRL*, XLV (1962–
63), pp. 319 ff.

that day could by anticipation be known and accepted at the present time—that those whose hearts were right with God could have the assurance of acquittal in His court here and now. But how in fact could human beings know themselves to be 'in the right' so far as God's assessment of them was concerned? If it was possible to be justified before God by observing the requirements of the Jewish law, as the Galatian Christians were now being taught, then what was the point of the death of Christ, which was central to the gospel? According to the gospel, His death procured His people's redemption and set them right with God; but there was no need for His death if this could have been achieved by the law. But we know, says Paul, 'that a man is not justified by the works of the law, but only through faith in Jesus Christ'—and his converts had proved this to be true in their own experience. So, he continues, 'we believed on Christ Jesus, that we might be justified by faith in Christ, and not by the works of the law: because by the works of the law shall no flesh be justified'[1] (Gal. ii. 16, RVmg.).

Faith, not works: that is one antithesis which Paul emphasizes to the Galatians. A companion antithesis in his argument is *Spirit, not flesh.* The new life which they had received when they believed the gospel was a life imparted and maintained by the Holy Spirit; it was unthinkable that the work of the Spirit, which belongs to a new order, should require to be supplemented by ordinances so completely bound to the old order of the 'flesh' as circumcision and all that went with it. The attempt to live partly 'after the Spirit' and partly 'after the flesh' was foredoomed to failure, because the two orders were in sharp opposition the one to the other: 'the flesh lusteth against the Spirit, and the Spirit against the flesh'[2] (Gal. v. 17).

Both these antitheses—works versus faith and flesh versus Spirit—recur in Romans in their logical sequence, the former

[1] An echo of Ps. cxliii. 2; cf. Rom. iii. 20 (p. 99).
[2] See pp. 152—156.

in chapters iii and iv, where the way of righteousness is under discussion, and the latter in chapters vii and viii, where the subject is the way of holiness.

Another *motif* of Galatians which appears also in Romans is the appeal to the precedent of Abraham. Since the Jewish ordinance of circumcision was based on the covenant made by God with Abraham (Gn. xvii. 10–14), those who insisted that Gentile converts to Christianity ought to be circumcised argued that otherwise they could claim no share in the blessings promised to Abraham and his descendants. To this Paul replies that the basis of Abraham's acceptance by God was not his circumcision, nor any comparable legal 'work', but his *faith*: 'Abraham believed God, and it was accounted to him for righteousness' (Gal. iii. 6, quoting Gn. xv. 6).[1] So the children of Abraham, who inherit the blessings promised to Abraham, are those who, like him, have faith in God and are accordingly justified by His grace. The gospel, in short, is the fulfilment of the promises made by God to Abraham and his offspring—promises which have not been annulled or modified by anything, such as the Mosaic law, which was instituted since they were made.

Moreover, Paul assures the Galatian Christians, those who submit to circumcision as a legal obligation put themselves under an obligation to observe the whole law of Moses, and become liable to the divine curse pronounced on those who fail to keep that law in its entirety.[2] But the liberating message of the gospel tells how 'Christ hath redeemed us from the curse of the law . . . that the blessing of Abraham might come on the Gentiles through Jesus Christ; that we might receive the promise of the Spirit through faith' (Gal. iii. 13 f.).

The principle of righteousness by law-keeping belongs to a stage of spiritual immaturity. But now that the gospel has come, those who obey it and believe in Jesus attain their spiritual majority as full-grown sons of God. The Spirit of

[1] Cf. Rom. iv. 3.
[2] A reference to Dt. xxvii. 26, quoted in Gal. iii. 10.

God who has taken up His abode in the hearts of believers is also the Spirit of His Son, and by His prompting they address God spontaneously as their Father in the same way as Jesus Himself did.[1]

Again, the gospel is a message of liberty in place of the yoke of bondage carried by those who rely upon the law to secure their acceptance by God. Why should those who have been emancipated by Christ give up their freedom and submit to servitude afresh? On the other hand, the freedom brought by the gospel has no affinity with anarchic licence. The faith of which the gospel speaks is a faith which manifests itself in a life of love, and thus fulfils 'the law of Christ '(Gal. v. 6, vi. 2).[2]

So Paul reasons with the churches of Galatia, arguing *ad hominem* as well as *ad hoc*. It has been suggested that 'justification by faith, while not necessarily incompatible with Paul's earlier doctrine, was actually formulated and expressed by him for the first time when he found it necessary to answer the arguments of the Judaizers in Galatia. It seems not at all unlikely that the term justification, which takes on its familiar Pauline meaning and importance only in Galatians and Romans, derived this importance and at least a part of this meaning not from Paul's regular theological vocabulary but from that of his opponents.'[3]

[1] Gal. iv. 6; cf. Rom. viii. 15 (see pp. 166 f.).
[2] Cf. Rom. xii. 9 ff., xiii. 8–10 (pp. 228 ff., 239 f.).
[3] C. H. Buck, *loc. cit.*, pp. 121 f. He says that this conclusion 'seems inescapable' after a comparison of 2 Cor. i–ix, where only the 'flesh-spirit' antithesis appears, with Galatians, where Paul uses both this and the 'works-faith' antithesis. Galatians is accordingly later than 2 Cor. i–ix, he finds, because if Paul had already formulated the antithesis 'faith versus works' in his mind before he wrote these chapters, he could scarcely have avoided using it at least once in view of the 'vehement anti-legal position' he takes up there. The situation with which he deals in 2 Cor. i–ix, however, is not on the same footing as that dealt with in Galatians and does not call in the same way for the use of the 'faith versus works' antithesis. I should date Galatians to a considerably earlier stage in Paul's ministry. Buck's view was anticipated in some important respects by W. Heitmüller, who held that Paul's 'doctrine of justification was for him entirely a polemic and apologetic doctrine, which first grew upon Paul the missionary in the course of his mission and served to defend his law-free preaching to the

But the gospel which Paul urges on the Galatian Christians in his letter was the gospel which he had brought them when first he visited their cities and preached the message of the cross to them so vividly that it was as if 'Jesus Christ Crucified' had been publicly placarded before their very eyes. More than that; it was the gospel which had revolutionized Paul's own life. Paul, as we know, was suddenly converted to the service of Christ from a life in which the law had been the centre round which everything else was organized. In his system of thought and practice there was no room to entertain even the possibility that the disciples' claim about Jesus might be true. His teacher Gamaliel might concede the possibility, if only for the sake of argument, but not so Paul. If one fact more than any other sufficed to disprove the disciples' claim that Jesus was the Messiah, it was the fact of His crucifixion. Whether Jesus merited such a death or not was a matter of minor importance; what was of real importance was the affirmation in the law: 'he that is hanged is accursed of God' (Dt. xxi. 23). The suggestion that one who died under the curse of God could be the Messiah was blasphemous and scandalous.

When Paul, in mid-career as a persecutor of the Church, was compelled to recognize that the crucified Jesus was risen from the dead and was all that His disciples had claimed for Him—Messiah, Lord, Son of God—his whole system of thought and life, previously organized around the law, must have been shaken to pieces. The confident judgment which he had formed about Jesus in accordance with that system was shown to be utterly wrong. But the fragments of the broken system soon began to organize themselves in a completely different pattern, round a new centre, the crucified and risen Jesus. Henceforth for Paul, to live was—Christ.

But what of the old argument, that the crucified One died under the divine curse? Was it no longer valid? It was still Gentiles against Jewish Christian attacks and perspectives' (*Luthers Stellung in der Religionsgeschichte des Christentums*, Marburg, 1917, pp. 19 f.). K. Holl traces this viewpoint back to O. Pfleiderer, C. von Weizsäcker, and W. Wrede (*Gesammelte Aufsätze* ii, Tübingen, 1928, pp. 18 f.).

valid, but received a new significance. By raising Jesus from the dead, God had reversed that curse. But why should Jesus have undergone the divine curse in the first place? Sooner rather than later Paul must have reached the conclusion set out in Galatians iii. 10–13—that Jesus submitted to the death of the cross in order to take upon Himself the curse which the law pronounced on all who failed to keep it completely (Dt. xxvii. 26). The *form* of this argument was such as Paul was quite familiar with in the rabbinical schools, but no Rabbi had ever formulated the *substance* of this bold argument—that the Messiah should undergo voluntarily the curse denounced upon the breakers of God's law in order to liberate them from that curse. But in this way the doctrine of a crucified Messiah, which had once been such a stone of stumbling to Paul,[1] became the corner-stone of his faith and preaching.

We cannot say how soon this reinterpretation took shape in his mind.[2] It may well have been assisted at an early stage by consideration of the portrayal of the Suffering Servant who, in Isaiah liii. 10–12, yields up his life as a guilt-offering for others and, by bearing the sin of many, procures righteousness for them.[3] But it cannot be too strongly emphasized that Paul's theology was not based primarily on study and speculation. It was based primarily on his own experience of God, who 'revealed his son' in him (Gal. i. 16) and flooded his inner being with divine love by the impartation of His Spirit (Rom. v. 5). All that he had sought so long by painstaking observance of the law was now his by God's gift—all that and much more.

[1] See Rom. ix. 32 f. (pp. 198 ff.).

[2] J. Weiss rightly thinks of the period of Paul's activity in Syria and Cilicia (Gal. i. 21), before he went to Antioch (Acts xi. 26), as formative in this regard. 'It cannot be too much insisted upon that the real development of Paul as a Christian and as a theologian was completed in this period which is so obscure to us, and that in the letters we have to do with the fully matured man . . . the "development" which some think they can discern in the period of the letters—ten years, at the most—is not worth considering at all' (*Earliest Christianity*, i, New York, 1959, p. 206). This last statement is too sweeping a judgment, but serves as a healthy corrective to excessive speculation on Paul's inner development.

[3] See pp. 118 f., 128, 132, 161, n. 1.

For now he could do the will of God with a free spontaneity such as he had never known under the law; he knew himself accepted by God, justified by His grace, blessed with a new power within, and called to a service which for ever thereafter gave zest and purpose to life.

'The just shall live by faith'—or, as Paul expounds it, 'it is he who is righteous by faith that will live'[1]—is not only the kernel of Galatians, and the text of Romans, but it was a foundation-principle in Paul's own life. Time and again he reverts to it, and not only in these two Epistles. When he reminds the Corinthians how Christ was 'made . . . sin' (i.e. a sin-offering) for us 'that we might be made the righteousness of God in him' (2 Cor. v. 21), or tells the Philippians of his ambition to 'gain Christ and be found in him, not having a righteousness of my own, based on law, but that which is through faith in Christ, the righteousness from God that depends on faith' (Phil. iii. 8 f., RSV), he shows quite plainly what was the ground of his hope and the motive-power of his apostolic ministry. The very contrast between his former activity as a persecutor and his new life as a bond-slave of Jesus Christ magnified the grace of God which had been bestowed so abundantly upon him, wiping his slate clean and making him what he now was.

The way of righteousness, then, which he sets forth to the Romans was a way which was well known to him, ever since his feet were planted on it outside the walls of Damascus. There is more autobiography in our Epistle than meets the eye—the autobiography of a man who has been justified by faith.[2]

---

[1] Hab. ii. 4, quoted in Gal. iii. 11 and Rom. i. 17 (see pp. 79 f.).

[2] See J. Buchanan, *The Doctrine of Justification* (1867; reprinted 1951). Paul whole-heartedly believed in the implanting of a righteous character, but as something logically subsequent to, and distinguished from, the conferment of a righteous status. Reformed theology has generally distinguished the two by calling the former 'sanctification' (the subject of Rom. vi–viii) and the latter 'justification' (the subject of Rom. i. 17, iii. 19–v. 21). Failure to observe this distinction leads to confusion in the interpretation of Paul. While we think of the distinction—between justification by faith as the initial act of God's grace and sanctification as the following and con-

'Justification by Faith means that salvation depends not on sacraments, not on what is done or not done by any priest or presbyter, but on the simple response of the believing heart to the Word of God in Jesus Christ. Observe what this really means; it is not just a theological figment. At one stroke it cuts at the root of the whole vast system of sacerdotalism, with its associated doctrine of works—penance, pilgrimage, fasting, purgatory, and all the rest. The Church is no longer a hierarchy of clergy performing indispensable rites for its members; no longer a caste of priests endued with mysterious, not to say magical powers at the word of a bishop; but the priesthood of all believing men, and a ministry authorised by the call of the Holy Spirit, by due examination of life and doctrine, and by the consent of the people concerned. . . . Accept this doctrine of Justification by Faith and the layman, the common man, John the Commonweal, at one stride comes into the centre.'[1]

tinuous work of His grace—as characteristically Lutheran and Reformed doctrine, there is ample evidence that justification by faith alone was held in the first half of the sixteenth century by several theologians in the Papal camp (especially in Italy), including the English Cardinal Reginald Pole. When G. Contarini wrote a treatise on justification by faith alone, Pole congratulated him on being the first to bring to light 'that holy, fruitful, indispensable truth'. (In fact, the Reformed doctrine of justification by faith had been anticipated at almost every point by Juliana of Norwich over a hundred years before.) It was the Council of Trent that checked this trend on the Papal side. Despite Pole's exhortation 'not to reject an opinion simply because it was held by Luther', the Council in 1546 defined justification in terms which confused it with sanctification and made it dependent on works as well as on faith, and anathematized point by point those who held the 'Reformed'—or rather the Pauline—doctrine. See *Acta Concilii Tridentini*, Sessio VI ('De iustificatione'); also L. von Ranke, *History of the Popes*, Book II (1908), Vol. I, pp. 109, 113, 158 ff. More recently it has been maintained, e.g. by the Roman Catholic theologians W. H. van der Pol and H. Küng (cf. especially the latter's *Rechtfertigung*, Paderborn, 1957, with its introduction by Karl Barth), that it was not the biblical doctrine of justification 'by faith alone' that the Council condemned, but the Reformers' 'external' interpretation of that doctrine, and that the Tridentine formulations (conditioned as they were by the polemical situation) have been misunderstood by Protestants as teaching a synergistic soteriology. See the critique of this account of the matter in G. C. Berkouwer, *Recent Developments in Roman Catholic Thought* (Grand Rapids, 1958), pp. 56 ff.

[1] Sir T. M. Taylor, *The Heritage of the Reformation* (1960), pp. 6 f. This whole pamphlet—embodying a speech delivered at the meeting of the General Assembly of the Church of Scotland held to commemorate the fourth centenary of the Scottish Reformation—is germane to the central argument of the Epistle to the Romans. See p. 237.

For this doctrine sets a man by himself face to face with God; and if it humbles him to the dust before God, it is that God may raise him up and set him on his feet. The man who has had such personal dealings with God, and has been raised to his feet by almighty power and grace, can never be enslaved in spirit to any other man. The doctrine of justification by faith underlies and undergirds the forms which democracy has taken in those lands most deeply influenced by the Reformation; it is a bastion of true freedom. Luther was charged with 'inciting revolution by putting little people in mind of their prodigious dignity before God'. How could he deny the charge? The gospel, as he had learned it from Paul, does precisely that.

Yet, crucial as the justification of sinners by faith alone is to the Pauline gospel, it does not exhaust that gospel. Paul sets his doctrine of justification, together with his other doctrines, in the context of the new creation that has come into being with and in Christ. That the acquittal of the day of judgment is pronounced here and now on those who put their faith in Jesus is part and parcel of the truth that for them 'the old order has gone, and a new order has already begun' (2 Cor. v. 17, NEB)—a truth made real in their present experience by the advent and activity of the Spirit.[1]

VI. 'FLESH' AND 'SPIRIT' IN ROMANS

a. 'Flesh'

To the reader of this Epistle William Tyndale gives the following wise advice: 'First we must mark diligently the manner of speaking of the apostle, and above all things know what Paul meaneth by these words—the Law, Sin, Grace, Faith, Righteousness, Flesh, Spirit and such like—or else, read thou it never so often, thou shalt but lose thy labour.'

Of these words two of the most important are the opposed terms 'flesh' and 'spirit', which in their distinctive Pauline

[1] Cf. W. D. Davies, *Paul and Rabbinic Judaism* (1948), pp. 222 f.

usage relate respectively to the old order superseded by Christ and the new order inaugurated by Him. Flesh and spirit wage incessant warfare the one against the other within the citadel of Mansoul. This warfare, as described in Paul's writings, is not the warfare between matter and mind, between the physical and rational elements in man, which we meet in Greek philosophy. The background of Paul's usage of these terms is the Old Testament, although their Old Testament usage is extended by Paul along lines peculiarly his own.[1]

In the Old Testament 'flesh' (Heb. *basar, she'er*) is the basic material of human (and animal) life. Leaving aside the frequent occurrences of 'flesh' in the sense of animal life (e.g. Gn. vi. 19) or the meat of animals which may be eaten (e.g. Ex. xii. 8), we observe that, as 'flesh', men are distinguished from 'the gods, whose dwelling is not with flesh' (Dn. ii. 11). When God announces that He will limit the duration of man's life, He says: 'My spirit shall not abide in man for ever, for he is flesh' (Gn. vi. 3, RSV). Man, in fact, is animated flesh; 'all flesh' (e.g. Gn. vi. 12; Is. xl. 5; Joel ii. 28) means 'all mankind' (when the context does not indicate the wider sense of 'all animal life'). 'Flesh' may denote human nature in its weakness and mortality: 'he remembered that they were but flesh' (Ps. lxxviii. 39). It can be used of the human body, as when a man is instructed to 'wash his flesh in water' (e.g. Lv. xiv. 9); or of the man himself in a more general sense, as in Psalm lxiii. 1, where 'my flesh longeth for thee' is synonymous with the preceding clause, 'my soul (Heb. *nephesh*) thirsteth for thee' (here both ' my soul' and 'my flesh' are little more than alternative ways of saying 'I').

It is against this Old Testament background, then, that we are to understand the Pauline usage of the term (Gk. *sarx*), with more particular reference to the Epistle to the Romans.

[1] An excellent treatment of these terms is given by E. Schweizer in Kittel's *Theologisches Wörterbuch zum Neuen Testament,* in the articles *pneuma* (Vol. VI, 1959), *sarx* and *sōma* (Vol. VII, 1960–). Part of the first article has appeared in English as *The Spirit of God* (Bible Key Words, 1960).

1. 'Flesh' is used in the ordinary sense of *bodily flesh* in Romans ii. 28, where the literal 'circumcision, which is outward in the flesh' (cf. Gn. xvii. 11) is contrasted with the spiritual circumcision of the heart.

2. 'Flesh' is used of *natural human descent or relationship*. Thus Christ is said in i. 3 to be David's descendant 'according to the flesh', as in ix. 5 He is said to belong to the nation of Israel 'as concerning the flesh'.[1] In iv. 1 Abraham is called 'our father, as pertaining to the flesh' (i.e. the ancestor of those of us who are Jews by birth), whereas spiritually he is the father of all believers (iv. 11 f., 16); his descendants by physical propagation are 'the children of the flesh' by contrast with 'the children of the promise' (ix. 8). People of Jewish birth are Paul's 'kinsmen according to the flesh' (ix. 3), or simply his 'flesh' (xi. 14).[2]

3. 'Flesh' is used in the sense of *mankind* in Romans iii. 20: 'by the deeds of the law there shall no flesh be justified.' This is a common Hebrew usage: Old Testament examples are 'O thou that hearest prayer, unto thee shall all flesh come' (Ps. lxv. 2); 'no flesh shall have peace' (Je. xii. 12); and we may compare our Lord's words, 'except that the Lord had shortened those days, no flesh should be saved' (Mk. xiii. 20). Paul appears to have been fond of this usage; although in Romans iii. 20 he is quoting Psalm cxliii. 2, the word 'flesh' does not appear in the Old Testament passage, yet he introduces the word into his quotation of it not only here but also in Galatians ii. 16. (Cf. 1 Cor. i. 29: 'that no flesh should glory in his presence.') Sometimes the same idea is expressed by the phrase 'flesh and blood' (e.g. Gal. i. 16: 'I conferred not with flesh and blood'—i.e. with any human being).

---

[1] In these two places, especially in the former, 'flesh' denotes not only natural descent but also the state of our Lord's existence before He was glorified (see pp. 72 f., 186).

[2] 'Flesh' appears in this sense in the Old Testament as, for example, when Abimelech says to his Shechemite kinsmen: 'remember also that I am your bone and your flesh' (Jdg. ix. 2).

4. 'Flesh' is used variously in the sense of *human nature*, as follows:

(i) *Weak human nature*. In Romans vi. 19 Paul explains his argument by the aid of an analogy from everyday life 'because of the infirmity of your flesh'; here by 'flesh' he refers more particularly to the *intelligence* of his readers. Again, in viii. 3 he speaks of the law as being unable to produce righteousness 'in that it was weak through the flesh'—i.e. the frail human nature which it had to work upon. (A good example of this sense of 'flesh' is provided by the saying of Jesus in Mt. xxvi. 41: 'the spirit indeed is willing, but the flesh is weak.')

(ii) *The human nature of Christ*. The humanity of Christ is something that He shares with all mankind. But our flesh is 'sinful flesh', because sin has established a bridgehead in our life from which it dominates the situation. Christ came in real flesh, but not in 'sinful flesh'; sin was unable to gain a foothold in His life. Therefore He is said to have come 'in the *likeness* of sinful flesh' (Rom. viii. 3). Having come thus He dealt effectively in His manhood with sin: He resisted its attempts to gain an entrance into His life and when in death He presented His sinless life to God as a sin-offering, God thus 'condemned sin in the flesh' (viii. 3)—i.e. He ratified the death-sentence passed on sin by means of the incarnation, sacrifice and victory of the man Christ Jesus.

(iii) *The 'old nature' in the believer*. When Paul speaks of 'my flesh', he means his sinful propensity inherited from Adam. There is nothing good in it (vii. 18); with it, he says, 'I . . . serve . . . the law of sin' (vii. 25).[1] It is still present with him, even if progressively disabled—and this in spite of the fact that it has been 'crucified'; compare Galatians v. 24, 'they that are Christ's have crucified the flesh with the affections and lusts', with Romans vi. 6, RV, 'our old man was crucified with him (Christ), that the body of sin might be done away.'

---

[1] The Corinthian Christians, though they were indwelt corporately and individually by the Spirit of God (1 Cor. iii. 16, vi. 19), were 'carnal' ('fleshly', Gk. *sarkinos, sarkikos*), not spiritual (1 Cor. iii. 1 ff.).

This apparent paradox is one that we meet repeatedly in the Pauline writings, where believers are enjoined time and again to be what they are—to be in actual practice what they are as members of Christ. Thus they are said to 'have put off the old man with his deeds' and to 'have put on the new man' (Col. iii. 9 f.), while elsewhere they are exhorted to 'put off . . . the old man' and 'put on the new man' (Eph. iv. 22, 24). The old man is what they were 'in Adam'; the new man is what they are 'in Christ'. Therefore to put on the new man is to put on Christ, and while Paul tells the Galatians that 'as many of you as have been baptized into Christ have put on Christ' (Gal. iii. 27), he tells the Romans to 'put . . . on the Lord Jesus Christ' (Rom. xiii. 14).

(iv) *Unregenerate human nature.* Though 'my flesh' is still present with me, I am no longer 'in the flesh'.[1] To be 'in the flesh' is to be unregenerate, to be still 'in Adam', in a state in which one 'cannot please God' (Rom. viii. 8). Believers were formerly 'in the flesh' (vii. 5), but now they 'are not in the flesh, but in the Spirit', if indeed the Spirit of God dwells within them—and if He does not, they do not yet belong to Christ (viii. 9).

5. Since, then, believers are no longer 'in the flesh', but 'in the Spirit', they should no longer live 'according to the flesh' —according to the pattern of their old unregenerate life[2]—but

---

[1] In Gal. ii. 20 ('the life which I now live in the flesh') 'in the flesh' means 'in mortal body'. The phrase is the same (Gk. *en sarki*) but the meaning is quite different from that discussed above.

[2] One important occurrence of this phrase 'according to the flesh' or 'after the flesh' (Gk. *kata sarka*) is in 2 Cor. v. 16: 'Wherefore henceforth know we no man after the flesh: yea, though we have known Christ after the flesh, yet now henceforth know we him no more.' These words are so regularly misapplied that it is worth emphasizing here that Paul does not deprecate any interest in the earthly life of Christ, or suggest that the other apostles' companionship with Him during His ministry was now irrelevant, and of no religious advantage; he contrasts rather his own present estimate of Christ with his estimate of Christ before his conversion, as NEB makes clear: 'With us therefore worldly standards have ceased to count in our estimate of any man; even if once they counted in our understanding of

'according to the Spirit' (see viii. 4 f., 12 f.). They have exchanged their unregenerate outlook ('the mind of the flesh') for one which properly belongs to the children of God ('the mind of the Spirit'), and it is their duty now to 'make not provision for the flesh, to fulfil the lusts thereof' (Rom. viii. 5–7, xiii. 14).[1]

6. The flesh is subject to the principle of 'sin and death' (Rom. vii. 23, viii. 2), and so is under sentence of death, for 'in Adam all die' (1 Cor. xv. 22). 'The mind of the flesh is death'; 'if ye live after the flesh, ye must die' (Rom. viii. 6, 13, RV). 'For he that soweth to his flesh shall of the flesh reap corruption'—or, in the NEB rendering, 'If he sows seed in the field of his lower nature, he will reap from it a harvest of corruption' (Gal. vi. 8).

The flesh, the human nature which is ours 'in Adam', is corrupted by sin; but the sins of the flesh have a much wider range in Paul's thought than they have tended to have in Christian moral theology. They include the sins that are specially associated with the body, but they also include sins which might more naturally be classified by us as sins of the mind. Thus, Paul's catalogue of 'the works of the flesh' in Galatians v. 19–21 comprises not only fornication and related forms of sexual vice, with drunkenness and revelry, but also sorcery, envy, quarrelsomeness, selfish ambition, and idolatry. Sin of any kind, in fact, is a work of the 'flesh'.

Sometimes the term 'body' is used instead of 'flesh'. Thus what are called 'the works of the flesh' in Galatians v. 19 are called 'the deeds of the body' in Romans viii. 13 in the same comprehensive sense. So also 'the body of sin' (Rom. vi. 6) is a synonym of 'flesh of sin' (Rom. viii. 3, RVmg.); we may

Christ, they do so now no longer.' It is in the light of Christ's exaltation, and of the new creation inaugurated by His triumph over death, that His earthly ministry must be evaluated; but in this light the importance of His earthly ministry is enhanced, not diminished.

[1] Cf. Gal. v. 16: 'Walk in the Spirit, and ye shall not fulfil the lust of the flesh.'

compare 'this body of death' (RSV) from which deliverance is sought in Romans vii. 24. (On the other hand, the 'body' of Rom. viii. 10, which is 'dead because of sin', is more simply this mortal body of flesh and blood.) We may also compare 'your members which are upon the earth' in Colossians iii. 5, which are to be treated as dead.[1]

b. 'Spirit'

In the Old Testament, 'flesh' is set over against 'spirit' (Heb. *ruach*, primarily 'wind', then 'vital vigour'). A classic passage is Isaiah xxxi. 3: 'The Egyptians are men, and not God; and their horses flesh, and not spirit.' God, by implication, is Spirit (cf. Jn. iv. 24); not only so, but the Spirit of God can energize men and impart to them physical power, mental skill, or spiritual insight that they would not otherwise have. The spirit in man is his breath, his disposition, his vitality.[2]

Similarly in the Pauline writings 'flesh' and 'spirit' are opposed terms. Believers in Christ are no longer 'in the flesh' but 'in the Spirit' (Rom. viii. 9); they 'walk not after the flesh, but after the Spirit' (Rom. viii. 4); they do not produce 'the works of the flesh' but 'the fruit of the Spirit' (Gal. v. 19, 22).

We are under the embarrassment of having to choose between a capital 'S' and a minuscule 's' each time we write the word; Paul was subject to no such embarrassment when he pronounced the Greek word *pneuma* during his dictation of this Epistle, and neither was Tertius as he wrote it.

---

[1] What Paul says about the 'flesh' in the sense of unregenerate human nature must not be taken as applying to the physical body. Of the 'flesh' in this sense he has nothing good to say; but the believer's body, while once used by the master-power of sin as an instrument of unrighteousness (Rom. vi. 13), can be presented to God as 'a living sacrifice' for the doing of His will (Rom. xii. 1), is indwelt by His Spirit (Rom. viii. 11; cf. 1 Cor. vi. 19 f.), and will one day be redeemed from mortality and invested with glory (Rom. viii. 23; cf. Phil. iii. 21). Paul does not share the Greek philosophers' contempt for the body as the fetter or prison-house of the soul.

[2] Cf. A. R. Johnson, *The Vitality of the Individual in the Thought of Ancient Israel* (1949), pp. 26 ff.

We can distinguish the following principal usages of 'spirit' in Paul:[1]

1. *The 'spiritual' part of man's constitution.* 'I serve' God 'with my spirit', says Paul (Rom. i. 9); with this we may compare vii. 6, where believers, no longer under law but under grace, 'serve in newness of spirit, and not in the oldness of the letter' (which, however, goes beyond i. 9 in its implications).[2] Circumcision 'in the spirit, and not in the letter'—i.e. the inward circumcision or purification of the heart, of which the prophets spoke (Je. iv. 4; cf. Dt. x. 16)—is contrasted with the literal circumcision of the flesh (Rom. ii. 29). Believers are exhorted to be 'fervent in spirit' (Rom. xii. 11). The spirit of believers moves in harmony with the Spirit of God (Rom. viii. 16).

The other New Testament writers use 'spirit' more or less as a synonym of 'soul'. This appears, for example, in the opening words of the *Magnificat*: 'My soul doth magnify the Lord, and my spirit hath rejoiced in God my Saviour' (Lk. i. 46 f.)—or we may compare our Lord's words in John xii. 27, 'Now is my soul troubled', with the Evangelist's statement in John xiii. 21 that 'he was troubled in spirit.' Paul himself uses 'spirit' in this more general sense when he asks: 'what man knoweth the things of a man, save the spirit of man which is in him?' (1 Cor. ii. 11). But for the most part 'spirit' and 'soul' are not only distinguished in Paul, but set in contrast to each other: the 'natural man' is literally the 'soulish' man (*psuchikos*, from *psuchē*, 'soul'), who is contrasted with the 'spiritual man'

[1] Among other usages, not listed below, there are a few occurrences of the word to denote 'spirit-beings' or 'spiritual powers' such as 'the spirit of the world' (1 Cor. ii. 12), 'the spirit that now worketh in the children of disobedience' (Eph. ii. 2) or the spirits (not always the Spirit of God) by whose inspiration prophets speak (1 Cor. xii. 10); or to denote a personal disposition, e.g. a 'spirit of slumber' (Rom. xi. 8).

[2] See p. 147. Cf. 2 Cor. iii. 6, where Paul and his colleagues are 'ministers of a new covenant; not of the letter, but of the spirit: for the letter killeth, but the spirit giveth life' (RV). The allusion to the new covenant of Je. xxxi. 31 ff., explicit in 2 Cor. iii. 6, is implicit in the other places where 'letter' and 'spirit' are thus set in contrast. See note on viii. 4 (pp. 161 f.).

(*pneumatikos*, from *pneuma*, 'spirit').[1] In Paul the human spirit may perhaps be described as the God-conscious element in man, which is dormant or dead until it is stirred into life by the Spirit of God. Or it may be thought of as the 'Christian personality' of 'men who, if we may put it so, are not only alive, but "Christianly" alive'.[2]

2. *The Spirit of God, or the Holy Spirit.* He is called 'the Spirit of holiness' in Romans i. 4, in relation to the resurrection of Christ; cf. viii. 11, where He is called 'the Spirit of him that raised up Jesus from the dead'. Under His enlightenment the conscience of man bears true witness (ix. 1). In the proclamation of the gospel He supplies the power to make the message effective in the hearers (xv. 19); those who are thus brought to faith in Christ are 'sanctified by the Holy Ghost' (xv. 16). Into the hearts of those who believe the gospel He comes pouring out the love of God (v. 5; cf. xv. 30); and by His power they are filled with peace, joy and hope (xiv. 17, xv. 13).

Since God has revealed Himself in Christ, the Spirit of God is the Spirit of Christ (viii. 9). So completely does the Spirit convey to believers the life and power of the risen and exalted Christ that *in practice* the two seem frequently to be identified (although in principle they are distinguished).[3] For example, the expressions 'if so be that the Spirit of God dwell in you' (viii. 9) and 'if Christ be in you' (viii. 10) are practically synonymous.

It is in chapter viii that the nature and implications of the Holy Spirit's indwelling and operation in the believer are most clearly set forth.[4]

---

[1] 1 Cor. ii. 14 f. Compare the distinction in 1 Cor. xv. 44 ff. between the present mortal body, which is 'a natural ("soulish") body' (*sōma psuchikon*), and the resurrection body, which is a 'spiritual body' (*sōma pneumatikon*).

[2] W. Barclay, *Flesh and Spirit* (1962), p. 14.

[3] Cf. 1 Cor. xv. 45b; 2 Cor. iii. 17a. N. Q. Hamilton speaks of this identification of the Spirit with the ascended Lord as 'dynamic' but not 'ontological' (*The Holy Spirit and Eschatology in Paul*, 1957, p. 6).

[4] See G. Smeaton, *The Doctrine of the Holy Spirit* (1882; reprinted 1958), pp. 71 ff.; E. F. Kevan, *The Saving Work of the Holy Spirit* (1953).

(i) *The Spirit imparts life.* His 'law' is the 'law of life'; to 'walk . . . after the Spirit' and so to have 'the mind of the Spirit' is to live[1] (viii. 4, 5, 6, 10), for He enables the believer to treat 'the deeds of the body'—the practices of the old unregenerate existence—as dead things, with no further power in his life. There can be no true life without Him: 'if any man have not the Spirit of Christ, he is none of his' (viii. 9). To be 'in (the) Spirit' (*en pneumati*) is the opposite of being 'in (the) flesh' (*en sarki*), and all believers are regarded as being 'in the Spirit' (viii. 9). In practice, then, to be 'in the Spirit' is to be 'in Christ' (or 'in Christ Jesus'); to be 'in the Spirit' is thus no individualist matter. For to be 'in Christ' is to be incorporated into Christ, to be a member of Christ, and so to be a fellow-member of all others who are similarly incorporated into Christ (xii. 5); this new solidarity which believers have 'in Christ Jesus' (viii. 1) is accordingly the same thing as Paul elsewhere describes as the 'fellowship of the Spirit' (Phil. ii. 1; cf. 2 Cor. xiii. 14) or the 'unity of the Spirit' (Eph. iv. 3).[2]

(ii) *The Spirit bestows freedom.* However men's spiritual bondage be viewed—as bondage to sin, bondage to the law, or bondage to death—it is the Spirit who liberates them. It is He who conveys to believers the power of the risen Christ, by which they are 'made free from sin' (Rom. vi. 18, 22); it is He who releases them from legal bondage, so that they now 'serve in newness of spirit, and not in the oldness of the letter' (vii. 6); it is He who imparts the new principle of 'life in Christ Jesus' which sets them free from 'the law of sin and death' (viii. 2). In all these instances we have illustrations of the principle concisely stated in 2 Corinthians iii. 17b: 'where the Spirit of the Lord is, there is liberty.'

(iii) *The Spirit supplies directive power in the lives of the 'sons of God'* (viii. 14). He is the 'Spirit that makes us sons' (viii. 15, NEB), by whose prompting believers approach God as children

---

[1] Cf. Gal. vi. 8b: 'he that soweth to the Spirit shall of the Spirit reap life everlasting.'

[2] This is placed beyond doubt by his statement in 1 Cor. xii. 13: 'in one Spirit were we all baptized into one body' (RV).

and call Him by the same familiar name of 'Father' as Jesus used when speaking to Him.[1]

(iv) *The Spirit intercedes for the people of God* (viii. 26 f.). So does Christ (viii. 34), but whereas Christ makes intercession in His place of exaltation in the presence of God, the Spirit makes intercession from within the lives of the believers whom He indwells.[2]

(v) *The Spirit is the sanctifying agency in the lives of believers.* 'Spirit' and 'flesh' are in undying opposition, and wage perpetual warfare the one with the other. But the Spirit is divinely powerful, and can put the 'flesh' progressively out of action in those lives which are yielded to His control and enabling grace. It is no quietist doctrine that Paul propounds: he knew his own spiritual life to be a struggle which would continue so long as he remained in mortal body—a struggle, however, in which victory and final glory were assured by the Spirit. And in the lives of those whom He is preparing for final glory His congenial work here and now is to reproduce in increasing measure the likeness of Christ.[3]

(vi) *The Spirit is the pledge of the future.* According to Old Testament prophecy, the outpouring of the Spirit of God would be a sign of the approaching day of the Lord (Joel ii. 28–32). This prophecy was quoted by Peter when the Spirit came down upon the disciples of Jesus on the day of Pentecost: 'This is that', he said, 'which was spoken by the prophet' (Acts ii. 16). The present interval 'between the times' is in a peculiar sense the age of the Spirit; in this age He not only makes effective in believers what Christ has accomplished for them, He not only communicates to them the power of the living

---

[1] Cf. Gal. iv. 6: 'because ye are sons, God hath sent forth the Spirit of his Son into your hearts, crying, Abba, Father' (see p. 166).

[2] This ascription of an intercessory ministry both to the exalted Christ and to the indwelling Spirit is paralleled by the twofold use of 'paraclete' or 'advocate' in the Johannine writings: 'Jesus Christ the righteous' is His people's 'advocate with the Father' (1 Jn. ii. 1), and the Holy Spirit is 'another . . . Advocate' (Jn. xiv. 16, NEB), sent by the Father to be with believers.

[3] Cf. 2 Cor. iii. 18.

and exalted Lord, but He enables them to live in the present enjoyment of the glory that is yet to be revealed.

Not only does the Spirit supply life here and now; His presence guarantees the resurrection life on a day yet to dawn. Thus the life of the age to come, 'eternal life', is conveyed to believers as the present 'gift of God . . . in Christ Jesus our Lord' (vi. 23, RV)—as an advance instalment, so to speak, of the coming resurrection life which will follow the redemption of the body (viii. 23).[1]

Not only does the Spirit enable believers here and now to realize their prerogative as 'the Lord's free-born children in the way of holiness'[2]; this too is an advance instalment of that 'liberty of the glory of the children of God' (RV) which, according to Romans viii. 21, is eagerly awaited not only by themselves but by all creation. The deliverance from bondage which they have already begun to enjoy in the Spirit will be consummated then; the 'adoption' (viii. 23) which will be realized fully with the resurrection is anticipated already by the aid of 'the Spirit of adoption' (viii. 15); and the glory of full conformity to the image of God's Son, for which they were foreordained (viii. 29), will be the full flowering of that sanctifying work on which the Spirit is even now engaged in their lives. The indwelling of the Spirit is thus presented in terms of 'proleptic eschatology'.[3] He is the 'firstfruits' of the final salvation (viii. 23),[4] the immediate 'down-payment' of that

[1] This redeemed body of the resurrection is described by Paul in 1 Cor. xv. 44 as 'a spiritual body'—that is, a body completely controlled by the Spirit. In 2 Cor. v. 5 the present gift of the Spirit is the 'earnest' of the coming day when believers will be 'clothed upon' with their 'house which is from heaven', when mortality will be 'swallowed up of life'.

[2] This phrase (of which W. B. Neatby said that 'the peculiar genius of Christianity has not often received a more striking expression') comes from the *Memoir of Anthony Norris Groves*[3] (1869), p. 418.

[3] See G. Vos, 'The Eschatological Aspect of the Pauline Conception of the Spirit', *Princeton Seminary Biblical and Theological Studies* (New York, 1912), pp. 209 ff.; *The Pauline Eschatology* (1952).

[4] Cf. Gal. v. 5: 'we through the Spirit wait for the hope of righteousness by faith.' So, in Eph. i. 13, 14 believers are said to have been 'sealed with that holy Spirit of promise, which is the earnest of our inheritance until the redemption of the purchased possession'.

inconceivably rich heritage which God has prepared for those who love Him.

VII. 'LAW' IN ROMANS

The term 'law' (*nomos*) occurs over seventy times in this Epistle, and not always in the same sense. Most often it means the law of God in one form or another, but there are a few places where it bears a different meaning. Here are its principal meanings, in ascending order of frequency.

1. *The Pentateuch.* When we are told that God's way of righteousness through faith is 'witnessed by the law and the prophets' (Rom. iii. 21b), 'the law' means the first five books of the Old Testament, as 'the prophets' is a comprehensive designation for the remaining books. This is a common New Testament usage, and reflects the Jewish application of the Hebrew word *torah* not only to the law in the stricter sense but to the five books which pre-eminently contain the law.

2. *The Old Testament as a whole.* In iii. 19 Paul says: 'we know that what things soever the law saith, it saith to them who are under the law.' 'What things soever the law saith' refers to a catena of biblical quotations in the preceding verses (10–18); but of these quotations five are from the Psalms and one from Isaiah. If it is 'the law' that says these things, 'the law' can mean only the Hebrew Bible—our Old Testament.

3. *A principle.* In iii. 27 Paul, having established that the grace of God justifies men and women through faith, says that, since this is the case, there is no room for boasting. 'By what law? of works? Nay: but by the law of faith.' Here 'the law of works' (not the same thing as 'the works of the law') and 'the law of faith' denote two contrasted principles by which men may seek to secure God's acceptance.

In vii. 21 Paul, considering the moral conflict that rages in the soul, discovers 'a law'—that is, a principle—'that, when I would do good, evil is present with me'. In the same context the moral conflict itself is viewed as a conflict between two laws or principles: first the law or principle which hands him over bound to the domination of sin (vii. 23, 25b), and second, 'the law of my mind' which acknowledges the goodness of God's law and desires to do it, but lacks the power to enforce what it acknowledges and desires (vii. 23). But when yet another principle begins to operate in the soul—'the law of the Spirit of life in Christ Jesus'—this proves stronger than 'the law (principle) of sin and death' and liberates the soul from the thraldom of the latter (viii. 2).

4. *The law of God.* To a man with Paul's heritage and training it was most natural to equate the law of God with the law of Moses—in other words, the law as God gave it to Israel through Moses (not to speak of the oral expansion of the written law, which in rabbinical tradition was given to Moses at Sinai as truly—in theory, at least—as the written law itself). This was the form in which Paul had come to know the law of God in his own experience. If (in opposition to many exegetes today) we regard Romans vii. 7–13 as a fragment of spiritual autobiography, Paul tells how it was his first awareness of the law that gave him his first consciousness of sin, and that he has the Mosaic law in mind is evident from the fact that the particular law which he selects to illustrate his point is one of the Ten Commandments—'Thou shalt not covet.'

When he deals with the situation of the Jews, who rejoiced in being the people of the law (ii. 17 ff., 23 ff.) and endeavoured to establish their acceptance with God by fulfilling the requirements of the law (ix. 31, x. 3 ff.), it is naturally the Mosaic law that he has in mind. When he speaks in v. 13 f., 20a, as though 'law' was unknown in the ages between Adam and Moses—that is, until God spoke at Sinai—we can trace the same equation of the law of Moses with the law of God. Indeed, when he is showing how Christians ought to live, and stressing the supremacy of the law of love, he formulates the law of love (as Jesus had done before him) in a commandment

53

from the Pentateuch, 'Thou shalt love thy neighbour as thyself' (xiii. 9, quoting Lv. xix. 18); and when he says that 'love is the fulfilling of the law' (xiii. 10) he illustrates what he means by 'law' by quoting a number of commandments from the Decalogue.

But in all this Paul is using the law of Israel as the outstanding and—to himself and many of his readers—the best-known manifestation of divine law. When, in vii. 1, he appeals to his readers as men who 'know the law' to agree with him 'that the law hath dominion over a man as long as he liveth', exegetes may debate whether he means Jewish law or Roman law, but it does not really affect his argument there, which is equally valid whether he had in mind Jewish or Roman law, or simply law in general. In whatever community a man lives, he is subject to the law of that community; and Paul, who maintained that 'there is no power but of God' (xiii. 1), would equally have maintained that there is no law but of God.

Again, when he argues that Jews and Gentiles are on an equal footing before God as regards their failure to do His will, he points out that, while Jews had a special revelation of God's will in their law, Gentiles were not deprived of all knowledge of His will; 'for when the Gentiles, which have not the law, do by nature the things contained in the law, these, having not the law, are a law unto themselves: which shew the work of the law written in their hearts, their conscience also bearing witness, and their thoughts the meanwhile accusing or else excusing one another' (ii. 14 f.). That is to say, the Gentiles had not been given the complete *torah*, or even the Ten Commandments, but they did have a sense of right and wrong; they had a built-in awareness of the real essence of God's law. So, when Paul says (iii. 20) that through law[1] comes our knowledge of sin, he says something that is true of Jews and Gentiles alike; and when he says in the same

---

[1] Very often (e.g. in more than half the occurrences in Romans) Paul uses *nomos* ('law') without a preceding article. This may at times be a reflection of the Hebrew treatment of *torah* as a proper noun, without the article; but it may also be regarded as an indication that Paul is thinking not only of *the* law *par excellence* but of law in general.

context that 'by legal works[1] no human being will be justified in God's sight', this too is equally valid for Jew and Gentile. Whether the 'legal works' are performed in accordance with a code promulgated by express divine authority, or in accordance with the dictates of conscience, the moral law within, Wordsworth's 'stern daughter of the voice of God', or in accordance with an accepted standard of decent behaviour— no matter, these are not the grounds on which men are accepted by God. Whichever of these forms 'law' may take, it is right to keep it; it is wrong, and indeed disastrous, to break or defy or ignore it; but it is vain to imagine that by keeping it we can accumulate a store of merit in the heavenly treasure-house. God has given law to men for a variety of purposes, and it has many uses; but when it is a question of His *justifying* men, He proceeds by a more excellent way.

The law, then, in whatever form it may appear, is God's law—'holy, and just, and good' (Rom. vii. 12). If, as Paul insists, it was not given to be the means of men's justification, why was it given? To this question the Epistle to the Romans provides a variety of answers, which may be arranged under four principal heads.

(i) *It was given to be a revelation of God and His will.* The distinction between right and wrong is not simply a matter of social convention; it is rooted in the being and character of God, and is written into the constitution of man, created as he has been in the image of God. The law is God's law, and, like God Himself, is 'true and righteous altogether' (Ps. xix. 9; cf. Rom. vii. 12, 16, 22).

(ii) *It was given for the health and preservation of the human race.* This particular purpose is served mainly by civil government, which (as is clearly stated in Rom. xiii. 1–7) is a ministry ordained by God to protect and encourage well-doing and to curb and punish wrong-doing.[2]

[1] Lit. 'works of law'.

[2] Compare the words ascribed to Rabbi Hanina in *Pirqe Aboth* iii. 2: 'Pray for the welfare of the government, since were it not for their fear of it men would swallow one another alive.'

(iii) *It was given to bring sin to light, and to lead men to repentance and reliance on the grace of God.* While in theory the man who keeps the law will live thereby (Rom. x. 5), in practice no-one is justified by the deeds of the law, because of universal failure to keep it perfectly (iii. 20a, 23). The innate human tendency to go contrary to the will of God manifests itself in concrete acts of disobedience when His will is revealed in the form of specific commandments (Rom. v. 13), so that 'by the law is the knowledge of sin' (Rom. iii. 20b, vii. 7). But the man who has experienced the law's power to bring his sin to light, together with its inability to procure him a righteous status in God's sight, is the more ready to cast himself in faith on the grace of God revealed in Christ as the sole means of his justification. Thus, as Paul puts it in another Epistle, 'the law was our custodian until Christ came, that we might be justified by faith' (Gal. iii. 24, RSV). But now that Christ has come, He 'is the end of the law, that every one who has faith may be justified' (Rom. x. 4, RSV)—that is to say, not only has He fulfilled the law Himself, by His perfect submission to the will of God, but since God's way of righteousness has been opened up in Him, He marks the supersession or 'end' of the law as even a theoretical means of justification. Those who are justified by faith in Him are 'not under law, but under grace' (Rom. vi. 14).

(iv) *It was given to provide guidance for the believer's life.* Thanks to the indwelling of the Spirit in the hearts of those who are 'in Christ Jesus', the righteous requirements of the law are fulfilled in them by a divine spontaneity as they live 'according to the Spirit' (Rom. viii. 3 f., RSV). But even so Paul thinks it necessary at a later point in the Epistle to lay down fairly detailed principles of guidance for the lives of Christians, that they may 'prove (by experience) what is the will of God, what is good and acceptable and perfect' (Rom. xii. 1 ff., RSV). These principles of guidance coincide with what he elsewhere calls 'the law of Christ' (Gal. vi. 2). While Paul himself was 'not under law but under grace' as regards his acceptance with

God, while he rejoiced in being 'discharged from the law' so as to 'serve not under the old written code but in the new life of the Spirit' (Rom. vii. 6, RSV), yet he could speak of himself as 'not being without law toward God but under the law of Christ' (1 Cor. ix. 21, RSV). But this law of Christ is the law of love which He Himself embodied and which He bequeathed as 'a new commandment' to His disciples. Moreover, the law of love sums up and brings to perfection the ancient prescriptions of the Decalogue. 'He who loves his neighbour has fulfilled the law. The commandments, "You shall not commit adultery, You shall not kill, You shall not steal, You shall not covet," and any other commandment, are summed up in this sentence, "You shall love your neighbour as yourself." Love does no wrong to a neighbour; therefore love is the fulfilling of the law' (Rom. xiii. 8–10, RSV).

Paul's gospel is thus fully absolved from the charge of antinomianism. When men have been justified by faith, right is still right and wrong is still wrong, and the will of God is still the rule of their lives. But to them the will of God is not enshrined in an external code of regulations: it is implanted within their hearts as a new principle of life. Like Paul, they are for evermore subject to 'the law of Christ'. The detailed resemblance between the ethical directions of Romans xii. 1–xv. 4 and our Lord's Sermon on the Mount (Mt. v–vii) amply entitles those directions to be described as 'the law of Christ'. The law of Christ is no more able to justify the sinner than the law of Moses was; whether expressed in the ethical directions of Romans xii. 1 ff. or in the Sermon on the Mount, Christ's law of love sets a loftier standard than even the Ten Commandments. 'The Sermon on the Mount is not, as many people fondly imagine nowadays, the fulfilment or essence of the Gospel, but it is the fulfilment of the Law.'[1] It presents the standard by which the disciples of Christ—in other words, those who have been justified by faith—ought to live. Those in whose hearts the love of God has been 'shed abroad' by the

---

[1] A. R. Vidler, *Christ's Strange Work* (1944), p. 14.

Holy Spirit are empowered by the same Spirit to fulfil the law of Christ by that love to God and man which is the reflection of God's own love, and their proper response to it.[1]

VIII. THE INFLUENCE OF ROMANS

In the summer of AD 386 Aurelius Augustinus, native of Tagaste in North Africa, and now for two years Professor of Rhetoric at Milan, sat weeping in the garden of his friend Alypius, almost persuaded to begin a new life, yet lacking the final resolution to break with the old. As he sat, he heard a child singing in a neighbouring house, *Tolle, lege! tolle, lege!* ('Take up and read! take up and read!').[2] Taking up the scroll which lay at his friend's side, he let his eyes rest on the words: 'not in rioting and drunkenness, not in chambering and wantonness, not in strife and envying. But put ye on the Lord Jesus Christ, and make not provision for the flesh, to fulfil the lusts thereof' (Rom. xiii. 13b–14). 'No further would I read,' he tells us, 'nor had I any need; instantly, at the end of this sentence, a clear light flooded my heart and all the darkness of doubt vanished away.'[3] What the Church and the world owe to this influx of light which illuminated Augustine's mind as he read these words of Paul is something beyond our power to compute.

In November 1515, Martin Luther, Augustinian monk and Professor of Sacred Theology in the University of Wittenberg, began to expound Paul's Epistle to the Romans to his students, and continued this course until the following September. As

---

[1] Cf. also P. Fairbairn, *The Revelation of Law in Scripture* (1869; reprinted Grand Rapids, 1957); C. H. Dodd, *The Bible and the Greeks* (1935), pp. 25 ff., *Gospel and Law* (1951); T. W. Manson, *Ethics and the Gospel* (1960); G. A. F. Knight, *Law and Grace* (1962); H. Kleinknecht and W. Gutbrod, *Law* (Bible Key Words, 1962).

[2] On the child's lips *tolle lege* may have been part of a game, meaning something like 'put and take'; but they conveyed another message to Augustine.

[3] *Confessions* viii. 29.

he prepared his lectures, he came more and more to appreciate the centrality of the Pauline doctrine of justification by faith. 'I greatly longed to understand Paul's Epistle to the Romans,' he wrote, 'and nothing stood in the way but that one expression, "the righteousness of God", because I took it to mean that righteousness whereby God is righteous and deals righteously in punishing the unrighteous. . . . Night and day I pondered until . . . I grasped the truth that the righteousness of God is that righteousness whereby, through grace and sheer mercy, he justifies us by faith. Thereupon I felt myself to be reborn and to have gone through open doors into paradise. The whole of Scripture took on a new meaning, and whereas before "the righteousness of God" had filled me with hate, now it became to me inexpressibly sweet in greater love. This passage of Paul became to me a gateway to heaven.'[1] The consequences of this new insight which Martin Luther gained from the study of Romans are writ large in history.[2]

In the evening of 24 May 1738, John Wesley 'went very unwillingly to a society in Aldersgate Street, where one was reading Luther's Preface to the Epistle to the Romans. About a quarter before nine,' he wrote in his journal, 'while he was describing the change which God works in the heart through faith in Christ, I felt my heart strangely warmed. I felt I did trust in Christ, Christ alone, for my salvation; and an assurance was given me that he had taken *my* sins away, even *mine*; and saved me from the law of sin and death.'[3] That critical

[1] *Luther's Works*, Weimar edition, Vol. 54, pp. 179 ff.

[2] Earlier still, in 1496, John Colet (later Dean of St. Paul's) returned from Italy to his own University of Oxford and (though he had no theological degree and was not even in deacon's orders) delivered a course of lectures on the Pauline Epistles, and primarily on Romans, which deeply impressed many who heard them. He made a clean break with the exegetical methods of the mediaeval schoolmen and expounded the text in accordance with the plain sense of the words, viewed in relation to the historical situation. Erasmus and Sir Thomas More were both influenced by Colet; to him Erasmus owed much of his insight into the true principles of biblical interpretation.

[3] *Works* (1872), Vol. I, p. 103.

moment in John Wesley's life[1] was the event above all others which launched the Evangelical Revival of the eighteenth century.

In August 1918, Karl Barth, pastor of Safenwil in Canton Aargau, Switzerland, published an exposition of the Epistle to the Romans. 'The reader', he said in his preface, 'will detect for himself that it has been written with a joyful sense of discovery. The mighty voice of Paul was new to me: and if to me, no doubt to many others also. And yet, now that my work is finished, I perceive that much remains which I have not yet heard. . . .' But what he had heard he wrote down—and that first edition of his *Römerbrief* fell 'like a bombshell on the theologians' playground'.[2] The repercussions of that explosion are with us still.

There is no telling what may happen when people begin to study the Epistle to the Romans. What happened to Augustine, Luther, Wesley and Barth launched great spiritual movements which have left their mark in world history. But similar things have happened, much more frequently, to very ordinary people as the words of this Epistle came home to them with power. So, let those who have read thus far be prepared for the consequences of reading further: you have been warned!

IX. ARGUMENT

Prologue

Paul to the Christians in Rome, greeting. I thank God for all that I hear about your faith, and I remember to pray for you constantly. I have often longed to pay you a visit, and now at last I am to have an opportunity of doing so. To preach the gospel in Rome—that is my ambition.

[1] See p. 167.
[2] The words are those of the Roman Catholic theologian Dr. Karl Adam.

A

1. I am in no way ashamed of the gospel—that message which God uses effectively for the salvation of all who believe. This is the message which reveals God's way of putting men and women right with Himself by the exercise of faith, in accordance with the statement of Scripture: 'It is he who is righteous by faith that will live.'

11. The necessity for such a message becomes clear as we contemplate the world of mankind. Not only do we see divine retribution working itself out among the pagans, whose wrong way of life is the fruit of wrong ideas about God; we see the Jewish nation too, in spite of their knowing the law of God and enjoying so many other privileges, failing to keep the law they know. In fact all mankind, Jews and Gentiles alike, are morally bankrupt before God; no-one can hope to be pronounced righteous by God on the basis of any work or merit of his own.

111. If men are to be pronounced righteous by God, it must be by His grace. And God in His grace has made it possible for man to be put in the right with Him, thanks to the redemptive work of Christ. On the ground of His sacrificial death, Christ is set before us as the One who makes full atonement for our sins; and we may appropriate the benefits of His atoning work by faith. Thus God maintains His own righteousness, and at the same time bestows righteousness on all believers in Jesus, regardless of whether they are Jews or Gentiles. The law of God is thus vindicated, and the sacred Scriptures are fulfilled.

If you consider Abraham, for example, you will find that this was the way in which he found favour with God: 'Abraham believed God', says the Scripture, 'and it was reckoned to him for righteousness.' (Nor is he an isolated case; we can see the same principle at work in the experience of David.) Mark this, too: these words were spoken of Abraham while he was still uncircumcised, showing that this way of righteousness by faith is for Gentiles as well as Jews: Abraham is thus the spiritual father of all believers, irrespective of their racial origin. And the statement that Abraham's faith was reckoned to him for righteousness means that if we believe in God, whose saving power has been revealed in the death and resurrection of Christ, it will similarly be reckoned to us for righteousness.

So then, by faith we receive God's gift of righteousness, and with it we receive also peace, joy, and the hope of glory. Thus we can endure affliction cheerfully, for God Himself is our joy. If His love, demonstrated in the sacrifice of Christ, has reconciled us to Himself, much more will the risen life of Christ procure our salvation in the day of ultimate judgment.

Once we formed part of an old solidarity of sin and death, when we lived 'in Adam' and shared the fruits of his disobedience. But now that old solidarity has been dissolved, to be replaced by the new solidarity of righteousness and life which is ours 'in Christ', the fruits of whose perfect obedience are shared by many. The law of Moses has nothing to do with this change of status; it was introduced simply that men's sinfulness might be brought into the open. But God's grace triumphed over men's sinfulness and now reigns supreme.

iv. Do I hear someone say, 'Let our sinfulness increase, then, that God's grace may be glorified yet more'? Perish the thought! For 'in Christ' we have entered upon a new life, and are dead so far as our old relation to sin is concerned. That, surely, was the meaning of our baptism. You may think of sin as a slave-owner, whose slaves we used to be. A slave is bound to obey his master's orders, but when he is dead, his master's orders do not affect him at all. Or, to change the figure slightly, when he is purchased by a new master, his former master has no further authority over him. So sin no longer has any authority over you, for now you belong to God, who has liberated you from your former slavery. Sin was a harsh master who dealt out death as his wages; God, by contrast, bestows on His servants the free gift of eternal life in Christ.

So, too, as regards the old bond of legal obligation. Those

who lived under the law were as much bound to it as a wife is bound to her husband. But as death breaks the marriage-bond, so the believer's death-with-Christ has broken the bond that formerly bound him to the law, and has set him free to be united to Christ. The law stimulated the very sins it forbade; those who are united to Christ produce the fruits of righteousness and life.

I know what I am talking about when I say that the law stimulates the very sins it forbids; it was the commandment 'Thou shalt not covet' that first brought the sin of covetousness to my notice and tempted me to commit it.

It is not the law that is at fault; it is the corrupt old nature which reacts in this way to the law. And that nature is still present, waging war against those elements in me that recognize the nobility of the law of God and desire to keep it. But my own strength is insufficient to win the victory over that old nature or to prevent it from forcing me to do its bidding. I remain divided at heart and defeated in life until I gratefully appropriate the victory that is mine through Jesus Christ my Lord.

Those who are in Christ receive His Spirit, and the Spirit of Christ sets in operation a new principle—the principle of life—which counteracts the old principle of sin and death. And those whose life is directed by the Spirit are able to fulfil the requirements of God as the law never enabled them to do. The Spirit enables the new nature to triumph over the old; the Spirit keeps the new life in being and action here and now, as one day He will transform our mortal bodies into immortal ones. The Spirit, thus directing our lives, enables us to live as the free-born sons of God; it is He who prompts us spontaneously to call God 'Father'. The day is coming when the sons of God, liberated from all that is mortal, will be manifested to the universe in the glory for which they were created; and on that day all creation will be liberated from its present frustration and share the glorious freedom of the sons of God.

For this day creation longs, and so do we, but amid our

present restrictions we have the aid and intercession of the Spirit, and the assurance that He co-operates in all things for our good, since our good is God's purpose. His purpose, which cannot fail, is to invest with glory all those whom He foreknew, foreordained, called and justified.

Let us therefore take courage, God is on our side; Christ is our almighty Saviour, and from His love no power in the universe, here or hereafter, can separate His people.

v. In all this, however, I have one unceasing sorrow: my own kinsmen, the nation specially prepared for the coming of the Saviour and the nation into which He was born, have failed to accept Him.

I do not mean that God's promises to Israel have been frustrated; throughout the course of history He has set His choice on some and passed others by. And my kinsmen have knowingly refused the way of righteousness by faith presented to them by God, preferring their own way of righteousness by law-keeping. They have not realized that Christ has put an end to the way of righteousness by law-keeping. The Gentiles have chosen the right way, while Israel has refused it.

Israel has refused it, I say, but not *all* Israel. As God had His faithful remnant in earlier days, so He has in our day a remnant chosen by His grace. And as then, so now the remnant is a promise of better things to come; Israel's refusal and consequent setting aside by God are only temporary. The Gentiles' enjoyment of gospel blessings will stimulate my kinsmen to jealousy; they will turn and embrace the gospel, and all Israel will rejoice in God's salvation.

You see, God's ultimate purpose for mankind is that all without distinction, Israel and the Gentiles alike, should enjoy these blessings. How wonderfully and wisely God works His purpose out! To Him be eternal glory!

B

In view of all that God has done for you in Christ, your lives should be lived out in His service. You are fellow-members of

64

the body of Christ; see that you discharge your respective functions for the well-being of the whole body corporate. And in all your relations with others, show the forgiving mercy of Christ.

Render all due obedience to the civil authorities; they in their way are servants of God. Let your one debt to others be the debt of love. And in the ominous times that impend, keep alert in spirit and live as Christians should.

Show great gentleness and consideration to your fellow-Christians. There are matters such as special days and certain kinds of food on which Christians do not all agree. Christian liberty is a fine thing, but it should not be asserted at the expense of Christian charity. Remember the example of Christ, how He always considered other people's interests before His own.

Epilogue

I write to you as the apostle to the Gentiles. I attach the highest importance to this ministry of mine; it fulfils the divine purpose of blessing for all nations, a purpose revealed in the Old Testament writings. I have discharged this ministry from Jerusalem to Illyricum, and now I propose to repeat the programme in Spain, and pay you a visit on my way there. First I must go to Jerusalem with a gift which the Gentile churches have contributed for the relief of their brethren there. Pray that all may go well in this respect.

Give a warm welcome to Phoebe, the bearer of this letter. Give my greetings to all my friends who are with you. Beware of those who bring divisive teachings; preserve the fine reputation you enjoy throughout the churches. My friends here send you their greetings. The grace of Christ be with you, and all glory be to God.

ANALYSIS

PROLOGUE (i. 1–15).
a. Salutation (i. 1–7).
b. Introduction (i. 8–15).

A. THE GOSPEL ACCORDING TO PAUL (i.16–xi. 36).

I. THE THEME OF THE GOSPEL: THE RIGHTEOUSNESS OF GOD REVEALED (i. 16, 17).

II. SIN AND RETRIBUTION: THE UNIVERSAL NEED DIAGNOSED (i. 18–iii. 20).
a. The pagan world (i. 18–32).
b. The moralist (ii. 1–16).
c. The Jew (ii. 17–iii. 8).
  i. Privilege brings responsibility (ii. 17–29).
  ii. Objections answered (iii. 1–8).
d. All mankind found guilty (iii. 9–20).

III. THE WAY OF RIGHTEOUSNESS: THE UNIVERSAL NEED MET (iii. 21–v. 21).
a. God's provision (iii. 21–31).
b. An Old Testament precedent (iv. 1–25).
c. The blessings which accompany justification: peace, joy, hope (v. 1–11).
d. The old and the new solidarity (v. 12–21).

IV. THE CHRISTIAN AND THE STATE (xiii. 1–7).

V. LOVE AND DUTY (xiii. 8–10).

VI. CHRISTIAN LIFE IN DAYS OF CRISIS (xiii. 11–14).

VII. CHRISTIAN LIBERTY AND CHRISTIAN CHARITY
(xiv. 1–xv. 6).
   a. Christian liberty (xiv. 1–12).
   b. Christian charity (xiv. 13–23).
   c. The example of Christ (xv. 1–6).

VIII. CHRIST AND THE GENTILES (xv. 7–13).

   EPILOGUE (xv. 14–xvi. 27).
   a. Personal narrative (xv. 14–33).
   b. Greetings to various friends (xvi. 1–16).
   c. Final exhortation (xvi. 17–20).
   d. Greetings from Paul's companions (xvi. 21–23 (24)).
   e. Doxology (xvi. 25–27).

COMMENTARY

PROLOGUE (i. 1–15)

a. Salutation (i. 1 7)

An ancient letter began with a simple salutation: 'X to Y, greetings.' Such a salutation forms the skeleton of the salutations with which most of the New Testament Epistles open, variously expanded and given a Christian emphasis.

The salutation to this letter takes a similar form: 'Paul . . . to all the beloved people of God at Rome . . . greetings.' But each part of the salutation is expanded—the sender's name, the recipients' name, and even the greetings.

1. *Paul, a servant of Jesus Christ, called to be an apostle.* The word translated servant is Gk. *doulos*, 'slave'; Paul is completely at his Master's disposal. His summons to be an apostle, a special commissioner of Christ, came directly, he claims, from 'Jesus Christ, and God the Father' (Gal. i. 1), who laid on him the responsibility of proclaiming the gospel in the Gentile world (Gal. i. 16).

Separated unto the gospel of God, that is, set apart for the ministry of the gospel, long before his conversion (cf. Gal. i. 15, where he speaks of himself as having been thus set apart from his birth). All the rich and diversified gifts of Paul's heritage (Jewish, Greek and Roman) and upbringing were foreordained by God with a view to his apostolic service. Cf. the risen Lord's description of Paul as 'a chosen vessel unto me, to bear my name before the Gentiles . . .' (Acts ix. 15). The 'gospel of God', His *euangelion*, is His joyful proclamation of the victory and exaltation of His Son, and of the consequent amnesty and liberation which men may enjoy through faith in Him. The

Old Testament background of the New Testament use of *euangelion* is found in the LXX of Isaiah xl–lxvi (especially Is. xl. 9, lii. 7, lx. 6, lxi. 1), where this noun or its cognate verb *euangelizomai* is used of the proclamation of Zion's impending release from exile. The New Testament writers treat this proclamation as foreshadowing the proclamation of the release from spiritual estrangement and bondage procured by the death and resurrection of Christ (see p. 208).

2. *Which he had promised afore by his prophets in the holy scriptures.* Cf. i. 17, iii. 21, iv. 3, 6 ff., for elaborations of this statement.

3. *Concerning his Son Jesus Christ our Lord.* This phrase, which expresses the subject-matter of 'the gospel of God', introduces a short confessional summary (verses 3, 4) which may have been as familiar to the Roman Christians as to Paul himself; it is likely, however, that Paul has recast its wording so as to bring out certain necessary emphases.

Which was made (better 'who was born', RV) *of the seed of David according to the flesh.* The Davidic descent of Jesus was clearly an element in earliest Christian preaching and confession. Jesus Himself appears to have laid no weight on it, but He did not refuse the designation 'Son of David' when it was applied to Him, as by blind Bartimaeus (Mk. x. 47 f.). His question about the scribal exegesis of Psalm cx. 1 (Mk. xii. 35–37) should not be construed as a repudiation of Davidic descent.

4. *Declared to be the Son of God with power.* The word rendered *declared* (*horizō*) has the fuller force of 'appointed' (it is used in Acts x. 42, xvii. 31 of Christ's appointment as Judge of all). Paul does not mean that Jesus *became* the Son of God by the resurrection, but that He who during His earthly ministry 'was the Son of God in weakness and lowliness' became by the resurrection 'the Son of God in power' (A. Nygren, *ad loc.*).

Similarly Peter at Pentecost concluded his proclamation of the resurrection and exaltation of Christ with the words: 'Therefore let all the house of Israel know assuredly, that God hath made that same Jesus, whom ye have crucified, both Lord and Christ' (Acts ii. 36). The phrase *with power* (*en dunamei*) appears also in Mark ix. 1, where the coming of the kingdom of God 'with power' is probably the direct sequel to the death and vindication of Jesus.

According to the spirit of holiness. There is an obvious antithesis between 'according to the flesh' and 'according to the spirit'. But when Paul states the second member of this antithesis, he makes it plain which 'spirit' he means by adding the genitive 'of holiness'. *The spirit of holiness* is the regular Hebrew way of saying 'the Holy Spirit'; and Paul here reproduces the Hebrew idiom in Greek. By the present antithesis of 'flesh' and 'spirit' he 'plainly . . . does not allude to the two natures of our Lord, but to *the two states* of humiliation and exaltation.'[1] It is one and the same Son of God who appears in humiliation and exaltation alike; but His Davidic descent, a matter of glory 'according to the flesh', is now seen nevertheless to belong to the phase of His humiliation, and to be absorbed and transcended by the surpassing glory of His exaltation, by which He has inaugurated the age of the Spirit. The outpouring and ministry of the Spirit attest the enthronement of Jesus as 'Son of God with power'.

By the resurrection from the dead. Better, 'by the resurrection of the dead' (RV). The phrase is literally 'in consequence of the resurrection of dead ones'; the plural 'dead ones' may be taken as an instance of what grammarians call the 'generalizing plural'. Exactly the same phrase appears, with reference to the resurrection of Christ, in Acts xxvi. 23 (RV, 'by the resurrection of the dead'). So here it is Christ's own resurrection that is referred to, and not (as some have thought) His raising of

[1] G. Smeaton, *The Doctrine of the Holy Spirit* (1882), p. 72. 'The antithetic terms "flesh", "spirit" do not divide His substance but unfold the economy of His manifestation' (W. Manson, 'Notes on the Argument of Romans' in *New Testament Essays in Memory of T. W. Manson*, 1959, p. 153).

Lazarus and others—still less the phenomenon described in Matthew xxvii. 52 f. But Christ's resurrection is denoted by a phrase which hints at the future resurrection of the people of Christ; His resurrection is the first instalment of 'the resurrection of the dead', as viii. 11 makes plain (cf. 1 Cor. xv. 20–23).

5. *Grace and apostleship.* This is probably a hendiadys, meaning 'the grace (or heavenly gift) of apostleship'; compare the references in xii. 6 to the 'gifts differing according to the grace that is given to us', and in xv. 15 to the 'grace' given to Paul by God to be a 'minister of Jesus Christ to the Gentiles'.

For obedience to the faith. Better, 'unto obedience of faith' (RV), i.e. to bring about the obedience that is based on faith in Christ. 'The faith' here is not the gospel, the body of doctrine presented for belief, but the belief itself. (Cf. xv. 18, xvi. 26.)

Among all nations. RV, 'among all the nations'. This phrase indicates Paul's special vocation to be the apostle to the Gentiles. The Greek word *ethnē* (like its Hebrew equivalent *goyim*) is variously rendered 'nations', 'Gentiles' or 'heathen' (for this last cf. Gal. i. 16, ii. 9, iii. 8, AV).

6. *Among whom are ye also.* This probably means not only that the Roman church was situated in the Gentile world but that its membership was now predominantly Gentile.

The called of Jesus Christ; or, 'called to be Jesus Christ's' (RV). (Cf. viii. 28, 30.)

7. *In Rome.* See textual note on pp. 25 f.

Called to be saints, i.e. 'saints by divine vocation', summoned by God to be His holy people, set apart for Himself. There are indications here and there in the New Testament that 'the saints' was a designation (very probably a self-designation) of those Jewish believers (cf. Rom. xv. 25; Eph. ii. 19) who looked on themselves as 'the saints of the most High' who were destined to receive royal and judicial authority from God (Dn. vii. 22, 27). Paul insists on applying the same designation to Gentile believers, concorporate with their brethren of Jewish race.

Grace to you and peace. The words 'Grace and peace', so common in Paul's salutations, probably unite the Greek and Jewish modes of greeting. The Greek says *Chaire!*—which literally means 'Rejoice!' The Jew says *Shalom!*[1]—'Peace!' Only, in uniting these two modes of greeting, Paul changes *chaire* to the similarly-sounding and more distinctively Christian word *charis*, 'grace'. The grace of God is His free love and unmerited favour to men, imparted through Christ; the peace of God is the well-being which they enjoy through His grace.

From God our Father, and the Lord Jesus Christ. This spontaneous and repeated collocation of Christ with God bears witness to the place which Christ had in the thoughts and worship of Paul and other early Christians.

b. Introduction (i. 8–15)

Having thus introduced himself and his theme, Paul explains why he is writing to them now. News that he has received about the high and renowned quality of their faith calls forth deep thanksgiving from Paul, and he assures them of their constant place in his prayers. The churches for which he had primary responsibility—those which he himself had founded—made heavy and continual calls upon his time and thought, but he could remember before God other churches too, and not least the church of the capital. He tells them of his long-standing desire and prayer for the opportunity of visiting them; and now, after earlier hindrances, it appeared that his prayer was about to be answered. He hopes not only to impart a blessing to the Roman Christians, but to receive one for himself through his fellowship with them. And while he has no thought of asserting his apostolic authority in Rome, he looks forward to preaching the gospel there and making some converts at Rome as in the rest of the Gentile world. The preaching of the gospel is in his blood, and he cannot refrain from it; he is

---

[1] Compare the Arabic *salaam*, which has the same meaning.

never 'off duty' but must constantly be at it, discharging a little more of that debt which he owes to all mankind— a debt which he will never fully discharge so long as he lives.

8. *I thank my God through Jesus Christ.* As it is through Christ that God's grace is conveyed to men (verse 5), so it is through Christ that men's gratitude is conveyed to God. The mediatorship of Christ is exercised both Godward and manward. (See p. 226, n. 1.)

Your faith is spoken of throughout the whole world. Cf. 1 Thessalonians i. 8, 'in every place your faith to God-ward is spread abroad.' In both passages Paul thinks more particularly of all the places where Christianity had been established (see also note on x. 18, p. 209).

9. *Whom I serve with my spirit.* NEB, 'to whom I offer the humble service of my spirit.'

Without ceasing I make mention of you always in my prayers. (Cf. Eph. i. 16; Phil. i. 3 f.; Col. i. 3; 1 Thes. i. 2; 2 Tim. i. 3; Phm. 4.) That Paul should pray regularly for his own converts is what we might expect, but it is evident from this passage that his prayers went beyond his immediate circle of personal acquaintance and apostolic responsibility.

10. *At length* (and 'oftentimes', verse 13). Of these earlier occasions when Paul had hoped or planned to visit Rome we have no independent information.

12. *That I may be comforted* (RSV, 'encouraged') *together with you.* This would correct any impression given by verse 11 that he would be the benefactor and they the beneficiaries. He hopes to receive help as well as to give it during his purposed visit to Rome.

13. *I would not have you ignorant, brethren.* A favourite Pauline expression, meaning 'I want you to know' (cf. xi. 25; 1 Cor. x. 1, xii. 1; 2 Cor. i. 8; 1 Thes. iv. 13).

Was let hitherto. RV, 'was hindered hitherto'; this archaic use of the word 'let' (cf. 2 Thes. ii. 7) survives in the semi-legal phrase 'without let or hindrance'.

14. *Both to the Greeks, and to the Barbarians.* To the Greeks, all non-Greeks were 'barbarians' (*barbaroi*, a word which probably imitated the unintelligible sound of foreign languages).

15. *At Rome.* See textual note on p. 26.

A. The Gospel according to Paul (i. 16–xi. 36)

I. THE THEME OF THE GOSPEL: THE RIGHTEOUSNESS OF GOD REVEALED (i. 16, 17)

'Believe me,' Paul goes on, 'I have no reason to be ashamed of the gospel I preach. No indeed; it is the powerful means which God employs for the salvation of all who believe—the Jew first, and the Gentile also. And why is this so? Because in this gospel there is a revelation of God's way of righteousness—a way of righteousness based on the principle of faith and presented to men for their acceptance by faith. It was of this righteousness that the prophet said: "He who is righteous by faith shall live." '

To understand the sense in which the gospel is said to reveal God's righteousness it is necessary to bear in mind some facts about the concept of righteousness in the Old Testament, which forms the chief background of Paul's thought and language.

'The ideas of right and wrong among the Hebrews are forensic ideas; that is, the Hebrew always thinks of the right and the wrong as if they were to be settled before a judge. Righteousness is to the Hebrew not so much a moral quality as a legal status. The word "righteous" (*ṣaddîq*) means simply "in the right", and the word "wicked" (*rashaʿ*) means "in the wrong". "I have sinned this time", says Pharaoh, "Jehovah is in the right (A.V. righteous), and I and my people are in the wrong (A.V. wicked)", Ex. ix. 27. Jehovah is always in the right, for He is not only sovereign but self-consistent. He is the fountain of righteousness . . . the consistent will of Jehovah is the law of Israel.'[1]

God is Himself righteous, and those men and women are righteous who are 'in the right'[2] in relation to God and His law. When, therefore, the righteousness of God is revealed in the gospel, it is revealed in a twofold manner. The gospel tells us first how men and women, sinners as they are, can come to be 'in the right' with God; and second how God's personal righteousness is vindicated in the very act of declaring sinful men and women 'righteous'. This second aspect of the matter is not dealt with immediately, but the former is expanded sufficiently to show that the principle on which God brings people into the right with Himself is the principle of faith, and for this statement Old Testament authority is adduced in the words of Habakkuk ii. 4, 'the just shall live by his faith'. Habakkuk ii. 4 may be called the 'text' of this Epistle; what follows is in large measure an exposition of the prophet's words.

16. *I am not ashamed of the gospel of Christ.* The genitive 'of Christ' is absent from the best attested text (cf. RV, RSV, NEB).

---

[1] W. R. Smith, *The Prophets of Israel* (1882), pp. 71 f. So, when Isaiah condemns the corrupt judges who 'justify the wicked for reward, and take away the righteousness of the righteous from him' (Is. v. 23), he refers to legal decisions; he does not mean that the righteous man is made intrinsically unrighteous. But God's word is a self-fulfilling word: when *He* declares a man righteous, that man *is* righteous. See also G. Quell and G. Schrenk, *Righteousness* (Bible Key Words, 1951).

[2] Or, to use a modern expression, 'in the clear'—with which we may compare the insistence by God in the Old Testament that He 'will by no means clear the guilty' (Ex. xxxiv. 7; see also note on Rom. iv. 5 on pp. 114 f.). Discussing a new Neo-Melanesian ('Pidgin') version of the New Testament for New Guinea, H. K. Moulton says: 'We salute strokes of genius such as the translation of "Justification": "God 'e say 'im alrite" ' (*The Bible in the World*, Jan.–Feb. 1963, p. 10).

'I am not ashamed' is an instance of the figure of speech called litotes: Paul means that he glories in the gospel and counts it a high honour to proclaim it.

17. *For therein is the righteousness of God revealed.* A remarkable anticipation of this twofold sense of 'the righteousness of God' —(a) His personal righteousness and (b) the righteousness with which He justifies sinners on the ground of faith—appears in the Qumran literature. 'By His righteousness my sin is blotted out. . . . If I stumble because of fleshly iniquity, my judgment is in the righteousness of God which shall stand for ever. . . . By His mercy He has caused me to approach and by His lovingkindnesses He brings my judgment near. By His true righteousness He judges me and by His abundant goodness He makes atonement for all my iniquities. By His righteousness He cleanses me from the impurity of mortal man and from the sin of the sons of men, that I may praise God for His righteousness and the Most High for His glory.'[1]

From faith to faith. NEB mg., 'It is based on faith and addressed to faith' seems preferable to NEB text, 'a way that starts from faith and ends in faith'. According to J. Murray, Paul's purpose in the repetition here and in iii. 22 ('through faith in Jesus Christ unto . . . all them that believe') is 'to accent the fact that not only does the righteousness of God bear savingly upon us *through faith* but also that it bears savingly upon *every one* who believes.'[2]

The just shall live by faith. These words from Habakkuk ii. 4 (where MT has '. . . by his faith'[3]) had already been quoted by Paul in Galatians iii. 11 to prove that it is not by the law that a man is justified before God. They appear again, together

[1] From the 'Hymn of the Initiants'; cf. G. Vermes, *The Dead Sea Scrolls in English* (1962), pp. 89–94.
[2] *The Epistle to the Romans*, I (Grand Rapids, 1959), p. 32; cf. also his Excursus, 'From Faith to Faith', pp. 363 ff.
[3] LXX reads 'the righteous one will live by my faithfulness' (or 'by faith in me'); one MS tradition, however, attaches the pronoun 'my' to 'righteous one', whence Heb. x. 38 (RV, RSV), 'my righteous one shall live by faith'.

with part of their context, in Hebrews x. 38 to encourage the readers of that Epistle to press on and not lose heart. Heb. *'emunah*, translated 'faith' in Habakkuk ii. 4 (LXX *pistis*) means 'steadfastness' or 'fidelity'; in the Habakkuk passage this steadfastness or fidelity is based on a firm belief in God and His word, and it is this firm belief that Paul understands by the term.

Habakkuk, crying out to God against the oppression under which his people groaned (late in the seventh century BC), received the divine assurance that wickedness would not triumph indefinitely, that righteousness would ultimately be vindicated, and the earth would 'be filled with the knowledge of the glory of the Lord, as the waters cover the sea' (Hab. ii. 14). This vision might be slow of realization, but it would certainly be fulfilled. Meanwhile, the righteous would endure to the end, directing their lives by a loyalty to God inspired by faith in His promise.

In the Qumran commentary on Habakkuk this oracle is applied to 'all the doers of the law in the house of Judah, whom God will save from the place of judgment because of their toil and their fidelity to the Teacher of Righteousness' (cf. G. Vermes, *op. cit.*, p. 237). In the Talmud (TB *Makkoth* 24a) 'the just shall live by his faith' is quoted alongside Amos v. 4, 'Seek ye me, and ye shall live', as an example of how the whole law may be summed up in one sentence. 'Perhaps "seek" (in Amos v. 4) means "seek the whole Torah"?' asked Rabbi Nachman ben Isaac. 'No', was the reply of Rabbi Shimlai; 'Habakkuk came after him and reduced it to one sentence, as it is written, "The just shall live by his faith".'

When Paul takes up Habakkuk's words and sees in them the central truth of the gospel, he appears to give them the sense, 'it is he who is righteous (justified) by faith that will live'. The terms of Habakkuk's oracle are sufficiently general to make room for Paul's application of them—an application which, far from doing violence to the prophet's intention, expresses the abiding validity of his message.

For Paul, as for many other Jews, 'life' (especially eternal life) and 'salvation' were practically synonymous. If Paul's self-designation as 'a Hebrew of Hebrews' (Phil. iii. 5, RV) means (as is probable) that he was the Aramaic-speaking child of Aramaic-speaking parents, he would very likely, when speaking his native tongue, employ the same word *ḥayyē*[1] for both 'life' and 'salvation'. 'It is he who is righteous (justified) by faith that will live' means, therefore, 'it is he who is righteous (justified) by faith that will be saved'. For Paul, life in the sense of salvation begins with justification but goes beyond it (cf. v. 9 f.); it includes sanctification (the subject of Rom. vi–viii) and is consummated in final glory (v. 2, viii. 30). In this comprehensive sense 'salvation' may well be regarded as the key 'to unlock the wards of Paul's theology'.[2]

II. SIN AND RETRIBUTION: THE UNIVERSAL NEED DIAGNOSED (i. 18–iii. 20)

a. The pagan world (i. 18–32)

Before Paul elaborates further the way in which God's way of righteousness is set forth in the gospel, he shows why it is so urgently necessary that the way to get right with God should be known. As things are, men are 'in the wrong' with God, and His wrath is revealed against them. There is a moral law in life that men are left to the consequences of their own freely chosen course of action, and unless this tendency is reversed by divine grace, their situation will go from bad to worse. Three times over the words of doom recur: 'wherefore God . . . gave them up . . .' (verses 24, 26, 28).

Paul's aim is to show that the whole of humanity is morally bankrupt, unable to claim a favourable verdict at the judg-

---

[1] In the Syriac New Testament this is the word used in the two phrases 'the words of this life' (Acts v. 20) and 'the word of this salvation' (Acts xiii. 26).

[2] A. M. Hunter, *Interpreting Paul's Gospel* (1954), p. 9, following C. A. A. Scott, *Christianity according to St. Paul* (1927), pp. 16 ff.

ment bar of God, desperately in need of His mercy and pardon.

He begins with an area of human life whose moral bankruptcy was a matter of general agreement among moralists of the day—the great mass of contemporary paganism. The picture which he draws of it is ugly enough in all conscience, but no uglier than the picture of it which we have from contemporary pagan literature. What is the cause, he asks, of this appalling condition which has developed in the world? Whence come these shameful perversions, this internecine enmity between man and man? It all arises, he says, from wrong ideas about God. And these wrong ideas of God did not arise innocently; the knowledge of the true God was accessible to men, but they closed their minds to it. Instead of appreciating the glory of the Creator by contemplating the universe which He created, they gave to created things that glory which belonged to God alone. Idolatry is the source of immorality. So the author of Wisdom had already said:

'For the idea of making idols was the beginning
of fornication,
and the invention of them was the corruption of
life' (Wisdom xiv. 12).

With Paul's language about the visible creation as a source of knowledge concerning the nature of its invisible Creator (verses 19, 20) we may compare the speech at Lystra in Acts xiv. 15–17 and especially that at Athens in Acts xvii. 22–31. There is a difference of emphasis between the speech at Athens and Paul's argument here, but no contradiction: there Paul was trying to gain a hearing from pagans, whereas here he is writing to established Christians. In the Athenian speech God's creation of the world and His providential arrangement of the seasons of the year and the habitable zones of the earth for man's well-being are intended to lead men to 'feel after him, and find him' (Acts xvii. 27). If, nevertheless, they acknowledge that He is an 'unknown God' to them, their self-confessed ignorance is not condoned as venial, although God in His mercy overlooked 'the times of ignorance' before the coming of Christ.

The culpable character of man's ignorance of God is emphasized still more here: it is a deliberate ignorance. Men had the knowledge of God available to them but 'did not like to retain God in their knowledge' (verse 28). The truth was accessible to them, but they suppressed it unrighteously and embraced 'the lie' in preference to it. Therefore 'God gave them up' to the consequences of their choice. And precisely here He has manifested His 'wrath'—that principle of retribution which must operate in a moral universe.

To a man so convinced as Paul was that the world was created and controlled by a personal God of righteousness and mercy, this retribution could not be an impersonal principle; it was God's own wrath. If it is felt that the word 'wrath' is scarcely suitable to be used in relation to God, it is probably because wrath as we know it in human life so constantly involves sinful, self-regarding passion. Not so with God: His 'wrath' is the response of His holiness to wickedness and rebellion. Paul would certainly have agreed with Isaiah in describing the execution of God's wrath as His 'strange work' (Is. xxviii. 21), to which He girds Himself slowly and reluctantly; indeed, he sets forth the revelation of God's wrath here as the background to His 'proper work' of mercy, which is so congenial to His character that He speeds with joyful haste to lavish it upon undeserving penitents.

But even if the picture of divine retribution, operating as a stern principle in human life, does provide a background to the everlasting mercy, it is a real and terrible background, and one that must seriously be reckoned with.

18. *The wrath of God is revealed.* Not in the gospel (in which the saving 'righteousness of God' is revealed) but in the facts of human experience: 'the history of the world is the judgment of the world' (Schiller). The revelation of 'the wrath to come' at the end-time (1 Thes. i. 10) is anticipated by the revelation of the same principle in the on-going life of the world. 'The idea that God is angry is no more anthropopathic than the thought that God is love. The reason why the idea of the divine anger is always exposed to misunderstanding is because among men anger is ethically wrong. And yet, even among men do we not speak of a "righteous anger"?'[1] The exposure of pagan idolatry and immorality in these verses follows lines laid down in such works of Jewish apologetic as the book of Wisdom quoted above (see especially Wisdom xii–xiv), and the *Epistle of Aristeas*; it recurs in the Christian apologists of the second century AD (e.g. the author of the *Epistle to Diognetus*, Aristides, Tatian, Athenagoras, and the *Preaching of Peter* mentioned by Clement of Alexandria (*Stromata* vi. 5)).

Who hold the truth in unrighteousness. Better 'who hold down the truth in unrighteousness' (RV); 'In their wickedness they are stifling the truth' (NEB). 'The truth' is more precisely defined in verse 25 as 'the truth of God'.

20. *From the creation of the world.* 'From' in the sense of 'ever since' (RSV).

Are clearly seen, being understood. Gk. *nooumena kathoratai*, where the former verb refers strictly to the intelligence and the latter to physical sight. 'Both the verbs . . . describe how, on contemplating God's works, man can grasp enough of His nature to prevent him from the error of identifying any of the created things with the Creator, enabling him to keep his conception of the Deity free from idolatry.'[2]

22. *They became fools.* As in the Wisdom literature of the Old Testament, folly (cf. 'their foolish heart' in verse 21) implies moral obtuseness rather than mere deficiency in intelligence.

23. *And changed the glory of the uncorruptible God into an image made like to . . . fourfooted beasts.* Cf. Psalm cvi. 20: 'Thus they

[1] E. Brunner, *The Mediator* (1934), p. 478.
[2] B. Gärtner, *The Areopagus Speech and Natural Revelation* (Copenhagen, 1955), p. 137.

changed their glory into the similitude of an ox that eateth grass' (a reference to the worship of the golden calf). Here the language is generalized. The threefold classification of animals (cf. Gn. i. 20–25) and the terms 'glory', 'image' and 'likeness' (RV; cf. Gn. i. 26) suggest that 'Paul's account of man's wickedness has been deliberately stated in terms of the Biblical narrative of Adam's fall.'[1]

24, 26, 28. *God gave them up.* Cf. Acts vii. 42 where, because of the idolatrous tendencies of the Israelites, 'God . . . gave them up to worship the host of heaven'. An impressive modern statement of this principle of divine retribution is provided by C. S. Lewis in *The Problem of Pain* (1940), pp. 115 f.; the lost, he says, 'enjoy forever the horrible freedom they have demanded, and are therefore self-enslaved'.

27. *That recompence of their error which was meet.* NEB renders rightly 'the fitting wage of such perversion'. In modern English 'error' is too weak a noun to render *planē* in a context like this; cf. Jude 11, where 'the error (*planē*) of Balaam' is the idolatry and fornication of Baal-peor into which the Israelites were seduced by his counsel (Nu. xxv. 1 ff., xxxi. 16).

28. *A reprobate mind.* NEB, 'their own depraved reason'.

To do those things which are not convenient. The word translated 'convenient' (*kathēkon*) was a technical term of Stoic philosophy, denoting what constituted proper or fitting conduct. Cf. Ephesians v. 4 where various 'unseemly' practices are described in AV as things 'which are not convenient'.

29. *Being filled with all unrighteousness* . . . The best-attested text omits 'fornication' from this catalogue of vices. 'Debate' means rather 'strife' (RV).

---

[1] M. D. Hooker, 'Adam in Romans i', *NTS*, VI (1959–60), p. 301.

30. *Despiteful.* That is, behaving with insulting and humiliating arrogance to those who are not powerful enough to retaliate.

31. *Implacable.* This adjective is absent from the best-attested text.

b. The moralist (ii. 1–16)

Paul's style is that appropriate to the type of composition which the ancients called the *diatribé*, in which questions or objections are put into the mouth of an imagined critic in order to be answered or demolished.

We can almost envisage him as he dictates his letter to Tertius, suddenly picking out the complacent individual who has been enjoying the exposure of those sins he 'has no mind to', and telling him that he is no better than anyone else. He imagines an interruption by some objector, and turns to refute his objection, first rebuking it with 'God forbid!' ('Perish the thought!') and then giving a reasoned reply to it. He starts a new phase of his argument with such a rhetorical question as 'What shall we say then?'[1] And all the time his thought races ahead of his words so that his words have to leap over a gap in order to catch up with his thought. We can only try to imagine how Tertius's pen kept up with the apostle's words. No wonder that, especially in impassioned moments, his Greek is full of breaks in construction and unfinished sentences.

We know that there was another side to the pagan world of the first century than that which Paul has portrayed in the preceding paragraphs. What about a man like Paul's illustrious contemporary Seneca, the Stoic moralist, the tutor of Nero?[2] Seneca might have listened to Paul's indictment and said,

---

[1] Cf. iii. 5, iv. 1, vi. 1, vii. 7, viii. 31, ix. 14, 30; and the similar 'Thou wilt say (to me) then' in ix. 19, xi. 19.

[2] See J. N. Sevenster, *Paul and Seneca* (Leiden, 1962).

'Yes, that is perfectly true of great masses of mankind, and I concur in the judgment which you pass on them—but there are others, of course, like myself, who deplore these tendencies as much as you do.'

Paul imagines someone intervening in terms like these, and he addresses the supposed objector: 'My good sir, in judging others you are passing judgment on yourself, whoever you may be, for in principle you do the same things as you condemn in them.' And how apt this reply would have been to a man like Seneca! For Seneca could write so effectively on the good life that Christian writers of later days were prone to call him 'our own Seneca'.[1] Not only did he exalt the great moral virtues; he exposed hypocrisy, he preached the equality of all men, he acknowledged the pervasive character of evil ('all vices exist in all men, though all vices do not stand out prominently in each man'), he practised and inculcated daily self-examination, he ridiculed vulgar idolatry, he assumed the role of a moral guide. But too often he tolerated in himself vices not so different from those which he condemned in others—the most flagrant instance being his connivance at Nero's murder of his mother Agrippina.

Even in this section of chapter ii, however, as more explicitly from verse 17 onwards, Paul is thinking chiefly of a Jewish critic. Such denunciation of pagan idolatry as we find in chapter i was common form in Jewish propaganda. Religious Jews found ample scope for passing adverse moral judgment on their Gentile neighbours.

That Paul has a Jewish critic more particularly in mind is evident from his repetition of the phrase 'to the Jew first, and also to the Greek' (see ii. 9, 10), in which he emphasizes that the Jews are the first to experience the judgment of God as well as the first to receive the good news of His saving grace (i. 16). This twofold primacy of the people of Israel, in salvation and judgment alike, was taught by the prophets in earlier

---

[1] *'Seneca saepe noster'*, says Tertullian; 'Seneca, so often one of ourselves' (*On the Soul* 20).

days; eight centuries before this Epistle was written, for example, we hear the word of God to His people through Amos: 'You only have I known of all the families of the earth: therefore I will punish you for all your iniquities' (Am. iii. 2).

We have seen how the portrayal of pagan idolatry in chapter i echoes the book of Wisdom. Similarly now, in turning to convict the Jews of *their* moral bankruptcy, Paul takes up themes from the same book. According to the author of Wisdom, God afflicted the Gentiles (such as the Egyptian oppressors of Israel in the days of Moses) by way of retribution for their wickedness, whereas the same afflictions were remedial in intention when they fell upon the Israelites:

'For thou didst test them as a father does in warning,
but thou didst examine the ungodly as a stern king
does in condemnation . . .
So while chastening us thou scourgest our enemies
ten thousand times more,
so that we may meditate upon thy goodness when we judge,
and when we are judged we may expect mercy'
(Wisdom xi. 10, xii. 22).

'Agreed,' says Paul; 'you do well to acknowledge God's goodness to you in spite of all your disobedience, but do you not realize that His goodness is intended to give you an opportunity to repent? Beware of despising His goodness and presuming on His mercy. If, instead of repenting, you maintain a hard and impenitent heart, then be sure that you are simply storing up for yourself an accumulation of divine wrath which will be discharged upon you at the judgment day.'

When divine judgment comes, it will be absolutely impartial. God 'will render to every man according to his deeds' (ii. 6). While, for Paul, forgiveness and eternal life are utterly of God's grace, divine judgment (as uniformly in the Bible) is always passed according to what men have done. Every material factor is taken into consideration. Men are held accountable for such knowledge of the truth as was accessible to them, not for what was not accessible. Jews, he says, will be judged on the basis of the written law, for *they* had access to that source of divine knowledge. Gentiles will be judged by another criterion, for among them too God did not leave Himself without witness. If the knowledge of God's character was available to them through the starry heavens above (cf. i. 20), it was also available to them through the moral law within. They did not have the law of Moses, as the Jews had, but they had the law of conscience, the distinction between right and wrong, engraved upon their hearts. When they violate that law, says Paul, they know that they are doing wrong, and by that knowledge they will be judged on the day when the inmost secrets of men's hearts are brought to light. Whether the will of God is known by the law of Moses or by the voice of conscience, knowledge of His will is not enough; it is the doing of His will that counts.

4. *The goodness of God leadeth thee to repentance.* Cf. Wisdom xi. 23: 'But thou art merciful to all, for thou canst do all things, and dost overlook men's sins, that they may repent.'

6. *Who will render to every man according to his deeds.* Cf. Job xxxiv. 11; Psalm lxii. 12; Proverbs xxiv. 12; Jeremiah xvii. 10, xxxii. 19 for Old Testament statements of this principle; it recurs in the New Testament in Matthew xvi. 27; 1 Corinthians iii. 8; 2 Corinthians v. 10; Revelation ii. 23, xx. 12, xxii. 12. See also Romans xiv. 12.

7. *To them who by patient continuance in well doing seek for glory and honour and immortality, eternal life.* Paul is not teaching salvation by works here, but emphasizing the impartiality of God as between Jew and Gentile; cf. Peter's surprised confession in Acts x. 34 f.: 'Of a truth I perceive that God is no respecter of persons: but in every nation (among Gentiles as well as Jews) he that feareth him, and worketh righteousness, is accepted with him.' God showed His acceptance of Cornelius, to whom these words were spoken, by sending Peter to him with the gospel, that he and his household might be saved (Acts xi. 14).

8. *Unto them that are contentious* ('factious', RV, RSV). The NEB rendering, 'for those who are governed by selfish ambition', does more justice to the basic sense of *eritheia*, which is derived from *erithos* ('hireling'). Even in antiquity, however, its meaning tended to be assimilated to that of *eris*, 'strife' ('contention', 'faction').

11. *There is no respect of persons with God.* 'Respect of persons' (lit. 'lifting the face', *prosōpolēmpsia*) is favouritism or partiality (cf. Dt. x. 17; 2 Ch. xix. 7; Jb. xxxiv. 19; Acts x. 34; Gal. ii. 6; Eph. vi. 9; Col. iii. 25; 1 Pet. i. 17). Our Lord stated the same truth when He said of the Father in heaven: 'he maketh his sun to rise on the evil and on the good, and sendeth rain on the just and on the unjust' (Mt. v. 45).

12. *As many as have sinned without law shall also perish without law.* Sin unchecked leads to perdition one way or another, but Gentiles will not be condemned for not conforming to a law-code which was not accessible to them. The principle is laid down that men are judged by the light that is available to them, not by light that is not available.

13. *The doers of the law shall be justified.* Paul may have in mind Leviticus xviii. 5, 'Ye shall therefore keep my statutes, and my judgments: which if a man *do*, he shall live in them'— a scripture which he quotes later in x. 5. The course of his argument indicates that while a man would be justified if he were a 'doer' of the law, yet, since no-one does it perfectly, there is no justification that way. The antithesis between merely hearing the law and doing it is elaborated in James i. 22–25. The expression 'the doers of the law' is found in Qumran literature; cf. p. 80 above.

15. *Which show the work of the law written in their heart.* A verbal parallel to the prophecy of the new covenant in Jeremiah xxxi. 33 (see p. 161); although Paul is not thinking of the new covenant here.

Their conscience also bearing witness. The word 'conscience' (*suneidēsis*) is not current in classical Greek. It belonged to the vernacular tongue and attained literary status only a short time before the beginning of the Christian era. It meant 'consciousness of right or wrong doing', but Paul uses it (and perhaps he was the first to do so) in the sense of an independent witness within, which examines and passes judgment on a man's conduct. In a Christian this examination and judgment are specially accurate because his conscience is enlightened by the Holy Spirit (cf. ix. 1).

c. The Jew (ii. 17–iii. 8)

i. Privilege brings responsibility (ii. 17–29). In ii. 17 Paul addresses the moralizer explicitly as a Jew. 'You bear the honoured name of Jew', he says, 'your possession of the law gives you confidence, you glory in the fact that it is the true God whom you worship and whose will you know.' Perhaps there is a further echo of Wisdom here:

'For even if we sin we are thine, knowing thy power;
but we will not sin, because we know that we are
accounted thine.
For to know thee is complete righteousness,
and to know thy power is the root of immortality'
(Wisdom xv. 2, 3).

'You approve the more excellent way,' Paul continues, 'for you have learned it from the law. You regard yourself as better taught than those lesser breeds without the law; you consider yourself a guide to the blind and an instructor of the foolish.

'But why not take an honest look at yourself? Have *you* no defects? You know the law, but do you keep it? You say "Thou

shalt not steal"; but do you never steal? You say "Thou shalt
not commit adultery"; but do you always keep that commandment? You detest idols, but do you never rob temples? You
glory in the law, but in fact your disobedience to the law brings
you and the God whom you worship into disrepute among the
pagans.

'To be a Jew will do a man good in the sight of God only
if he keeps the law. A Jew who breaks the law is no better than
a Gentile. And conversely, a Gentile who keeps the law's
requirements is as good in the sight of God as any law-abiding
Jew. Indeed, a Gentile who keeps the law of God will condemn
a Jew who breaks it, no matter how well-versed that Jew may
be in the sacred Scriptures, no matter how canonically circumcised he is. You see, it is not a matter of natural descent
and an external mark like circumcision. The word "Jew"
means "praise", and the true Jew is the man whose life is
praiseworthy by God's standards, the man whose heart is pure
in God's sight, whose circumcision is the inward circumcision
of the heart. He is the true Jew, I say—the truly praiseworthy
man—and his praise is not a matter of human applause, but
of divine approval.'

17. *Behold, thou art called a Jew.* For 'behold' (*ide*) the better
attested reading is 'but if' (*ei de*); cf. RV, RSV.

18. *Knowest his will.* Lit., 'knowest the will'; God's will is
'the will' *par excellence.* Cf. 1 Maccabees iii. 60, RV: 'as may be
the will in heaven, so shall he do.'

Approvest the things that are more excellent. The word *diapheronta*
means primarily 'things that differ' and then also 'things that
differ from others by surpassing them', i.e. 'things that excel'.
AV, RV and RSV accept this latter sense here; NEB prefers the
former sense ('you are aware of moral distinctions'). The same
phrase appears in Philippians i. 10 (AV, 'that ye may approve
things that are excellent'; NEB, 'may thus bring you the gift
of true discrimination').

20. *The form of knowledge and of the truth.* That is, the formulation or embodiment of knowledge and truth.

22. *Dost thou commit sacrilege?* Lit., 'do you rob temples?' The Greek verb is *hierosuleō*. What Paul has in mind is difficult to say; perhaps he refers to some scandalous incident like that of AD 19 recorded by Josephus (*Antiquities* xviii. 81 ff.), when four Jews of Rome, led by one who professed to teach the Jewish faith to interested Gentiles, persuaded a noble Roman lady, a convert to Judaism, to make a munificent contribution to the temple at Jerusalem, but appropriated it for their own uses. When the matter came to light, the Emperor Tiberius expelled all resident Jews from Rome (see p. 13). An incident like this brought the honoured name of 'Jew' into disrepute among the Gentiles.

24. *For the name of God is blasphemed among the Gentiles through you, as it is written.* The reference is to Isaiah lii. 5: 'my name continually every day is blasphemed' ('despised', RSV). The sad plight of the Jews in exile caused the Gentiles to speak lightly of their God, imagining that He was unable to help His people. Now it is not His people's misfortune, but their misconduct, that causes the Gentiles to conclude that the God of such people cannot be of much account. Members of the Qumran community were warned to be careful in their dealings with Gentiles, 'lest they blaspheme'.[1]

25. *Circumcision verily profiteth, if thou keep the law.* Cf. Galatians v. 3: 'every man that is circumcised . . . is a debtor to do the whole law.' Circumcision, performed as a legal requirement, puts a man under liability to keep all the rest of the law, whether it be accepted in later life, as by proselytes (which is what Paul has in view in Galatians), or administered to Jewish infants (which is what he has in mind here). But as neither

[1] G. Vermes, *The Dead Sea Scrolls in English*, p. 114.

93

category of circumcised persons can keep the whole law but must inevitably default on their liability, he adds: *but if thou be a breaker of the law, thy circumcision is made uncircumcision.*

This lesson had already been taught in part by Jeremiah: 'Behold, the days are coming, says the Lord, when I will punish all those who are circumcised but yet uncircumcised—Egypt, Judah, Edom, the sons of Ammon, Moab . . . for all these nations are uncircumcised, and all the house of Israel is uncircumcised in heart' (Je. ix. 25 f., RSV). Israel's neighbours for the most part practised circumcision (the Philistines were a notorious exception); but the circumcision of Israel's neighbours was not a sign of God's covenant, as Israelite circumcision was intended to be. Yet, if Israel and Judah departed in heart from God, their physical circumcision would be in God's sight no better than that of their neighbours—so far as any religious value was concerned, it was no circumcision at all. Cf. Deuteronomy x. 16: 'Circumcise therefore the foreskin of your heart, and be no more stiffnecked.'

But Paul goes further than Jeremiah: not only is circumcision reckoned as uncircumcision, if it is not accompanied by heart-devotion; but uncircumcision is reckoned as spiritual circumcision, if nevertheless obedience to God is practised.

27. *Shall not uncircumcision which is by nature, if it fulfil the law, judge thee?* That is, the shortcomings of an unworthy Jew will be shown up by the example of a Gentile who, with none of the distinctive Jewish privileges, nevertheless pleases God.

29. *Whose praise is not of men, but of God.* The Jews derived their name from their ancestor Judah (Heb. *Yehudah*), whose name is associated in the Old Testament with the verb *yadah*, 'praise'; cf. his mother's words at his birth, 'Now will I praise the Lord' (Gn. xxix. 35), and his father's deathbed blessing, 'Judah, thou art he whom thy brethren shall praise' (Gn. xlix. 8).

94

ii. Objections answered (iii. 1–8). Here Paul imagines someone breaking into his argument and saying: 'Well then, if it is being a Jew inwardly that counts, if it is the "circumcision" of the heart that matters, is there any advantage in belonging to the Jewish nation, or in being physically circumcised?' We might have expected Paul to answer this supposed question quite categorically: 'None at all!' But, rather to our surprise, he replies: 'Much every way.' Of course it is an advantage to belong to the Jewish nation. Think of all the privileges[1] granted by God to that nation—privileges in which other nations had no part. It would be asking too much of Paul to expect him to deny his ancestral heritage, especially as now he had found in the gospel to which his life was devoted the fulfilment of the age-old hope of his nation.

Among the ancestral privileges of Israel, Paul reckons as of first importance the fact that they were the custodians of 'the oracles of God'. To have the revelation of God's will and purpose committed to them was a high honour indeed. But if it was a high honour, it carried with it a great responsibility. If they proved unfaithful to their trust, their case was worse than that of the nations to which God had not revealed Himself.

Now in fact Israel had not proved faithful to their trust. And this might have been put as an objection to Paul when he argued that it was a great advantage to belong to the nation which had received the oracles of God. But his reply is that men's faithlessness never alters God's faithfulness or frustrates His purpose. The unfaithfulness of men simply sets His truth in relief: His righteousness is always vindicated over against their unrighteousness.

Then a further objection is dealt with. Someone may say: 'If my faithlessness sets God's faithfulness in bolder relief; if my unrighteousness establishes His righteousness; why should He find fault with me? He is really the gainer by my sin; why should He exact retribution for it?' This objection seems so

[1] A further list is given in Rom. ix. 4 f.

foolish to Paul that he apologizes for mentioning it. The answer is plain: God is the moral Governor of the universe, the Judge of all the earth; how could He exercise that function which is inseparable from His Godhead if He did not exact retribution for sin?

The supposed objector, however, is persistent, and repeats his argument in different words: 'If my falsehood makes God's truth shine more brightly by contrast, it redounds to His glory; why then does He insist on condemning me as a sinner? The end—God's glory—is good; why is the means—my sin—counted wrong? Surely the end justifies the means?'

'As a matter of fact,' says Paul, 'that is precisely what some people say my gospel amounts to; but their charge is not only slanderous, it stands self-condemned because it is such a contradiction in terms.' The gospel of justification by faith, apart from 'works of righteousness', has always called forth this criticism, but the criticism is amply refuted by the fact that the same gospel insists unequivocally that the 'fruits of righteousness' must follow justification.

4. *Let God be true, but every man a liar.* The second clause may echo the psalmist's dismayed outcry, 'All men are liars' (Ps. cxvi. 11). 'Let every man be convicted of falsehood,' says Paul, 'rather than impugn the veracity of God.'

That thou mightest be justified in thy sayings, and mightest overcome when thou art judged. 'That thou mightest be vindicated when thou speakest, and mightest win the case when thou *enterest into judgment*' (*krinesthai* should be taken as middle voice here, not passive). The quotation is from Psalm li. 4, where MT means simply '. . . when thou judgest' (so AV, RV; cf. RSV, 'so that thou art justified in thy sentence and blameless in thy judgment').

8. *Let us do evil, that good may come.* It is easy to see how Paul's gospel could be misrepresented as though it taught this. Those, whether Jews or Christians, who regarded religion as essentially a matter of law (however liberally 'law' might be interpreted), could not but conclude that a doctrine of justification 'apart from the deeds of the law' undermined the place of law in man's approach to God, and therewith undermined religion and morality.

Whose damnation is just. This may mean either 'To condemn such men as these is surely no injustice' (NEB) or 'such an argument is quite properly condemned' (J. B. Phillips). The relative pronoun translated 'whose' may refer back either to the people who say such things or to the things they say. For the real answer to the accusation see vi. 2 ff. On the English word 'damnation' see notes on xiii. 2, xiv. 23 (pp. 237, 253).

d. All mankind found guilty (iii. 9-20)

'Well then,' the interlocutor proceeds, 'you have said that it *is* an advantage to belong to the Jewish nation. Does it not follow that we are superior to those Gentiles who have not the privileges that we have?' 'No indeed,' says Paul; 'we may have received greater advantages, but we are in fact in no better case than they are. They have sinned, it is true; but then, so have we. All men, Jews and Gentiles alike, are bound to plead guilty before the bar of God. The situation is well summed up in the words of Scripture.'

Here Paul adduces a catena of six Old Testament quotations in which the general sinfulness of men is summed up. The catena comes in here to clinch a case already established by various arguments. If the quotations were examined one by one, it would be necessary to relate them to their historical contexts; some at least of them had a particular rather than a universal reference. But the general picture which they present here rounds off the case which Paul has been building up. And if he supposes an objection to his use of these quotations, the objection is not that he has detached them from their historical contexts, but that they refer to the wicked Gentiles only, not to Israel. 'No,' he replies, 'these quotations are taken from the Jewish scriptures, and therefore the people whom they have primarily in view are Jews.' What is written in the law (here meaning the Hebrew Bible as a whole) applies naturally to the people of the law. The law brings out men's sinfulness but does nothing to cure it. Jews as well as Gentiles, then, have to confess themselves morally bankrupt. If there is any hope for either group, it must be found in the mercy of God, and not in any claim that men or nations may try to establish upon Him. Because of the universal fact of sin, the way of acceptance with God by reason of our works of righteousness is closed—the notice is clearly worded: 'No Road This Way.'

9. *No, in no wise* (*ou pantōs*). There is a *prima facie* clash between Paul's answer here to 'are we (Jews) better than they (Gentiles)?' and his answer in verse 2 to 'what advantage then hath the Jew?'—'Much every way.' But 'Much every way' has reference to the privileges which the Jews, as the elect nation, enjoyed; 'No, in no wise' relates to their standing before God. Privileges or no privileges, Jews and Gentiles stand equally in need of His grace.

10–12. *There is none righteous . . . there is none that doeth good, no, not one.* Quoted from Psalm xiv. 1c, 2b–3 (repeated in Ps. liii. 1c, 2b–3).

13. *Their throat is an open sepulchre; with their tongues they have used deceit.* Quoted from Psalm v. 9.
The poison of asps is under their lips. Quoted from Psalm cxl. 3.

14. *Whose mouth is full of cursing and bitterness.* Quoted from Psalm x. 7.

15–17. *Their feet are swift to shed blood . . . the way of peace have they not known.* Quoted from Isaiah lix. 7 f.

18. *There is no fear of God before their eyes.* Quoted from Psalm xxxvi. 1.

19. *What things soever the law saith.* The reference is to the preceding quotations; but since none of them is taken from the Law in the stricter sense (the Pentateuch)—they are all drawn from the Psalter, with one exception, which comes from Isaiah—'law' here must mean the Hebrew Scriptures in general. See p. 52.

20. *By the deeds of the law there shall no flesh be justified in his sight.* A free quotation and amplification of Psalm cxliii. 2: 'enter not into judgment with thy servant (cf. Ps. li. 4, quoted in verse 4 above); for in thy sight shall no man living be justified.' Cf. Galatians ii. 16 ('a man is not justified by the works of the law'), iii. 11 ('no man is justified by the law in the sight of God'). Paul adds the reason why no-one can be justified in God's sight 'by the deeds of the law'; it is that *by the law is the knowledge of sin.* This point is repeated and expanded in v. 20, vii. 7 ff. See pp. 56, 128, 147 ff.

III. THE WAY OF RIGHTEOUSNESS: THE UNIVERSAL NEED MET (iii. 21–v. 21)

a. God's provision (iii. 21–31)

But now a new way to acceptance with God has been opened up, a completely different way from that of legal obedience. Yet this is no new-fangled way, thought up by ourselves; it has ample witness borne to it in advance in the Old Testament writings—in the Law and the Prophets. It is the way of faith in Jesus Christ, and it lies open to all who believe in Him, Jew and Gentile alike. We have already seen that there is no difference between these two divisions of mankind, since both Jews and Gentiles have sinned and fall short of God's glory, the true end for which God created them. But by this new way both Jews and Gentiles can be brought into a right relationship with God, can have the assurance of acceptance by Him

99

and receive His free pardon. They receive it freely, by His sheer grace; they receive it because of the redemptive work accomplished by Christ. It is Christ whom God has set forth before our eyes as the One whose sacrificial death has atoned for our guilt and removed the imminent retribution which our rebellion against God has incurred. What Christ has thus procured for us we can make effectively our own by faith.

This, then, is the way in which God has demonstrated His righteousness—He has vindicated His own character and at the same time He bestows a righteous status on sinful men. This is why God, in His patient dealing with men, could pass over the sins which they committed before the coming of Christ, instead of exacting the full penalty; He was showing them mercy in prospect of the demonstration of His righteousness at this present epoch. And this demonstration shows us how God remains perfectly righteous Himself while He pardons those who believe in Jesus and puts them in the right before His judgment bar.

If this is so, who has any right to boast? All ground of boasting in one's personal righteousness is removed, not by the law of works but by the principle of faith. Where Jew and Gentile alike are justified by God's grace, through no merit of their own, none can say: 'I achieved this by my own effort.' The conclusion of Paul's argument is that a man is set right in God's sight by faith, quite apart from the works prescribed by the law. If acceptance by God could be attained only by keeping the Jewish law, then God would be in a special sense the God of the Jews. But He is as much the Gentiles' God as the God of the Jews, for in the gospel one and the same way of righteousness is opened up for both. He will accept Jews by virtue of their faith, and He will accept Gentiles on exactly the same basis.

For Paul, the division between Jews and Gentiles was the basic division in the human race. He himself was a Jew by birth and upbringing and had been taught to look upon non-

Jews as benighted sinners, lacking the knowledge of God's law by which alone it was possible to gain acceptance in His sight. And indeed the cleavage between Jew and Gentile was one of the most unbridgeable in the ancient world. There are other cleavages which may bulk larger in our eyes today—cleavages of race, nationality, class and colour, whose recalcitrance presents us with far more acute problems than the division between Jew and Gentile. But Paul's argument is as valid in the light of contemporary cleavages as it was in the face of those of his own day: there is no difference between east and west, black and white, for all are equally in need of the free mercy of God, and all may receive His mercy on the same terms.

The Roman poet Horace, laying down some lines of guidance for writers of tragedies in his day, criticizes those who resort too readily to the device of a *deus ex machina* to solve the knotty problems which have developed in the course of the plot. 'Do not bring a god on to the stage', he says, 'unless the problem is one that deserves a god to solve it' (*nec deus intersit, nisi dignus uindice nodus inciderit*).[1]

Luther took up these words and applied them to the forgiveness of sins: here, he said, is a problem which needs God to solve it (*nodus Deo uindice dignus*).[2] True, for sinful man cannot solve it, though he desperately needs a solution to it; it is his problem; it is he who has to be forgiven. And what Paul tells us here is that the problem has been worthily solved by the grace of God, who has set forth Christ as the solution, the means of forgiveness, the guarantor of our acceptance. All that is required of sinful man is that he should embrace by faith what God's grace has provided.

It may be asked, however, whether God's law is not nullified by this principle of faith. Far from it, says Paul. By this

---

[1] Horace, *Ars Poetica*, 191 f.
[2] I owe the quotation from Luther to T. R. Glover, *Jesus in the Experience of Men* (1921), p. 72.

principle of faith the law is upheld, sin is condemned, righteousness is vindicated, and—the Old Testament Scriptures are fulfilled. This he now proceeds to show.

21. *The righteousness of God.* God's way of righteousness or justification. See the quotation from Luther on p. 59.

22. *By faith of Jesus Christ.* That is, 'through faith in Jesus Christ' (RV, RSV); the genitive is 'objective'.

Unto all and upon all them that believe. The best-attested text omits 'and upon all' (cf. RV, RSV, NEB).

There is no difference. As here there is no distinction between Jews and Gentiles (or between any other categories of mankind) in respect of sin, so in Romans x. 12 'there is no difference' between them in respect of the mercy of God.

23. *All have sinned.* The two words (*pantes hēmarton*) are identical with those at the end of Romans v. 12, but whereas there the context suggests that the reference is to the participation of all in 'man's first disobedience', here we have rather a statement of the fact that all men, as individuals, have sinned.

Come short of the glory of God. The traditional interpretation of Isaiah xliii. 7, 'I have created him for my glory' (which is said, in the context, of 'every one that is called by my name'), applies it to mankind in general. Through sin man falls short of the ideal which God had in view when He brought him into being. Cf. Romans v. 2.

24. *Being justified freely by his grace.* Paul's hope, before he became a Christian, was that by dint of perseverance in observing the law of God, he might at length be pronounced righteous by God when he stood before His judgment-seat. But in this way of righteousness apart from the law, the procedure is reversed: God pronounces a man righteous at the beginning of his course, not at the end of it. If He pronounces him righteous at the beginning of his course, it cannot be on the basis of works which he has not yet done; such justification is, on the contrary, 'an act of God's free grace, wherein he pardoneth all our sins, and accepteth us as righteous in his sight' (*Westminster Shorter Catechism*).

And when it comes to the question of our *acceptance* by God, how much more satisfying it is to know oneself 'justified freely by his grace' than to hope to be justified by 'the deeds of the law'. In the latter case, I can never be really satisfied that I have 'made the grade', that my behaviour has been sufficiently meritorious to win the divine approval. Even if I do the best I can (and the trouble is, I do not always do that), how can I be certain that my best comes within measurable distance of God's requirement? I may hope, but I can never be sure. But if God in sheer grace assures me of His acceptance in advance, and I gladly embrace His assurance, then I can go on to do His will without always worrying whether I am doing it adequately or not. In fact, to the end of the chapter I shall be an 'unprofitable servant', but I know whom I have believed:

'He owns me for His child;
I can no longer fear.'

In Isaiah xl–lv Israel's deliverance from their exile in Babylonia is their 'justification'—and God's. 'Only in the Lord . . . is righteousness and strength' (Is. xlv. 24, RV), and His righteousness and strength are shown in His people's deliverance: 'In the Lord shall all the seed of Israel be *justified*, and shall glory' (Is. xlv. 25); 'this is the heritage of the servants of the Lord, and their righteousness is of me, saith the Lord' (Is. liv. 17). Why is their deliverance their justification? Had they not deserved their punishment of exile? Yes; Jerusalem had 'received of the Lord's hand double for all her sins' (Is. xl. 2); but God's free grace restored them, and their restoration was both His victorious vindication of His name among the nations (Is. xlii. 13, xlviii. 9–11) and His people's salvation.

Through the redemption that is in Christ Jesus. The redemption (*apolutrōsis*[1]) is the act of buying a slave out of bondage in order to set him free. Here too the merciful dealings of God with Israel provide an Old Testament background to Paul's language, whether we think of Israel's redemption from Egyptian bondage (Ex. xv. 13; Ps. lxxvii. 15, lxxviii. 35) or their later deliverance from the Babylonian exile (Is. xli. 14, xliii. 1). The grace of God which 'justifies' those who believe has been actively manifested in the redemptive work of Christ.

'As I was walking up and down in the house, as a man in a most woful state, that word of God took hold of my heart, Ye are "justified freely by his grace, through the redemption that is in Christ Jesus" (Rom. iii. 24). But oh, what a turn it made upon me! Now was I as one awakened out of some troublesome sleep and dream, and listening to this heavenly sentence, I was as if I had heard it thus expounded to me: Sinner, thou thinkest that because of thy sins and infirmities I cannot save thy soul, but behold my Son is by me, and upon him I look, and not on thee, and will deal with thee according as I am pleased with him' (John Bunyan, *Grace Abounding*, §§257–258).

25. *Whom God hath set forth to be a propitiation through faith in his blood.* Note the more accurate punctuation in RV, 'whom God set forth to be a propitiation, through faith, by his blood'; the two phrases 'through faith' and 'in his blood' are independently epexegetic of 'propitiation'. The key word is 'propitiation', the AV and RV rendering of *hilastērion*. This may be taken either as the accusative singular masculine of the adjective *hilastērios* ('propitiatory'), in agreement with 'whom' (*hon*); or, more probably, as the neuter substantive *hilastērion*, used in LXX to denote 'place of propitiation', 'place where sins

---

[1] Cf. E. K. Simpson, *Words Worth Weighing in the Greek New Testament* (1946), pp. 8 f. In LXX this word and its cognates are frequently used of redemption by one who is under a special obligation because of kinship or some comparable relation to the person redeemed—by a *go'el*, to use the Hebrew word (e.g. Lv. xxv. 47—49).

are blotted out'. The commonest LXX usage of the word is as the equivalent of Heb. *kapporeth*, the golden slab or 'mercy seat' which covered the ark in the holy of holies (so more than twenty times in the Pentateuch). In Ezekiel xliii. 14 ff. it is used (5 times) to render Heb. *'azarah*, the 'ledge' (so RSV; AV and RV have 'settle') around the altar of burnt-offering in Ezekiel's temple.

The noun *hilastērion* is related to the verb *hilaskomai*, which in pagan Greek means 'placate' or 'make gracious', but in LXX takes on the meaning of Heb. *kipper* ('make atonement') and cognate words, among which is included *kapporeth*, 'mercy seat', 'place where sins are atoned for *or* wiped out'. Exception has been taken to the use of the verb 'propitiate' and the substantive 'propitiation' in rendering these Greek words into English in the New Testament, on the ground that these English terms smack of placating or appeasing.[1] We may compare the avoidance of these terms here in RSV ('whom God put forward as an expiation by his blood, to be received by faith') and NEB ('God designed him to be the means of expiating sin by his sacrificial death, effective through faith'). But if *hilaskomai*, *hilastērion* and their cognates acquired a new meaning from their biblical context, we may expect that by dint of long usage the English words 'propitiate' and 'propitiation' have acquired a biblical meaning in the same way. In any case, misunderstanding is excluded by Paul's insistence that it is God, not sinful man, who has provided this *hilastērion*. The Old Testament similarly ascribes the initiative in this matter to God's grace: 'For the life of the flesh is in the blood: and *I have given it to you* upon the altar to make atonement (Heb. *kipper*; LXX *exilaskomai*) for your souls; for it is the blood that maketh atonement by reason of the life' (Lv. xvii. 11, RV). It is an Old Testament passage like this, incidentally, which explains Paul's usage of the expression 'his blood' in the

---

[1] Cf. C. H. Dodd, *ad loc.*; also in *The Bible and the Greeks* (1935), pp. 82 ff.; for a defence of the rendering 'propitiation', cf. L. Morris, *The Apostolic Preaching of the Cross* (1955), pp. 125 ff.

present verse and justifies the NEB interpretation of it as 'his sacrificial death'.

The death of Christ, then, is the means by which God does away with His people's sin—not symbolically, as in the ritual of Leviticus xvi in which the material mercy-seat figured, but *really*. And *really* in a twofold sense; the sin has been removed not only from the believer's conscience, on which it lay as an intolerable burden, but from the presence of God. We may compare the way in which the writer to the Hebrews associates the sacrifice of Christ with the realization of Jeremiah's prophecy of the new covenant: 'their sins and their iniquities will I remember no more' (Heb. viii. 12, quoting Je. xxxi. 34).

Once we do justice to the initiative of divine grace in the efficacy of Christ's self-offering, there is no reason why we should exclude from the meaning of *hilastērion* the averting of divine wrath, if the context so warrants. And the context does warrant the inclusion of the averting of divine wrath in the meaning of *hilastērion* in Romans iii. 25. Paul has already said in i. 18 that 'the wrath of God (NEB, "divine retribution") is revealed from heaven against all ungodliness and unrighteousness of men'; how then is this 'wrath' to be removed? The *hilastērion* which God has provided in Christ not only removes the ungodliness and unrighteousness of men but at the same time averts the wrath or retribution which is the inevitable sequel to such attitudes and actions in a moral universe.

On the whole, it seems best to take *hilastērion* here as a substantive, alluding to the mercy-seat as the place where atonement was made in Old Testament days, before the Babylonian exile. Paul 'informs us that in Christ there was exhibited in reality that which was given figuratively to the Jews' (Calvin).[1]

---

[1] Cf. J. N. Darby's New Translation: 'whom God has set forth a mercy-seat'. For a strong argument in favour of this interpretation see T. W, Manson, 'Hilastērion', *JTS*, XLVI (1945), pp. 1 ff. Cf. also E. K. Simpson, *Words Worth Weighing in the Greek New Testament*, pp. 10 ff.; W. D. Davies. *Paul and Rabbinic Judaism* (1948), pp. 237 ff. Against this interpretation see G. A. Deissmann, *Encyclopaedia Biblica*, III (1902), cols. 3033–3035 (*s.v.* 'Mercy Seat').

The contrast between the old *hilastērion* and the new is pointed by the words 'whom God hath set forth'. The old *hilastērion* was concealed behind the curtain which separated the holy of holies from the outer sanctuary, and was seen by none except the high priest, on the annual day of atonement. But in Christ 'the mercy-seat is no longer kept in the sacred seclusion of the most holy place: it is brought out into the midst of the rough and tumble of the world and set up before the eyes of hostile, contemptuous, or indifferent crowds' (T. W. Manson). The phrase *through faith* indicates how the saving benefits of the gospel mercy-seat are appropriated. The accompanying phrase *in his blood* is not dependent on *faith*, as AV implies; it refers to the sacrificial death of Christ as the means by which the one effective atonement for sin is made (cf. Rom. v. 8 f.: 'while we were yet sinners, Christ died for us . . . being now justified by his blood, we shall be saved from wrath through him').

Paul has thus pressed into service the language of the law-court ('justified'), the slave-market ('redemption') and the temple ('mercy-seat') to do justice to the fullness of God's gracious act in Christ. Pardon, liberation, atonement—all are made available to men by His free initiative, and may be appropriated by faith. And faith in this sense is not a kind of work that is specially meritorious in God's sight; it is that simple and open-hearted attitude to God which takes Him at His word and gratefully accepts His grace.

To declare his righteousness for the remission (*paresis*, 'passing over') *of sins that are past, through the forbearance of God*. That is, 'to demonstrate that God was not unrighteous when He passed over sins committed in earlier days, in the period of His forbearance'. The redemption accomplished by Christ has retrospective as well as prospective efficacy; He is the 'mercy-seat' for all mankind—'the propitiation for our sins', as a later New Testament writer puts it (using a word from the same stock as *hilastērion*), 'and not for ours only; but also for the whole world' (1 Jn. ii. 2, RV). With the description of the ages before Christ as the period of God's forbearance may be compared Paul's proclamation to the Athenians: 'The times of ignorance therefore God overlooked; but now . . .' (Acts xvii. 30, RV). Although the moral problem here may not be as obvious to the modern mind as it was to Paul's, yet to pass over wrong is as much an act of injustice on the part of a judge as to condemn the innocent, and 'shall not the Judge of all the earth do right?'

26. *That he might be just, and the justifier of him which believeth in Jesus.* In the self-offering of Christ, God's own righteousness is vindicated and the believing sinner is justified. For Christ occupies a unique position as God's representative with man and man's representative with God. As the representative Man He absorbs the judgment incurred by human sin; as the representative of God He conveys God's pardoning grace to men. The phrase 'just, and the justifier' recalls Isaiah xlv. 21 ('a just God and a Saviour'); Zechariah ix. 9 ('just, and having salvation').[1]

28. *Without the deeds of the law.* That is, 'apart from the works of the law'. Paul does not mean that the works of the law should not be kept, but that even when a man keeps them tolerably well, he is not thereby justified in God's sight. He is cutting the ground from beneath the feet of those who say, 'I always do the best I can . . . I try to live a decent life . . . I pay twenty shillings in the pound, and what more can God expect of me?'

Luther underlines 'without the works of the law' by adding the adverb 'alone': 'man becomes righteous without works of

---

[1] R. St. J. Parry (*Cambridge Greek Testament*, 1912, *ad loc.*) translates Paul's phrase 'just even when He justifies him that hath faith in Jesus'. R. V. G. Tasker approves this rendering because it brings out the tension between the justice and mercy of God involved in the mystery of atonement ('The Doctrine of Justification by Faith in the Epistle to the Romans', *EQ*, XXIV, 1952, pp. 37 ff., esp. pp. 43 f.).

the law, through faith alone.'[1] For this 'addition' to the text
he was severely criticized by some. He attached little importance to such critics whom he described as 'making a tremendous fuss because the word *sola*, "alone", is not in Paul's
text, and this addition . . . to God's Word is not to be tolerated'.
But in the sense in which Luther intended the word 'alone' it
summarized accurately the apostle's meaning: it is by faith
alone, and not by legal works, or by any other fancied means
of justification, that men receive the righteous status which
God by His grace bestows.[2] When this is grasped, it can be seen
that men have no ground for self-congratulation as they
contemplate the way of salvation; it is *sola gratia, sola fide, soli
Deo gloria* ('by grace alone, through faith alone; to God alone
be the glory').

Yet, while men are justified in this sense by faith alone, 'the
faith which justifies is not alone'; it is, as Paul says in Galatians
v. 6, 'faith which worketh by love'—and just how it so works
is set out in practical detail in chapters xii–xv of this Epistle.
But this belongs to a later stage of the argument; at present the
important thing to emphasize is that it is by faith, not by what
he *does*, that a man receives the justifying grace of God.

31. *We establish the law.* If Paul had expressed himself in
Hebrew, he would have used the verb *qiyyem*. This is the verb
used in the frequent rabbinical assertion that Abraham 'fulfilled the law'. Paul may have some such assertion in mind,
so he goes on to argue that Abraham did indeed fulfil or
'establish' the law, but according to the testimony of Scripture
he established it through receiving God's gift of righteousness
by faith.

---

[1] 'So halten wir nun dafür, dass der Mensch gerecht werde ohne des
Gesetzes Werke, allein durch den Glauben.' A parallel to this use of 'faith'
in the sense of 'faith alone' is adduced from Diogenes Laertius in W. Bauer,
Griechisch-Deutsches Wörterbuch zu den Schriften des NTs[5] (Berlin, 1958), *s.v.*
pistis.
[2] Cf. the rendering of RVmg. and NEB in Gal. ii. 16: '*but only* through
faith in Christ Jesus'. See p. 38, n. 2.

b. An Old Testament precedent (iv. 1–25)

Paul has already said that this 'righteousness of God apart from law' is attested by the Law and the Prophets—i.e. by the Old Testament. This must now be shown, and Paul undertakes to show it principally from the story of Abraham, with a side-glance at the experience of David.

Of all the righteous men in the Old Testament record, none could surpass Abraham—'Abraham my friend', as God calls him in Isaiah xli. 8. God's own testimony to Abraham is recorded in Genesis xxvi. 5: 'Abraham obeyed my voice, and kept my charge, my commandments, my statutes, and my laws.' What about Abraham, then? If it is a man's works that justify him in God's sight, Abraham would have a better chance than most—and he would be entitled to take some credit for it. But that is not God's way. God's way is clearly indicated in the record of Genesis xv. 6: when the divine promise came to Abraham, in spite of the extreme improbability of its fulfilment by all natural considerations, 'he believed in the Lord; and he counted it to him for righteousness'. Paul had already made this statement the basis of an *ad hominem* argument to the churches of Galatia, when they were disposed to abandon the principle of faith for that of legal works. Now he makes it the text for a more systematic exposition of the principle of faith.

Abraham's acceptance with God was clearly not based on his works, good as they were. Paul's argument is not merely textual and verbal, dependent on a selection of Genesis xv. 6 in preference to other texts from those chapters in Genesis which might have pointed in the other direction. For Abraham's good works, his obedience to the divine commandments, were the fruit of his unquestioning faith in God; had he not first believed the promises of God he would never have conducted his life from then on in the light of what he knew of God's will. No, when God gave Abraham a promise (in the fulfilment of which, incidentally, the whole gospel was bound up), he simply took God at His word, and acted accordingly.

Now mark the difference, Paul goes on. When a man works for some reward, that reward is his due; when he simply puts his trust in God, it is by pure grace that his faith is reckoned to him for righteousness.

Nor is Abraham an isolated instance of the principle of justification by faith; another Old Testament example lies ready to hand in the case of David. Paul now quotes the opening words of Psalm xxxii in which the psalmist, in joyful relief at the assurance of divine pardon, exclaims:

> 'How happy are those whose transgressions have been for-given, whose sins have been covered over!
> How happy is the man to whose account the Lord reckons no sin!'

Here, plainly, is someone else, of whose sin there could be no question, who yet has received God's free pardon and who is pronounced 'not guilty' before the tribunal of heaven. And if we examine the remainder of the psalm to discover the ground on which he was acquitted, it appears that he simply acknow-ledged his guilt and cast himself in faith upon the mercy of God.

To return now to Abraham, a further crucial question arises. What relation, if any, lies between Abraham's being justified by faith and the rite of circumcision? For a Jew, this was a point of great importance: circumcision was the outward and visible sign of God's covenant with Abraham. No uncircum-cised man could claim any share in that covenant; circumcision was held to entitle Jews or Gentile proselytes[1] to all its privi-leges, apart from those who by wilful repudiation of the divine commandments cut themselves off from the covenant people.

---

[1] Even proselytes, who might have been regarded as Abraham's children by adoption, were not permitted to call him 'our father'; in the synagogue liturgy they called the patriarchs *'your* fathers' when Jews by birth referred to them as *'our* fathers'.

One might, therefore, think of a Jew as replying to Paul's argument here: 'Granted that Abraham's faith in God was credited to him for righteousness, this principle is applicable only to Abraham and his circumcised offspring.' But Paul has a ready answer to this. What was Abraham's condition when he was justified by faith? Was he circumcised, or uncircumcised? To this there could be only one answer. He was uncircumcised. The covenant of circumcision was not introduced until a later stage in Abraham's life (Gn. xvii. 10 ff.)—at least fourteen years later, according to the Genesis chronology.[1] When at last Abraham was circumcised, his circumcision was but the external seal of that righteous status which God had bestowed upon him long before, by virtue of his faith. Quite plainly it was faith, not circumcision, that God required of him. Here then is hope for the Gentiles: the case of Abraham shows that circumcision or uncircumcision is irrelevant to a man's status before God.

Abraham, accordingly, is the true father of all who, like him, believe in God and take Him at His word. He is the father of uncircumcised believers, for he was himself uncircumcised when his faith was reckoned to him for righteousness; he is the father of circumcised believers too, not so much on the ground of their circumcision as on the ground of their faith.

If circumcision had nothing to do with Abraham's justification by God, with all the promised blessings that accompanied it, the law had even less to do with it. For, as Paul had pointed out to the Galatians, the law was given 430 years later than God's promise to Abraham and could not invalidate it or restrict its scope (Gal. iii. 17). If, long after the promise was given, it had been made conditional on obedience to a law which was not mentioned in the original terms of the promise, the whole basis of the promise would have been nullified. The promise was a promise of blessing, and is fulfilled in the gospel.

[1] Thirteen years after Ishmael's birth (Gn. xvii. 25; cf. xvii. 1, 24, with xvi. 16). And the narrative sequence of Genesis implies that the conception of Ishmael (Gn. xvi. 3 f.) was the sequel to the promise of Gn. xv. 4, that Abraham would yet have a son of his own to be his heir.

The Mosaic law does indeed pronounce a blessing on those who keep it, but at the same time it invokes a curse on those who break it. And in view of the universal failure to keep the law, the curse is more prominent and relevant than the blessing: *the law worketh wrath* (verse 15). A sinful tendency may indeed be present in the absence of any law; but it takes a legal enactment to crystallize that tendency into a positive transgression or breach of law. And for each such transgression the law fixes an appropriate penalty; this is inherent in the principle of retribution which is inseparable from the idea of law. The law need not fix rewards for those who keep it, but it does necessarily lay down penalties for those who break it. A gracious promise such as God made to Abraham belongs to a totally different realm from law.

No; Abraham's justification and attendant blessings were based on his faith in God; they were not earned by merit or effort on his part (as would have been the case had they been conditional on law-keeping) but bestowed on him by God's grace. And the principle on which God thus dealt with Abraham extends to his descendants—not to his natural descendants as such, for they have become subject to the obligations of the law, but to his spiritual descendants, those who follow the example of Abraham's faith. This, says Paul, is what God meant when he gave him the name Abraham in place of Abram, as he was formerly called, and said: 'I have made thee a father of many nations.' These comprise all, Jews and Gentiles alike, who believe in God; Abraham is the father of all believers.

Consider, too, the quality of Abraham's faith. It was faith in the God who brings the dead to life, who calls non-existent things as though they actually existed—and gives them a real existence by doing so. When God told him that his descendants would be as numerous as the stars, Abraham was still childless. Not only so, but he was beyond the age at which a man may reasonably hope to be a father, and Sarah his wife was even more certainly beyond the age of motherhood. Abraham did not shut his eyes to these unfavourable circumstances; he took them all into careful consideration. But when he set over against them the promise of God, he found that the certainty of God's ability and will to fulfil His promise outweighed them all. Having nothing to go upon but the bare word of God, he relied on that, in the face of all the opposite indications which pressed upon him from every side. In fact his faith was strengthened by the very force of the obstacles which lay in its path. And his faith won him the favour of God.

Now, adds Paul, the statement that Abraham's faith was counted to him for righteousness does not apply to Abraham alone; the principle which it enshrines holds good for all believers in God, and especially for believers in God as He is reveáled in the gospel—the God who raised Jesus from the dead. Jesus had been delivered up to death because of His people's sins; but God raised Him up to procure their justification.

1. *What shall we say then that Abraham . . . hath found?* The answer, as Paul proceeds to show, is: 'justification by faith, through God's grace'.

Abraham our father ('forefather', RV, RSV), *as pertaining to the flesh.* In view of the qualifying phrase (cf. i. 3, ix. 3, 5), 'our' means 'of us Jews'; in another sense (iv. 11 f., 16 f.), Abraham is the father of all believers, whether they be Jews or Gentiles by birth.

3. *Abraham believed God, and it was counted unto him for righteousness.* Cf. Galatians iii. 6 for Paul's earlier quotation and application of Genesis xv. 6.

5. *To him that . . . believeth on him that justifieth the ungodly, his faith is counted for righteousness.* Abraham was not ungodly; he was a man of outstanding piety and righteousness. But the principle on which Abraham was justified, being one that excludes the idea of accumulating merit by works of piety and righteousness, is one that is equally available to the ungodly, who have no such works to rely on. So the tax-collector in the parable went home 'justified' rather than the Pharisee, not because his merit was greater (it was incomparably less) but because, realizing the futility of self-reliance, he cast himself entirely on God's grace (Lk. xviii. 9 ff.). The description of God as one 'that justifieth the ungodly' is so paradoxical as to be startling—not to say shocking. In the Old Testament the acquittal of the guilty and the condemnation of the innocent are alike repeatedly denounced as the acts of unjust judges. Indeed, for the better guidance of judges in the administration of justice the God of Israel offers Himself as their example. 'I will not justify the wicked', He says in Exodus xxiii. 7; in the LXX version the same Greek words are used to convey what God forbids in the law as Paul here uses to declare what God in fact does in the gospel. No wonder that he thought it necessary above to maintain that God, in justifying sinners, nevertheless preserves His own character untarnished. Once they are justified, indeed, the ungodly cease to be ungodly, but it is not on the basis of any foreseen amendment of their ways that they are justified. If we fail to appreciate the moral problem involved in God's forgiving grace, it may be because we have 'not yet considered how serious a thing is sin'.[1] The solution to the paradox is provided in Romans v. 6.

6. *David also.* Psalm xxxii is ascribed to David in the titles of both MT and LXX. There is a formal link between Psalm xxxii. 1 f., quoted in verses 7, 8, and Genesis xv. 6, quoted in verse 3, in that the verb 'impute' (RV, 'reckon') is common to both passages. In rabbinical exegesis such a link was held to encourage the interpretation of the one passage by the other, by the principle called *gezerah shawah* ('equal category'). Paul uses this principle here, but the link is not a merely formal

---

[1] Cf. Anselm's words to Boso in *Cur Deus Homo* i. 21: '*nondum considerasti quanti ponderis sit peccatum.*'

one: the non-imputation of sin, in which the psalmist rejoices, amounts to the positive imputation of righteousness or pronouncement of acquittal, for there can be no verdict of 'not proven' in God's law-court.

11. *The sign of circumcision.* That is to say, the sign which consisted of circumcision; the phrase 'of circumcision' represents the Greek 'genitive of definition'. In Genesis xvii. 11 God tells Abraham that circumcision is to be a sign or 'token of the covenant betwixt me and you'. Paul's exegesis identifies this covenant with that of Genesis xv. 18, in which (fourteen years at least before Abraham was circumcised) God showed Abraham effectively how He counted his faith to him for righteousness. Circumcision is thus treated as a subsequent and external seal of that righteous status which Abraham already possessed as God's gift; it neither created nor enhanced that righteous status.

13. *That he should be the heir of the world.* This is not a formal quotation of any recorded promise to Abraham, but an interpretation of those promises which make reference to 'all families of the earth' (Gn. xii. 3) and 'all the nations of the earth' (Gn. xviii. 18, xxii. 18). When Abraham's heritage is delimited in geographical terms it lies between Egypt and the Euphrates (Gn. xv. 18; cf. xiii. 14 f.), but in the spiritual and permanent sense in which the promises made to him are interpreted in the New Testament, his inheritance cannot be confined within such earthly frontiers (cf. Heb. xi. 10, RV: 'he looked for the city which hath the foundations, whose builder and maker is God').

Or to his seed. The promise to Abraham in Genesis xii. 3, 'in thee shall all families of the earth be blessed', is repeated to him in Genesis xxii. 18 in the form 'in thy seed shall all the nations of the earth be blessed'. In Galatians iii Paul takes up both forms of the promise and shows how the word 'seed' in the second form, being a collective singular, can and does refer primarily to Christ (verse 16) and consequently also to the people of Christ (verse 29). Here his point is that, whichever form of the promise we consider, its validity has nothing to do with the law (which came centuries later, as is noted in Gal. iii. 17) or with the righteousness which depends on keeping the law.

14. *If they which are of the law be heirs, faith is made void.* Because the inheritance promised to Abraham would now depend on a new principle, which depends on works, not faith.

And the promise made of none effect. Because if its fulfilment depends on law-keeping, men's inability to keep the law will ensure that the promise will in fact never be fulfilled.

15. *Because the law worketh wrath.* That is, law inevitably imposes penalties for failure to keep it.

For where no law is, there is no transgression. Here, as in v. 13 ('sin is not imputed when there is no law'), Paul appears to be enunciating a current legal maxim (like the Roman maxim *nulla poena sine lege*).

16. *Therefore it is of faith, that it might be by grace.* A concise statement of the principle that what God provides by His free grace can be appropriated by men only through faith. What, on the contrary, is earned by works (not faith) is bestowed as a matter of merit (not grace).

17. *I have made thee a father of many nations.* In Genesis xvii. 5 the Hebrew runs literally 'I have made thee *father of a multitude* (*'ab hamon*) of nations', where the first part of *hamon* ('multitude') is linked with the last syllable of the new name *Abraham*.

Before him whom he believed. These words are logically connected with the clause in verse 16, that 'the promise might be sure to all the seed'—i.e. 'that the promise might be valid for all Abraham's spiritual posterity (whether Jews or Gentiles by natural birth) in the sight of God, in whom Abraham placed his trust'.

Who quickeneth the dead. This is a general designation of God in Jewish devotion, but is used here with special reference to Abraham's 'own body now as good as dead . . . and the deadness of Sarah's womb' (verse 19, RV).

And calleth those things which be not as though they were. The reference here is to the 'many nations' which were to spring from Abraham; not only had they no existence as yet, but (since Abraham and Sarah had now entered a childless old age) nothing seemed less likely than that they should ever exist.

18. *So shall thy seed be.* Quoted from Genesis xv. 5, where God tells Abraham (while he is still childless) that his descendants will be as innumerable as the stars.

19. *He considered not his own body now dead.* The word 'not' should be omitted as a late and inferior reading; the point is that Abraham *did* take into consideration every relevant factor, including his great age and the high improbability, by all natural reckoning, that he would ever have a son when his body was now 'as good as dead' (so the same participle, *nenekrōmenos,* is rendered in Heb. xi. 12, AV, with regard to this very situation). Yet, having considered all these factors, he concluded that the certainty of the divine promise outweighed every natural improbability.

25. *Who was delivered for our offences.* This may be a quotation from some primitive confession of faith; the language appears to be based on Isaiah liii. The verb 'deliver' in this sense (*paradidōmi*) occurs twice in the LXX version of that chapter: in Isaiah liii. 6, 'the Lord has delivered him (the Suffering Servant) up for our sins' and in Isaiah liii. 12, 'because of their sins he (the Servant) was delivered up'. (This last clause deviates considerably from the Hebrew text, 'and he made intercession for the transgressors'; see note on Rom. viii.

34, p. 180.) This use of the verb in relation to Jesus' being
handed over to death suggests that when it is used in 1
Corinthians xi. 23 in Paul's narrative of the institution of the
Eucharist the meaning is not so much, as AV has it, 'the same
night in which he was betrayed' (viz., by Judas) but rather
'in which he was delivered up' (viz., by God).

A verbal resemblance may also be traced between this
clause and the Targum of Jonathan on Isaiah liii. 5, in which
we find an Aramaic clause (*'ithmesar ba'awayathana*) which, if it
stood by itself, might be rendered 'he was delivered up for our
iniquities'. In the Targum, however, it is not the Servant-
Messiah but the temple that is the subject of the clause: the
Servant-Messiah 'will build the sanctuary which was profaned
by our trespasses and delivered up for our iniquities'.

And . . . raised again for our justification. The preposition 'for' in
both clauses of this verse represents *dia* ('because of'); Christ
was 'delivered up' to atone for His people's sins and was
raised up to guarantee their justification. (We must not
interpret the two clauses so woodenly as to suggest that His
resurrection had nothing to do with the atonement for their
sins and His death nothing to do with their justification; the
latter idea is ruled out by Rom. v. 9.)

c. The blessings which accompany justification: peace, joy, hope (v. 1–11)

Having set out God's way of justifying sinners, and established
it on the basis of Old Testament precedent, Paul now enumer-
ates the blessings which accrue to those whose faith has been
counted to them for righteousness. The first of these is peace
with God. Men and women who were formerly in a state of
rebellion against Him have now been reconciled to Him by
the death of Christ. It was the purpose of God, as he tells us
in another Epistle, to 'reconcile all things unto himself' by
Christ, but pre-eminently to reconcile those who were formerly
'alienated and enemies' to Him at heart (Col. i. 20–22). And
that in fact the death of Christ *has* accomplished this reconcilia-

tion has been a matter of plain experience in the lives of successive generations of believers. The reconciliation is something which God has already effected through the death of Christ, and men are called upon to accept it, to enter into the good of it, to be at peace with God.

This peace carries with it free access to God; the former rebels are not merely forgiven in the sense that their due punishment has been remitted, but they are brought into a place of high favour with God—'this grace wherein we stand'. It is through Christ that they have entered into this state of grace, and through Him, too, that they 'rejoice in hope of the glory of God'. Peace and joy are twin blessings of the gospel; as an old Scots preacher put it, 'peace is joy resting; joy is peace dancing'.

Three objects of joy are mentioned in this paragraph; the first is our hope of the glory of God. More about this coming glory will come into view when we reach the eighth chapter. But the glory of God is the end for which He created man, and it is through the redemptive work of Christ that this end will be achieved. So long as His people remain in mortal body, it remains a *hope*, but it is a sure hope, one that is certain of fulfilment, because those who cherish it have already received a guarantee of its realization in the gift of the Holy Spirit, who fills their hearts with the love of God.

The second object of joy is an unexpected one: 'we even rejoice in our afflictions', says Paul (verse 3). If this seems strange to us, let us remind ourselves that in the New Testament affliction is viewed as the normal experience of a Christian. The apostles warned their converts that 'we must through much tribulation enter into the kingdom of God' (Acts xiv. 22); and when tribulation came their way, as it regularly did, they could not complain that they had not been prepared for it. But affliction and tribulation were not only regarded as an inevitable feature of the Christian lot, they were looked upon as a token of true Christianity: they were a sign that God counted those who endured them worthy of His kingdom (cf. 2 Thes. i. 5). Besides, they had a salutary moral effect on those who suffered them, for they helped them to cultivate endurance and steadfastness of character, and when such endurance and steadfastness were linked to Christian faith, Christian hope was the more stimulated.

And, above all, believers learned to rejoice in God Himself (verse 11). The hope of glory was a joyful hope, and those who knew why they were suffering trial and persecution could rejoice amid their troubles, and even because of them; but no joy is comparable to the joy that is found in God Himself— the joy of those who echo the words of the psalmist: 'God my exceeding joy' (Ps. xliii. 4).

And why not rejoice in God? His people have been reconciled to Him by the death of Christ, and experience daily deliverance from evil through the resurrection life of Christ, while the end to which they confidently look forward is no longer the outpouring of divine wrath but the unveiling of divine glory. And from first to last they ascribe their blessings to God's love. It was because of that love that Christ laid down His life for them while they were weak, sinful and completely unattractive. The love of men and women will go to death itself for those who are the natural objects of that love, but not for the unlovely and unloving. Yet this is where the love of God shines brightest: God confirms *His* love to us in the fact that Christ died for us while we were in a state of rebellion against Him. So entirely at one are the Father and the Son that the self-sacrifice of the one can be presented as a token of the love of the other. And indeed, throughout the New Testament the death of Christ is the supreme manifestation of the love of God: 'Herein is love,' says John, 'not that we loved God, but that he loved us, and sent his Son to be the propitiation for our sins' (1 Jn. iv. 10). What a perversion of the divine character is perpetrated by those who sometimes talk as if Christ died for men in order to make God love them! That a change in the relation between God and man is brought by the death of Christ is clearly taught here and elsewhere; but no change was involved in the reality of God's love.

Love, joy, peace and hope, then, the true fruit of the Spirit, mark the lives of those who have been justified by faith in God. The guilty past has been cancelled, the glory of the future is assured, and here and now the presence and power of the Spirit of God secure to the believer all the grace he needs to endure trial, to resist evil, and to live as befits one whom God has declared righteous.

1. *We have peace with God* (so AV, RVmg., RSV; cf. NEBmg.). RV and RSVmg. read 'let us have peace with God'. The question is which of two alternative Greek readings we are to follow— the indicative *echomen* ('we have') or the subjunctive *echōmen* ('let us have'). Both are well attested, but the attestation is rather stronger for the subjunctive (which is exhibited not only by the first hand in the Alexandrian codices *Aleph* and B but also by the western codex D and the Latin version) than for the indicative (to which the text in *Aleph* and B was corrected by a later hand and which is exhibited by the western codex G). The variation in reading may go back to a primitive stage in the transmission of the text, earlier than the publication of the *corpus Paulinum* (see p. 24); the replacement of the one form by the other would be facilitated by the fact that, with a strong stress accent on the first syllable (as in Modern Greek) the distinction between the long and the short vowel in the second syllable would tend to disappear, so that the two forms would have almost identical pronunciations. In the course of dictation, therefore, the speaker might intend the one form and the scribe write down the other.[1] There can be no doubt that 'we have peace with God' suits Paul's argument better (cf. verse 11, RV, 'we have now received the reconciliation'); however, in view of the textual evidence, we might accept the

[1] This is not the only place in Romans where precisely this kind of textual variation appears, although this is the only place where it materially affects the sense. For example, in vi. 2 over against the future indicative *zēsomen* ('shall we live?') we have as a variant reading in many MSS the aorist subjunctive *zēsōmen* ('are we to live?').

subjunctive if we understand it to mean, with NEB, 'let us continue at peace with God.'[1]

2. *By whom also we have access by faith into this grace wherein we stand.* RVmg., RSV and NEB omit 'by faith', which is absent from a number of early eastern and western authorities. Even if not expressed, it is implied (cf. xi. 20, 'thou standest by faith'). Cf. Ephesians ii. 18: 'through him we both (Jewish and Gentile believers alike) have access by one Spirit unto the Father.' 'Access' denotes the privilege of approaching or being introduced into the presence of someone in high station, especially a royal or divine personage. Here Christ is viewed as ushering believers into their new state of grace and acceptance before God (cf. Eph. iii. 12).

And rejoice in hope of the glory of God, from which through sin we had fallen short (iii. 23). The verb 'rejoice' (like 'glory' in verse 3), so far as the form goes (*kauchōmetha*) might be either indicative ('we rejoice') or subjunctive ('let us rejoice').

5. *Hope maketh not ashamed.* Cf. Isaiah xxviii. 16, LXX (quoted in ix. 33, x. 11): 'Whosoever believeth on him shall not be ashamed.' A hope which fails of realization does make one ashamed, but the hope which is based on the promise of God is assured of fulfilment.

The love of God (i.e. God's love to us) *is shed abroad in our hearts by the Holy Ghost which is given unto us.* This reference to the Holy Spirit's work in the believer anticipates the fuller account which is given in chapter viii. The present work of the Spirit is the pledge of that glory for which the believer hopes.

6. *In due time.* That is, at the time of greatest need, when nothing but His death would help.

Christ died for the ungodly. This explains the paradox of iv. 5, that God 'justifieth the ungodly'.

---

[1] Cf. J. B. Phillips' version: 'let us grasp the fact that we *have* peace with God.'

7, 8. *Peradventure for a good man some would even dare to die. But . . . while we were yet sinners, Christ died for us.* 'A good man' is literally 'the good man' (RV), where the definite article indicates a particular type of man. There is little distinction between 'righteous' and 'good' in this verse; 'good' represents *agathos*, not *chrēstos* ('kindly'). Some would take 'good' as neuter here, as though it denoted a good cause rather than a good man. Paul's general argument is clear enough: 'even for one who is just or good you will scarcely find anyone willing to lay down his life—well, perhaps a few people might go so far as to do so—but God's love is seen in Christ's laying down *His* life for those who were neither just nor good, but ungodly sinners.'

9. *Being now justified by his blood.* His 'blood', as in iii. 25, denotes the laying down of His life as a sacrifice; 'by his blood' here is synonymous with 'by the death of his Son' in verse 10.

We shall be saved from wrath through him. Cf. 1 Thessalonians i. 10, where Jesus is called 'our Deliverer from the coming wrath'; in both places the outpouring of judgment at the end-time is probably in view. See also 1 Thessalonians v. 9: 'God hath not appointed us to wrath, but to obtain salvation by our Lord Jesus Christ.' Those who have been pronounced righteous by God can rejoice already in their deliverance from His wrath.

10. *When we were enemies, we were reconciled to God by the death of his Son.* Cf. Colossians i. 21 f.: 'And you, that were sometime alienated and enemies in your mind by wicked works, yet now hath he reconciled in the body of his flesh through death.' The hostility and estrangement which requires to be removed lies in man, not God; it is He who takes the initiative in good will by providing 'the redemption that is in Christ Jesus'.

Much more, being reconciled, we shall be saved by his life. This statement is expanded in vi. 8 ff. 'His life' is His resurrection life.

11. *By whom we have now received the atonement.* 'Atonement' in AV here has its etymological sense of 'at-one-ment', making 'at one', i.e. reconciling. Tyndale appears to have been the first to use 'atonement' in this theological sense. But that is a sense which the English word no longer bears; render therefore (with RV, RSV and NEB) 'reconciliation', which is the proper equivalent of *katallagē*. Where reconciliation is mentioned in the New Testament, God or Christ is always the Reconciler, and man is the object (or among the objects) of the reconciliation. God has 'reconciled us to himself by Jesus Christ', and men are summoned in Christ's name to be 'reconciled to God' (2 Cor. v. 18, 20). The situation may be compared to that of a king proclaiming an amnesty for rebellious subjects, who are urged to accept his gracious pardon while it is extended to them. God's abhorrence of sin does not make him the enemy of sinners or seek their ill; His desire is for 'all men to be saved, and to come unto the knowledge of the truth' (1 Tim. ii. 4).

d. The old and the new solidarity (v. 12–21)

The portrayal of Christ as the 'last Adam', the counterpart of the 'first Adam', is a prominent feature of Paul's Christology. It is not peculiar to him among the New Testament writers, and it may not even have been original with him, but he develops it more fully than any other, especially in this section of Romans and in his discussion of resurrection in 1 Corinthians xv. 22, 45–49.

The idea of God's man as the fulfiller of God's purpose is a recurring one in the Old Testament; he is 'the man of thy right hand, . . . the son of man whom thou madest strong for thyself' for whose prosperity and victory prayer is offered in Psalm lxxx. 17. When one man fails in the accomplishment of God's purpose (as, in measure, all did), God raises up another to take his place—Joshua to replace Moses, David to replace Saul, Elisha to replace Elijah. But who could take the place of *Adam*? Only one who was competent to undo the effects of Adam's sin and become the inaugurator of a new humanity. The Bible—and, indeed, the history of the world—knows of one man only who has the necessary qualifications. Christ stands forth (in Carlyle's translation of Luther's hymn) as

'the Proper Man
Whom God Himself hath bidden.'

And for those whom He has put right with God the old solidarity of sin and death, which was theirs in association with the first Adam, has given way to a new solidarity of righteousness and life in association with the 'last Adam'.

Paul rounds off his argument thus far by drawing a parallel and antithesis between Adam and Christ. Adam is for him a 'figure'—a counterpart or type—of Christ. As death entered the world through Adam's disobedience, so new life comes in through Christ's obedience. As Adam's sin involves his posterity in guilt, so Christ's righteousness is credited to His people.

To Paul, Adam was of course a historical individual, the first man. But he was more: he was what his name means in Hebrew—'mankind'. The whole of mankind is viewed as having existed at first in Adam. Because of his sin, however, Adam is mankind in alienation from God: the whole of mankind is viewed as having originally sinned in Adam. In the fall narrative of Genesis iii 'all subsequent human history lies encapsuled'; its incidents are re-enacted in the life of the race and indeed, to some extent, of each member of the race.

Paul was thoroughly conversant with the Hebrew concept of corporate personality, and his thought could readily oscillate on the one hand between the first man Adam and sinful mankind, and on the other hand between Christ, 'the second man', and the community of the redeemed. And very properly so: our solidarity with our fellows is a reality which we tend to overlook in the assertion of our individual independence. 'No man is an island, entire of itself; every man is a piece of the continent, a part of the main. If a clod is washed away, Europe is the less as well as if a promontory were or a manor of thy friends. Every man's death diminishes *me*, because I am involved in mankind. And therefore never send to know for whom the bell tolls: it tolls for thee.' John Donne's oft-quoted words express a permanent truth. Because we live in separate bodies we tend to think that all other aspects of our personality are equally separate and self-contained, but they are not. Here, however, two different kinds of solidarity are distinguished. A new creation has come to birth: the old 'Adam-solidarity' of sin and death has been broken up to be replaced by the new 'Christ-solidarity' of grace and life. Yet the break is not a sharp and clear-cut one: at present there is an overlap between the two. 'As in Adam all die' applies in the physical realm to believers just as much as 'even so in Christ shall all be made alive' does, so long as this mortal life endures. But here and now they do have the assurance that because they are 'in Christ' they will indeed 'be made alive', because here and now through faith in Him they have received from God that justification which brings life in its train. 'In God's sight,' said Thomas Goodwin, seventeenth-century President of Magdalen College, Oxford, 'there are two men—Adam and Jesus Christ—and these two men have all other men hanging at their girdle strings.'

The obedience of Christ to which His people owe their justification and hope of eternal life is not to be confined to His death. His death is here viewed as the crown and culmination of that 'active obedience' which characterized His life throughout its course. It was a perfectly righteous life that He offered up in death on His people's behalf. The righteous life in itself would not have met their need had He not carried His obedience to the point of death, 'even the death of the cross'; but neither would His death have met their need had the life which He thus offered up not been a perfect life. In his language here Paul echoes the words of the fourth Servant Song: 'by his knowledge shall my righteous servant justify many (lit. "make the many righteous"); for he shall bear their iniquities' (Is. liii. 11).

So, if the fall of Adam brought all his posterity under the dominion of death, the obedience of Christ has brought a new race triumphantly into the realm of grace and life.

'But,' says someone, 'in all this discussion of Adam and Christ, have you not forgotten Moses? Where does he come in? Surely the introduction of the law between Adam and Christ means that there are three ages, inaugurated respectively by Adam, Moses and Christ, and not just two, inaugurated respectively by Adam and Christ?'

'No', says Paul. 'The law has no permanent significance in the history of redemption. It was introduced as a temporary measure for a practical purpose. Sin was present in the world ever since Adam's fall, but the law served the purpose of bringing sin right out into the light of day, that sin might be more clearly recognized for what it really is. More than that: the law actually had the effect of increasing the amount of open sin in the world. It is not merely that in the presence of specific laws sin takes the form of specific transgressions of those laws; the presence of law can positively stimulate sin, as a prohibition may tempt people to do what is prohibited whereas they might never have thought of doing it if the ordinance forbidding it had not been brought to their attention.' Paul here shows sound insight into human nature. There is a point of real substance in the story of the old lady who objected to the recitation of the Ten Commandments in church 'because they put so many ideas into people's minds'.

But the law introduced no new principle into the situation; it simply revealed more fully the principle of sin which was already present. The gospel, on the other hand, has introduced a completely new principle—the principle of God's grace. However fast the operation of law stimulates sin and causes it to increase, faster still does the grace of God increase and remove the accumulated load of sin.[1]

12. *As by one man sin entered into the world, and death by sin.* The 'one man' is Adam; the reference is to the fall narrative of Genesis iii. Cf. Wisdom ii. 23 f.:

'God created man for incorruption,
and made him in the image of his own eternity,
but through the devil's envy death entered the world
and those who belong to his party experience it.'

The same point is made by the outcry in 2 Esdras vii. 118: 'O Adam, what have you done? For though it was you who sinned, the fall was not yours alone, but ours also who are your descendants.' Ben Sira characteristically draws a misogynistic moral from the narrative: 'From a woman sin had its beginning, and because of her we all die' (Ecclus. xxv. 24; see p. 150). But none of these writers sees anything of the deeper significance in the fall of man which is now unfolded by Paul.

Death passed upon all men, for that all have sinned. Render with RSV: 'and so death spread to all men because all men sinned'— sinned, that is to say, in Adam, not subsequently, in imitation of Adam's sin, which is the meaning of the words in iii. 23 (and cf. verse 14 below).[2] The construction, and the underlying thought, is paralleled in 2 Corinthians v. 14 (RSV): 'one has

---

[1] Two recent monographs on Rom. v. 12–21 are K. Barth, *Christ and Adam* (English translation, 1956), and J. Murray, *The Imputation of Adam's Sin* (Grand Rapids, 1959). Professor Murray also devotes Appendix D of his commentary on Romans, I (pp. 384 ff.) to an able critique of 'Karl Barth on Romans 5'. Another telling critique of Barth's monograph, from a standpoint far removed from Professor Murray's, is R. Bultmann's essay, 'Adam and Christ according to Romans 5', in *Current Issues in New Testament Interpretation*, ed. W. Klassen and G. F. Snyder (1962), pp. 143 ff. See also C. K. Barrett's Hewett lectures, *From First Adam to Last: A Study in Pauline Theology* (1962).

[2] The statement in 2 Baruch liv. 19, 'every man has been the Adam of his own soul', while it is an interesting anticipation of Pelagius's teaching, cannot be used to illustrate Paul's argument here (but see p. 149).

died for all; therefore all have died'—where, however, it is the racial effect of the death of Christ, not of the sin of Adam, that Paul has in view. It is not simply because Adam is the ancestor of mankind that all are said to have sinned in his sin (otherwise it might be argued that because Abraham believed God all his descendants were automatically involved in his belief[1]); it is because Adam *is* mankind. Although the Vulgate rendering of 'for that' (Gk. *eph' hō*) by 'in whom' (Lat. *in quo*) may be a mistranslation, it is a true interpretation.[2]

Paul does not conclude his sentence with a 'so' clause to match the 'as' clause of verse 12. His reference to death as spreading to all men because of sin leads him to introduce the long parenthesis of verses 13–17, and when it is finished, instead of providing the principal clause for which the reader has been waiting, he repeats the 'as' clause of verse 12 in different words in verse 18 and follows up the new 'as' clause with a balancing 'even so' clause. An apodosis in correlative terms to the 'as' clause of verse 12 would be worded more or less like this: 'even so by one man God's way of righteousness was introduced, and life by righteousness.'

13. *Until the law sin was in the world.* Once sin had gained an entrance into the human family, death followed. The sentence on Adam, 'in the day that thou eatest thereof thou shalt surely die' (Gn. ii. 17), was executed upon his descendants, even although, until the law was given, there was no positive commandment for them to transgress as there was for Adam.

But sin is not imputed when there is no law. (Cf. iv. 15.) Yet sin was all-pervasive, and mortal in its effect, even in the absence of any positive commandment with penalty attached. Sin manifests itself in the form of specific transgressions when there are specific commandments to be transgressed. Later Jewish

---

[1] See p. 113.

[2] 'It is therefore better to take the *eph' hō* (Old Latin *in quo*) as bringing out the corporate solidarity of human guilt—"all men sinned in Adam" ' (W. Manson in *New Testament Essays in Memory of T. W. Manson*, p. 159).

tradition regarded the commandments to Noah in Genesis ix. 1–7 as laws binding on all the Gentiles, but we do not know whether Paul so regarded them.

14. *Who is the figure of him that was to come.* That is, Adam, the first man, is a counterpart or 'type' (*tupos*) of Christ, whom Paul elsewhere calls 'the last Adam' and 'the second man' (1 Cor. xv. 45, 47). It is noteworthy that the only Old Testament character to be called explicitly a 'type' of Christ in the New Testament is Adam.[1] And there is a fitness in this, even if the typological relation between them is one of contrast rather than resemblance: in Paul's thought Christ replaces the first man as the archetype and representative of a new humanity:

> 'Adam, descended from above,
> Federal head of all mankind.'

15. *If through the offence of one many be dead, much more the grace of God . . . hath abounded unto many.* For 'many' RV rightly renders 'the many' in both clauses (cf. verse 19), 'the many' being the great mass of mankind (like the twofold 'all' in 1 Cor. xv. 22). See also Romans xi. 32 (pp. 223 f.). It is a natural inference from these words 'that the grace procured by Christ belongs to a greater number than the condemnation contracted by the first man'. So Calvin put it—which may surprise those who imagine that he envisaged the elect as a small minority. Calvin did indeed know of some who envisaged the elect as a minority, and who accordingly argued that Paul was here 'merely debating a point'; and he felt that their argument could not be disproved. His own reasoning was, however, 'that if Adam's fall had the effect of producing the ruin of many, the grace of God is much more efficacious

---

[1] There are, of course, other Old Testament characters whom New Testament writers treat implicitly, if not expressly, as 'types' of Christ; Melchizedek in the Epistle to the Hebrews is a notable example. But the typological relationship between Christ and Adam is on a plane all its own.

in benefiting many, since admittedly Christ is much more powerful to save than Adam was to ruin'.

In the statement that the grace of God abounded to 'the many' (RV), the expression 'the many' is probably a deliberate echo of Isaiah liii. 11, where the Servant of the Lord justifies 'the many' (MT, LXX). Hence 'the many' is also used by way of balance in the first part of the verse of those who died in Adam; compare also the twofold occurrence of 'the many' in verse 19 (RV), where 'through the obedience of the one shall the many be made righteous' is even more clearly an echo of Isaiah liii. 11.[1]

16. *And not as it was by one that sinned, so is the gift. . . .* The free gift is not on the same scale as the effect of Adam's sin. Through the action of one sinner sentence of condemnation was passed; but the free gift, bestowed after many repetitions of the primal sin, issues in God's reversal of that adverse judgment and His conferment of a righteous status upon many sinners.

17. *The gift of righteousness,* i.e. the gift of justification, the righteousness which God bestows on believers.

Shall reign in life by one, Jesus Christ. When death reigns, men are its helpless victims; when Christ reigns, men share His risen life and royal glory (cf. viii. 17).

18. *By the offence of one . . . by the righteousness of one.* RV renders 'through one trespass . . . through one act of righteousness'. This is grammatically as permissible as the AV rendering, but the AV rendering gives a better parallel to verse 19: 'by one man's disobedience . . . by the obedience of one'. 'The righteousness of one' is strictly 'one man's act of righteousness'

---

[1] See Leslie C. Allen, 'Isaiah liii. 11 and its Echoes', in *Vox Evangelica: Biblical and Historical Essays by Members of the Faculty of London Bible College* (1962), pp. 24 ff.

(*dikaiōma,*[1] with a different sense from that which it has in verse 16), as contrasted with 'one man's act of transgression'. The 'act of righteousness' is the crowning act of Christ's life-long obedience (verse 19), when He yielded up His life.

Unto justification of life. Since Paul has used *dikaiōma* in this sentence with the meaning 'act of righteousness', he does not use it again (as he did in verse 16) in the sense of 'justification', but employs *dikaiōsis,* which he had already used in this sense in iv. 25. 'Justification of life' is justification which issues in life (just as condemnation issues in death).

19. *As by one man's disobedience many were made sinners, so by the obedience of one shall many be made righteous.* For 'many' read 'the many' (so RV, NEB); cf. verse 15. 'O the sweet exchange, O the inscrutable creation, O the unlooked-for benefits, that the sin of many should be put out of sight in one Righteous Man, and the righteousness of one should justify many sinners!' (*Epistle to Diognetus* ix. 5). His obedience achieved more than Abraham's could ever have done; by His passion and triumph He has won the right and power to beat back the hostile cosmic forces—to 'retrieve the cosmic situation', as C. K. Barrett puts it[2]—and ensure for His people participation in His victory.

20. *The law entered* (*pareiserchomai,* 'came in beside', RV; 'intruded into this process', NEB) *that the offence might abound.* Cf. Galatians iii. 19: 'Wherefore then serveth the law? It was added because of transgressions ("to make wrongdoing a legal offence", NEB), till the seed should come to whom the promise was made.' In this sense the law is a parenthetic dispensation in the course of God's dealings with mankind.

---

[1] This word is also used in Rom. i. 32 (of God's righteous judgment), ii. 26 and viii. 4 (of the righteous requirements or regulations of the law), v. 16 (of justification).

[2] *From First Adam to Last,* p. 93.

IV. THE WAY OF HOLINESS (vi. 1–viii. 39)

a. Freedom from sin (vi. 1–23)

i. A supposed objection (vi. 1, 2). 'Well,' someone might say, 'if God's grace so abounded over sin, why should we not go on sinning so as to give His grace the opportunity of abounding all the more?'

This is not a completely hypothetical objection, for in fact there have always been people to insist that this is the logical corollary of Paul's teaching about justification by faith; and unfortunately, in every generation, people claiming to be justified by faith have behaved in such a way as to lend colour to this criticism. James Hogg's *Private Memoirs and Confessions of a Justified Sinner* (1824) provides the outstanding literary example of such deliberate antinomianism; a notable historical instance may be seen in the Russian monk Rasputin, the evil genius of the Romanov family in its last years of power. Rasputin taught and exemplified the doctrine of salvation through repeated experiences of sin and repentance; he held that, as those who sin most require most forgiveness, a sinner who continues to sin with abandon enjoys, each time he repents, more of God's forgiving grace than any ordinary sinner. The case-books of many soul-physicians[1] would reveal that this point of view has been commoner than is often realized, even when it is not expressed and practised so blatantly as it was by Rasputin.

Some of Paul's own converts gave him much cause for concern on this very score. It was bad enough to have his theological opponents misrepresenting his gospel as being tantamount to 'Let us do evil, that good may come' (iii. 8); it was worse when his converts played into their hands by behaving as though the gospel gave them licence to do whatever they liked. Paul's Corinthian correspondence shows how much trouble his converts gave him in this regard: it is plain

---

[1] Cf. Hannah Whitall Smith, *Religious Fanaticism* (1928).

that some of them imagined that sexual irregularities, for example, were matters of very small importance. From the terms in which he directs the Corinthian church to excommunicate a man who was living in an incestuous relation, it appears that some members of the church, far from expressing any disapproval of this scandalous state of affairs, thought that it was rather a fine assertion of Christian liberty (1 Cor. v). No wonder that other Christians maintained that the only way to inculcate the principles of sound morality in such people was to require them to keep the law of Moses—indeed, to impose that law upon them as a condition of salvation, over and above the requirement of faith in Christ. But Paul's own experience had taught him that all the law-keeping in the world could not bring the assurance of pardon and peace with God, whereas faith in Christ did so at once. He could never consider legalism as the remedy for libertinism; he knew a more excellent way. When a man yielded his life to the risen Christ and the power of His Spirit, his inward being was radically transformed, a new creation took place. That man received a new nature which delighted to produce spontaneously the fruit of the Spirit, those graces which were manifested in their perfection by Christ Himself. To many people this appeared impracticably optimistic (and so it still appears to many), but Paul trusted the Spirit of Christ in his converts, and in the long run his trust was vindicated, though he had to endure many heartbreaking disappointments in his spiritual children until at last he could see 'Christ... formed' in them (Gal. iv. 19).

In the division of the Epistle to the Romans on which we have now entered we see him expound this teaching at length in reply to the argument that one ought really to go on sinning, so that God's grace might abound the more.[1]

ii. The meaning of baptism (vi. 3–14). 'Anyone who can argue like that,' says Paul, 'shows that he has not begun to

---

[1] For a popular exposition of Paul's argument here see J. O. Buswell, Jr., *Ten Reasons Why a Christian does not live a Wicked Life* (Chicago, 1959).

understand the gospel. Life in sin cannot coexist with death to sin.' But what is meant by this 'death to sin'?

'Listen,' he says; 'do you not remember what happened when you were baptized?' From this and other references to baptism in Paul's writings, it is certain that he did not regard baptism as an 'optional extra' in the Christian life, and that he would not have contemplated the phenomenon of an 'unbaptized believer'.[1] We may agree or disagree with Paul, but we must do him the justice of letting him hold and teach his own beliefs, and not distort his beliefs into conformity with what we should prefer him to have said. (This applies to many other subjects than Paul's baptismal doctrine!)

In apostolic times it is plain that baptism followed immediately upon confession of faith in Christ. The repeated accounts of baptism in Acts give ample proof of this; the incident of the twelve disciples at Ephesus (Acts xix. 1–7) is the exception that proves the rule. Faith in Christ and baptism were, indeed, not so much two distinct experiences as parts of one whole; faith in Christ was an essential element in baptism, for without it the application of water, even accompanied by the appropriate words, would not have been baptism.

But when believers were baptized, what happened? This, says Paul. Their former life came to an end; a new life began. They were, in fact, 'buried' with Christ when they were plunged in the baptismal water, in token that they had died so far as their old life of sin was concerned; they were raised again with Christ when they emerged from the water, in token that they had received a new life, which was nothing less than participation in Christ's own resurrection life. 'Shall we continue in sin, that grace may abound?' But how could they, if the life which they now lived, even while yet in mortal body, was the life which was theirs by union with the risen Christ? The very idea was a moral contradiction in terms.

[1] His references to baptism in 1 Cor. i. 14–17 do not mean that he regarded the sacrament itself as unimportant, but that the identity of the baptizer was unimportant. He takes it for granted that all the members of the Corinthian church were baptized (1 Cor. i. 13, vi. 11, x. 1 ff.).

But how is this going to work out in practice? 'Yield your-selves to God,' says Paul; 'present your bodies to Him as instruments for the doing of His will. Formerly you were enslaved to sin, but your old relationship to sin has been broken—broken irrevocably, by death. What death? The death which you have died with Christ. Now that you are united to Him by faith, His death has become yours; your "old self" has been "crucified" on His cross. Christ had to do with sin, as well as you; He had to do with it as sin-bearer, you have had to do with it as sinners. As the bearer of His people's sins, He died; but now He lives His resurrection life. He no longer bears His people's sins; when once He had died for their sins, He rose from the dead, and now death can touch Him no more. If you consider yourselves to have died in His death, and risen to a new life in His resurrection, sin will dominate you no more.

'You now live under a régime of grace, and grace does not stimulate sin, as law does; grace liberates from sin and enables you to triumph over it. How then can you think of going on in sin, just because you now live under a régime of grace and not of law? Anyone who talks like that has not the remotest inkling of what divine grace means.'

3. *Baptized into Jesus Christ.* Cf. Galatians iii. 27: 'as many of you as have been baptized into Christ have put on Christ'— i.e. have been incorporated into Him, have become members of His body (cf. 1 Cor. xii. 13), and so have shared by faith-union with Him those experiences which were His historically, His crucifixion and burial, His resurrection and exaltation. Further light on Paul's doctrine of baptism is provided in 1 Corinthians x. 2, where the Israelites who left Egypt are said to have been 'all baptized unto Moses in the cloud and in the sea'. Baptism thus seals the believer's exodus, his deliverance from the bondage of sin.

4. *Buried with him by baptism into death.* Cf. Colossians ii. 12:

'buried with him in baptism'. Burial sets the seal on death; so the Christian's baptism is a token burial in which the old order of living comes to an end, to be replaced by the new order of life-in-Christ.

Christ was raised up from the dead by the glory of the Father. The 'glory' here is more especially God's glorious power—'the working of his mighty power, which he wrought in Christ, when he raised him from the dead' (Eph. i. 19 f.; cf. Col. ii. 12).

6. *Our old man is crucified with him.* 'The man we once were has been crucified with Christ' (NEB). This 'crucifixion' is not a present experience but a past event, expressed by the aorist tense in Greek; those who are united by faith to Christ are reckoned as having been crucified with Him when He was crucified. Cf. Galatians ii. 20: 'I have been crucified (perfect tense) with Christ; it is no longer I who live, but Christ who lives in me; and the life I now live in the flesh I live by faith in the Son of God, who loved me and gave himself for me' (RSV). Similarly in Galatians vi. 14 Paul speaks of 'the cross of our Lord Jesus Christ, by which the world has been crucified (perfect tense) to me, and I to the world' (RSV). In these two passages from Galatians the perfect tense denotes a present state produced by the past event of Romans vi. 6. Moreover, in Galatians vi. 14 there is probably a side-glance at an alternative meaning of the verb 'crucify' (*stauroō*), namely 'fence off'; so that Paul's words may also imply: 'that cross forms a permanent barrier between the world and me, and between me and the world.' For 'the old man' cf. Colossians iii. 9 and Ephesians iv. 22, quoted on p. 44. He belongs to the 'present evil age' from which the death of Christ delivers His people (Gal. i. 4, RSV).

That the body of sin might be destroyed. 'For the destruction of the sinful self' (NEB), i.e. that the 'flesh', the unregenerate nature with its downward tendency, the 'old Adam' in which sin found a ready accomplice, might be rendered inoperative.

This 'body of sin' is more than an individual affair; it is rather that old solidarity of sin and death which all share 'in Adam', but which has been broken by the death of Christ, with a view to the creation of the new solidarity of righteousness and life of which believers are made part 'in Christ'. It is not the human body in the ordinary sense that is to be destroyed or put out of action; baptism does not have this effect. With the phrase 'the body of sin' cf. 'the body of this death' in vii. 24 or 'sinful flesh' in viii. 3.

7. *He that is dead is freed from sin.* Lit. 'he who has died has been justified from sin', the point of which is paraphrased by NEB: 'a dead man is no longer answerable for his sin.' Death pays all debts, so the man who has died with Christ has his slate wiped clean, and is ready to begin his new life with Christ freed from the entail of the past.

10. *He died unto sin once,* i.e. 'once for all' (RVmg., RSV, NEB); the Greek word is *ephapax,* which is used repeatedly in the Epistle to the Hebrews to emphasize the finality of the sacrifice of Christ. In His death He dealt effectively and conclusively with sin, winning a victory 'that needs no second fight, and leaves no second foe'.

11. *Reckon ye also yourselves to be dead indeed unto sin, but alive unto God.* In other words, live as though you had already entered the resurrection life. This 'reckoning' is no vain exercise but one which is morally fruitful, because the Holy Spirit has come to make effective in believers what Christ has done for them, and to enable them to become in daily experience, as far as may be in the present conditions of mortality, what they already are 'in Christ' and what they will fully be in the resurrection life. This is the subject of viii. 1–27.
Through Jesus Christ our Lord. Read simply 'in Christ Jesus' (the additional phrase 'our Lord' may have found its way into later texts under the influence of v. 21, vi. 23).

12. *That ye should obey it in the lusts thereof.* The best-attested text omits 'it in'. (Cf. xiii. 14.)

14. *Sin shall not have dominion over you: for ye are not under the law, but under grace.* The law demanded obedience, but grace supplies the power to obey; hence grace breaks the mastery of sin as law could not. See pp. 161 ff.

iii. The slave-market analogy (**vi. 15–23**). Paul then uses the analogy of the slave-market to illustrate his point. A slave is bound to obey his master. But there is a point beyond which his master has no authority over him—and that point is death. When the slave is dead, his master can go on giving orders to the corpse until he is blue in the face, but the corpse will pay no attention. 'Once', says Paul, 'you were slaves of sin. Sin was your master, and you were forced to do all the evil things that sin ordered you to do; you had no power to say "No". But now you have died so far as your relation to sin is concerned, and you need pay no more heed to the dictates of sin.

'Or, to put it another way, a slave's former owner has no more authority over him if he becomes someone else's property. That is what has happened to you. You have passed from the service of sin into the service of God; your business now is to do what God desires, not what sin dictates. There is a big difference indeed between the kind of thing you will do as servants of God and the kind of thing you used to do as servants of sin. And not only is there a difference in character between the two kinds of service; there is a great difference between the ends of these forms of service. Sin pays wages to its servants— the wages being death. God gives us not wages, but something better and much more generous; in His grace He gives life eternal as a free gift—that life eternal which is ours by union with Christ.'

What do we think of this argument? Is it a legal fiction, or an exhortation to pull ourselves together and make a new start, a good resolution that we will do better in the future? 'Reckon yourselves dead in relation to sin, but alive in a new relation to God by virtue of your incorporation in Christ', says Paul (verse 11). Is this just an exertion of the will, or an effort of the imagination? No, it is not. It is something that has proved its reality in the lives of many, and they have no difficulty in understanding what Paul means. For the God of whom he speaks is the living God, and when men and women present themselves to Him, to be used in His service, He accepts them as His servants and gives them the power to do His will. The Christ of whom Paul speaks is the Christ who truly died and rose again, and in the lives of those who put their trust in Him 'He breaks the power of cancelled sin.'

15. *Shall we sin, because we are not under the law, but under grace?* This is the same antinomian argument as in verse 1, in a slightly different form of words, suggested by verse 14. The man who is 'under grace' is the man who shares the life of Christ. As the life of Christ was and is characterized by spontaneous and glad obedience to the Father's will, so the life of those who are 'in Christ' will be characterized by the same obedience. 'Love God, and do as you please' is a maxim which, in those who have God's love shed abroad in their hearts by the Holy Spirit, can only result in their doing those things which please God. To make being 'under grace' an excuse for sinning is a sign that one is not really 'under grace' at all.

16. *His servants ye are to whom ye obey.* 'To whom' (AV) is an over-literal translation of the Greek dative. 'You are slaves of the master whom you obey' (NEB).

17. *But God be thanked, that ye were the servants of sin, but . . .* If the AV is read aloud, emphasis must be put on the verb 'were' (as if to say, God be thanked that that is now a thing of the past). Render with RV: 'But thanks be to God, that, whereas ye were servants of sin, ye became obedient. . . .'

Ye have obeyed from the heart that form of doctrine which was delivered you. The 'form of doctrine' or 'pattern of teaching' (NEB) is probably the summary of Christian ethics, based on the teaching of Christ, which was regularly given to converts in the primitive Church to show them the way of life which they ought thenceforth to follow. It is the body of teaching which Paul elsewhere calls 'the tradition' or 'the traditions' (cf. 1 Cor. xi. 2, RV; 2 Thes. ii. 15, iii. 6)—the noun (*paradosis*) is cognate with the verb translated 'deliver' (*paradidōmi*). It may be inferred from various summaries of this teaching in the Epistles that it was arranged in catechetical form at an early period.[1] But the 'pattern of teaching' was embodied in Christ Himself to whom they now belonged. (See also pp. 242 f.)

18. *Being then made free from sin.* That is, having been liberated from the tyranny of sin, not 'justified' from sin as in verse 7.

19. *I speak after the manner of men because of the infirmity of your flesh.* That is, I am using a human analogy or mode of speech (cf. 1 Cor. xv. 32) to help the weakness of your understanding (see p. 43).
To iniquity unto iniquity. That is, 'to greater and greater iniquity' (RSV).

20. *Ye were free from righteousness.* That is, sin and not righteousness was your master then.

21. *The end of those things is death.* Cf. i. 32 for 'the judgment of God, that they which commit such things are worthy of death'.

22. *Ye have your fruit unto holiness.* 'The return you get is sanctification' (RSV)—and this, in fact, is the subject of the present section of the Epistle (chapters vi–viii). Those who have been justified are now being sanctified; if a man is not

[1] Cf. E. G. Selwyn, *The First Epistle of Peter* (1946), pp. 363 ff.

being sanctified, there is no reason to believe that he has been justified.

b. Freedom from law (vii. 1-25)

i. The marriage analogy (vii. 1-6). We can well understand the need of freedom from sin, but why should Paul be so concerned about freedom from the law? The law is God's law, the law forbids sin, the law prescribes righteousness. More than that, men of God in Israel in earlier days had found the law to be a safeguard against sin. 'Great peace have they who love thy law', said one psalmist, 'and nothing shall trip them up' (see Ps. cxix. 165); another could say: 'The law of the Lord is perfect, converting the soul' (Ps. xix. 7).

But Paul speaks differently, and he speaks out of his own experience. With the law of God in itself he has no fault to find: it is 'holy, and just, and good' (vii. 12). What is really at fault is the conception of religion as law-keeping, the idea that by painstaking conformity to a law-code one can acquire merit in God's sight.

When Peter, at the Council of Jerusalem, described the law as 'a yoke . . . which neither our fathers nor we were able to bear' (Acts xv. 10), he speaks as a typical member of the Jewish rank-and-file, one of the *ammê ha'areṣ*. And he is thinking, probably, not only of the written law, but of its oral amplification handed down through generations of scribes. Of this oral law tradition said that Moses received it on Sinai and 'delivered it to Joshua, Joshua to the elders, the elders to the prophets, and the prophets to the "men of the great synagogue" '. Simon the Just, one of the last survivors of the 'great synagogue', delivered it to Antigonus of Socoh, and after him it was delivered in turn to four successive pairs of scholars, generation after generation, and after them it was received by Hillel and Shammai, founders of the two great rabbinical schools which were dominant in the time of Christ and the apostles.

Only those who dedicated themselves wholeheartedly to the keeping of the law, interpreted according to 'the tradition of the elders', had any hope of success; but for them it was a real hope. The rich young lawyer who told Jesus that he had kept all the commandments from his early days was not a liar or a hypocrite (Lk. xviii. 21). When Paul, twenty years and more after his conversion, looks back to his earlier career as a Pharisee and says that he was, 'touching the righteousness which is in the law, blameless' (Phil. iii. 6), he is speaking in terms of sober fact. Yet he found in Christ a new life and a new power, a new joy and a new peace, such as he had never known before, together with a new 'righteousness'—'not . . . a righteousness of mine own, even that which is of the law, but that which is through faith in Christ, the righteousness which is of God by faith' (Phil. iii. 9, RV).

But in this section of the Epistle to the Romans he tells us more clearly than anywhere else just how he found the law so inadequate as a way to secure a righteous standing before God. He has hinted at it before: 'by the law', he has said, 'is the knowledge of sin' (iii. 20); 'sin shall not have dominion over you', he has told his Christian readers, 'for ye are not under the law, but under grace' (vi. 14). But what had their not being under law to do with their freedom from the dominion of sin? Had he said 'sin shall not have dominion over you, for ye are not under *sin* . . .' we could have understood him more easily, although we might have regarded the statement as tautologous. But Paul knew what he wanted to say, and chose his words with care. Freedom from sin and freedom from law are two things which went closely together in his experience. If in chapter vi he illustrates freedom from sin in terms of the relation between a slave and his master, in vii. 1–6 he illustrates freedom from law in terms of the relation between a wife and her husband.

Marriage, he says, is a lifelong relationship. A wife is bound to her husband as long as he lives; if, during his lifetime, she leaves him for another man, she is branded as an adulteress. But if he dies, she is free to become the wife of another without incurring any disrepute. Death breaks the marriage-bond—

and death breaks a man's relation to the law. When Paul applies the analogy, we are conscious of a reversal of the situation; the believer in Christ is compared to the wife, and the law is compared to the husband, but whereas in the illustration it was the husband who died, in the application it is not the law that has died, but the believer; the believer has died with Christ—and yet it is still the believer who, no longer bound to the law, is free to be united with Christ. If, however, we put the matter in simpler terms, we can express Paul's meaning easily enough: as death breaks the bond between a husband and wife, so death—the believer's death-with-Christ—breaks the bond which formerly yoked him to the law, and now he is free to enter into union with Christ. His former association with the law did not help him to produce the fruits of righteousness, but these fruits are produced in abundance now that he is united with Christ. Sin and death were the result of his association with the law; righteousness and life are the product of his new association; for (as Paul puts it elsewhere), 'the letter killeth, but the spirit giveth life' (2 Cor. iii. 6).

Such an attitude to the law must have seemed preposterous to many of his readers then (it has seemed preposterous to many of his readers since); but Paul goes on to explain it in the light of his own experience, and gives us a most illuminating piece of spiritual autobiography—partly in the past tense, and partly in the present.

1. *I speak to them that know the law.* Better, with NEB, 'I am speaking to those who have some knowledge of law.' It is immaterial for the present stage of the argument whether they knew it in the form of Jewish law or Roman law; in either case it was true that 'a person is subject to the law so long as he is alive, and no longer' (NEB).

2. *The woman which hath an husband is bound by the law to her husband so long as he liveth.* For 'by the law' read rather (with RV, RSV, NEB) 'by law'; again, the statement is generally true whether one thinks of Jewish law or Roman law.

The law of her husband. The law (Jewish or Roman) which binds her to her husband and makes him her master.

3. *She shall be called an adulteress.* (Cf. Mk. x. 12.) The Greek verb used here is the intransitive *chrēmatizō*, 'be publicly known as' (used in Acts xi. 26 of the giving of the name 'Christians' to the disciples of Jesus).

4. *That ye should be married to another, even to him who is raised from the dead.* Since He was raised from the dead, He will die no more (vi. 9); therefore this new marriage relationship will not be broken by death, as the old one was.

That we should bring forth fruit unto God. It is somewhat far-fetched to think that the marriage metaphor is being continued, so that the 'fruit' here spoken of is viewed as the off-spring of the new marriage. The fruit, like the 'fruit unto holiness' of vi. 22, is a righteous life, characterized by those 'good works, which God hath before ordained that we should walk in them' (Eph. ii. 10).

5. *When we were in the flesh.* That is, when we were un-regenerate (see p. 44).

The motions of sins, which were by the law, did work in our members to bring forth fruit unto death. That is, 'the sinful passions evoked by the law worked in our bodies, to bear fruit for death' (NEB). How the law can evoke sinful passions appears in verses 7–13. The 'fruit unto death' consists of those evil works whose 'end' is death, according to vi. 21.

6. *But now we are delivered from the law, that being dead wherein we were held.* Better, '. . . having died to that wherein we were holden' (RV). It is by virtue of this death (death-with-Christ and death-to-sin) that we have been 'delivered' (or rather, to give the legal flavouring of the RV rendering, 'discharged') from our former liability under the law.

In newness of spirit. That is, in the new life which believers live 'in (the) Spirit'; for the latter phrase, cf. viii. 9.

And not in the oldness of the letter. The old, pre-Christian life, for those who, like Paul, had been brought up as observant Jews, was characterized by submission to an external code. But now the Spirit supplies within that regulative principle which once the law, and that imperfectly, supplied from without. This antithesis between 'spirit' and 'letter' points to the new age as that in which Jeremiah's new covenant is realized (Je. xxxi. 31 ff.); cf. viii. 4 (p. 161) and see further on p. 47 with n. 2.

ii. The dawn of conscience (vii. 7–13). How then did the law prove a stimulus to sin in Paul's own experience?

Once upon a time, he tells us, he had no consciousness of sin. In his earliest days he did not make the acquaintance of the law; he lived a carefree life. But 'shades of the prison-house begin to close upon the growing boy'; the day came when Paul had to take upon himself the obligation to keep the law. The occasion might be his *bar mitzwah* ceremony,[1] or the period immediately preceding or following it. The obligation to keep the law involved first of all the obligation to know and obey the Ten Commandments. Prohibitions, as a matter of common knowledge, tend to awaken a desire to do the thing that is forbidden; the smoker may forget how much he wants to smoke until he sees a sign which says 'No Smoking'.

Here, then, were the Ten Commandments, all but one of them charged with prohibitions: 'Thou shalt not . . .' Paul was not greatly tempted to worship a graven image or to commit murder, adultery or theft. The commandment which caused the trouble was the tenth, which deals with an inward attitude rather than with an overt action or word. 'Thou shalt not covet' was Paul's stumbling-block. The commandment in

---

[1] The ceremony in which a Jewish boy at the age of thirteen becomes a 'son of the commandment', i.e. assumes personal responsibility to keep the law.

its Old Testament formulation specifies a number of objects which a man must not covet—his neighbour's house, wife, servants, animals, or property in general. Paul was not necessarily stimulated to covet any of these; the trouble went deeper. Covetousness itself is a sin; it is indeed a basic element in most forms of sin. As Paul puts it elsewhere (Col. iii. 5), covetousness is plain idolatry. It may be illicit desire; it may be desire for something lawful in itself, but desire of such a self-regarding intensity that it usurps the place which God alone ought to have in man's soul.

'So,' says Paul, 'I should never have come to know what covetousness was but for the commandment which says "Thou shalt not covet". But that commandment provided sin with a bridge-head from which it launched an attack on me, and as a result it brought all kinds of covetousness to birth within me. Without a law to stir it into life sin lay dormant; but when I became aware of the law, sin sprang to life and laid me low. Here is a paradox indeed! The law was given that man might keep it and live; but it was death, not life, that this law brought to me.'

It should be pointed out that this autobiographical interpretation of verses 7–13 (and of the following verses too) does not command the general acceptance today that it formerly did; one recent writer speaks of it as 'now relegated to the museum of exegetical absurdities'.[1] But it is the most natural way to understand this section, and the arguments against it are not conclusive. Paul, of course, did not think of his own experience as unique; he describes it here because it is true in a greater or lesser degree of the human race. 'Here Paul's autobiography is the biography of Everyman' (T. W. Manson). Covetousness in one form or another is common to mankind; and it may well be that here, as in Romans v. 12 ff., Paul has Adam's transgression in mind as well as his own. Covetousness played a part in Adam's downfall. When Paul speaks of sin as 'deceiv-

---

[1] P. Demann, quoted by F. J. Leenhardt, *The Epistle to the Romans*, p. 181; cf. J. Munck, *Paul and the Salvation of Mankind* (1959), pp. 11 f.

ing' or 'beguiling' him (verse 11), we are reminded of Eve's complaint in Genesis iii. 13: 'The serpent beguiled me, and I did eat.' But Paul would not have re-told the fall story in the first person singular had he not recognized it as an authentic description of his own experience, as well as of the experience of all mankind. In this respect, at least, he knew himself to be 'the Adam of his own soul'.[1]

7. *I had not known sin, but by the law.* Cf. iii. 20: 'by the law is the knowledge of sin.' The function of the law is thus propaedeutic; by revealing to men their sinfulness and inability, it reveals to them also their need of that deliverance which only God's grace can effect.

Thou shalt not covet. (Ex. xx. 17; Dt. v. 21.) It is natural for human beings to want things; when it is brought to their attention that certain things which they want are forbidden them by law, there is a tendency to want them all the more, to set their hearts upon them.

8. *Sin, taking occasion by the commandment.* In this and the following verses sin is personified as a powerful enemy. The word rendered 'occasion' is *aphormē*, a base for military operations.

Wrought in me all manner of concupiscence. 'Concupiscence' here is simply 'covetousness' (RV, RSV). NEB says 'all kinds of wrong desires'. C. K. Barrett points out that covetousness, the breach of the law, is the perversion of love, which is 'the fulfilling of the law' (Rom. xiii. 10).[2]

9. *I was alive without the law.* So Adam was not conscious of any sinful inclination until his obedience was tested by the commandment 'thou shalt not eat'. But Paul understands the inwardness of the fall narrative all the better in the light of his own experience.

Sin revived. Better, 'sin sprang to life' (NEB).

[1] 2 Baruch liv. 19; see p. 129.   [2] *From First Adam to Last*, pp. 80, 116 f.

10. *The commandment, which was ordained to life.* A reference to Leviticus xviii. 5, quoted in Romans x. 5 (cf. ii. 13).

11. *Deceived me.* The verb (*exapataō*) is the same as that used in 2 Corinthians xi. 3 ('the serpent beguiled Eve') and 1 Timothy ii. 14 ('the woman being deceived was in the transgression'); cf. the simple verb *apataō* in Genesis iii. 13, LXX. But the parallel with the fall story must not be pressed too far, for Paul's doctrine is that mankind sinned 'in Adam' and not in Eve, and in Genesis iii, as is pointed out in 1 Timothy ii. 14, 'it was not Adam who was deceived' (NEB).

13. *Was then that which is good made death unto me?* Cf. 2 Esdras ix. 36 f.: 'For we who have received the law and sinned will perish, as well as our heart which received it; the law, however, does not perish but remains in its glory.'

But sin, that it might appear sin, working death in me by that which is good. That is: it was not the law, ordained as it was that the man who obeyed it should live thereby, that brought me into a state of death. The law is good; it could not bring about this evil state of affairs. No; the villain of the piece is Sin; Sin seized the opportunity afforded it when the law showed me what was right and what was wrong, without supplying the power to do the former and avoid the latter (a power which law was never designed to supply). Sin forced me against my better judgment to do what the law showed me to be wrong, and thus involved me in condemnation and death. And in consequence I appreciated, as I should not otherwise have done, just how sinful, how contrary to God and goodness, Sin actually is.

iii. The conflict within (vii. 14–25). In this section Paul continues to speak in the first person singular, but he leaves the past tense and uses the present. Not only so, but there is an inward tension here which was absent from verses 7–13. There, sin assaulted him by stealth and struck him down; here, he puts up an agonizing resistance, even if he cannot beat down the enemy. There, he described what happened to him when he lived in 'this present age'; here, 'the age to come' has already arrived, although the old age has not yet passed away. He is a man living simultaneously on two planes, eagerly longing to live a life in keeping with the higher plane, but sadly aware of the strength of indwelling sin that keeps on pulling him down to the lower plane.

In a lecture on Paul's description of himself as being 'sold under sin', Dr. Alexander Whyte said:

> 'As often as my attentive bookseller sends me on approval another new commentary on Romans, I immediately turn to the seventh chapter. And if the commentator sets up a man of straw in the seventh chapter, I immediately shut the book. I at once send the book back and say "No, thank you. That is not the man for my hard-earned money".'

What did he mean?

This, that Paul's poignant description in verses 14-25 of someone who loves the law of God and longs to do it, but is forced by a stronger power than himself to do things which he detests, is no 'abstract argument but the echo of the personal experience of an anguished soul'.[1] Paul himself knows what it means to be torn this way and that by the law of his mind which approves the will of God, and the law of sin and death which pulls the other way.

The Christian, in fact, lives in two worlds simultaneously, and so long as this is so he lives in a state of tension. Temporally he lives in this world; as a man of flesh and blood he is subject to the conditions of mortal life; he is a 'son of Adam', like all his fellow-men, and with them he is subject to the law that 'in Adam all die'. Spiritually, however, he has passed from death to life, from the realm of darkness to the kingdom of light; he

---

[1] M. Goguel, *The Birth of Christianity* (1953), pp. 213 f. Goguel assigns the experience here described to the years immediately following Paul's conversion.

has shared in Christ's death, burial and resurrection, in which he has been raised 'to walk in newness of life', a citizen of the new world, a member of the new creation, no longer 'in Adam' but 'in Christ'.

The day will come when this present order will pass, when the new age will be established in glory, and then the tension between the two ages will be resolved. But so long as Christians live 'between the times', Paul's words in another Epistle retain their full relevance: 'the flesh lusteth against the Spirit, and the Spirit against the flesh: and these are contrary the one to the other; so that ye cannot do the things that ye would' (Gal. v. 17).[1]

Here then is the self-portrait of a man who is conscious of the presence and power of indwelling sin in his life; it is a tyrant whose dictates he hates and loathes, but against whose power he struggles in vain. When he is compelled by *force majeure* to obey the tyrant's dictates, he does not acknowledge the ensuing acts as his own; they are the very opposite of what he desires to do. What he desires to do is the law of God, he delights in it, he recognizes that it is 'holy, and just, and good'. But, for all his desire to obey God's law, he is compelled by the malignant power within to disobey it. 'The good that I would, I do not: but the evil which I would not, that I do.'

This unequal struggle against 'the law of sin which is in my members' (as Paul calls it) has been the real experience of too many Christians for us to state confidently that Paul cannot be speaking autobiographically here—and in the present tense too. Paul can entreat his friends 'by the meekness and gentleness of Christ' (2 Cor. x. 1); but did this meekness and gentleness come to him naturally? There is good reason to believe that a man of his imperious zeal found it no easy matter to 'crucify the flesh'—to win the victory over a hasty tongue, a premature judgment, a resentment at any encroachment on the sphere of his apostolic service. The man who made it his daily business to discipline himself so as not to be disqualified

[1] For the counterpart in Romans to Gal. v. 16, see p. 156.

in the contest of holiness, the man who pressed on to the goal of God's upward calling in Christ Jesus, knew that that 'immortal guerdon' was to be run for 'not without dust and heat'. He was too constantly given to portraying the way of holiness as a race to be run, a battle to be fought, for us to imagine that victory came to him 'sudden, in a minute'.

True, but victory did come to him. The present passage leads up to a paean of triumph, although it begins with a sad confession of inability. The inability persists only so long as 'I myself'—that is, I in my own strength—fight the battle. So long as I do that, says Paul, I may serve the law of God with my mind, but my body willy-nilly goes on rendering obedience to the law of sin. Must I always know defeat? Must I always carry this incubus on my back? Will deliverance never come? Thank God it will, through Jesus Christ our Lord.[1]

14. *I am carnal, sold under sin.* The nature which I have inherited 'in Adam' finds the law uncongenial. The law is 'spiritual' because it is God's law; but this nature of mine is unspiritual (*sarkinos*, 'fleshly'), enslaved to a power which my will repudiates. There is something in man—even regenerate man—which objects to God and seeks to be independent of Him; this 'something' is what Paul here calls his 'flesh' (cf. verse 18), a prey to the tyranny of indwelling sin. The phrase 'sold under sin' is reminiscent of Wisdom i. 4, where it is said that wisdom will not 'dwell in a body that is held in pledge by sin' (RV).

15. *For that which I do I allow not.* 'I do not even acknowledge my own actions as mine' (NEB).

For what I would, that do I not; but what I hate, that do I. It is customary to quote as classical parallels Horace's *quae nocuere sequar, fugiam quae profore credo,* 'I pursue the things that have

---

[1] For an examination of the rival interpretations of Rom. vii. 14–25, with a solution which goes far to do justice to the strongest arguments on either side, see three articles by C. L. Mitton, 'Romans vii reconsidered', *ExT*, LXV (1953–54), pp. 78 ff., 99 ff., 132 ff.

done me harm; I shun the things I believe will do me good' (*Epistles* i. 8. 11); or Ovid's *uideo meliora proboque; deteriora sequor*, 'I see and approve the better course, but I follow the worse one' (put into the mouth of Medea in *Metamorphoses* vii. 20 f.). C. K. Barrett (*ad loc.*) points out an even closer verbal parallel in Epictetus, according to whom (ii. 26. 4) the thief does not do what he wishes; but he also points out, and very pertinently, that neither Ovid nor Epictetus (nor, we may add, Horace) is saying exactly what Paul says. Paul has within him an independent witness, the voice of conscience (cf. note on ii. 15, p. 91), which, by condemning his failure to keep the law, bears testimony to the law as being 'holy, and just, and good'.

17, 20. *It is no more I that do it, but sin that dwelleth in me.* But as soon as my will consents to it, then it is I who do it, even if it was not so before:

18. *To will is present with me; but how to perform that which is good I find not.* Read with RV: 'to will is present with me, but to do that which is good is not' (the best attested text omits 'I find').

22. *I delight in the law of God after the inward man.* And therefore I can sing 'O how love I thy law!' and everything else in the hundred-and-nineteenth psalm; yet am I not hereby justified. The 'inward man' is the 'new man' in Christ that is daily being renewed in the Creator's image (cf. 2 Cor. iv. 16; Col. iii. 10).

23. *The law of sin.* The evil principle, or the tyranny of indwelling sin.

24. *O wretched man that I am!* 'Believers are perfect as to their justification, but their sanctification is only begun. It is a progressive work. When they believed in Christ, they knew but very little of the fountain of corruption that dwells in them. When Christ made Himself known to them as their Saviour, and the Beloved of their souls, the carnal mind seemed to be dead, but they found out afterwards that it was not dead. So some have experienced more soul trials after their conversion than when they were awakened to a sense of their lost condition. "O wretched man that I am! who shall deliver me from the body of this death?" is their cry till they are made perfect in holiness. But He that hath begun a good work in them will perform it until the day of Jesus Christ.'[1]

Who shall deliver me from the body of this death? One can find no lack of verbal parallels to this exclamation in classical literature and elsewhere. Philo—a truer disciple of Plato than of the prophets—speaks of the body as 'that composition of clay, that moulded statue, that house so close to the soul, which it never lays aside but carries like a corpse from the cradle to the grave—what a grievous burden!' (*On Husbandry* 25.) Epictetus speaks of himself as 'a poor soul shackled to a corpse' (fragment 23). Some commentators have tried to illuminate Paul's words by reference to Virgil's account of the Etruscan king Mezentius, who tied his living captives to decomposing corpses (*Aeneid* viii. 485 ff.). But Paul is not thinking of the body of flesh and blood; the evil was more deeply rooted. 'The body of this death', or 'this body of death' (RSV), is, like the 'body of sin' (vi. 6), that heritage of human nature subject to the law of sin and death which he shares with all sons of Adam, that *massa perditionis* in which the whole of the old creation is involved, and from which, for all his longing and struggling, he cannot extricate himself by his own endeavours.

25. *I thank God through Jesus Christ our Lord.* It is astonishing to find this outbreak of triumph hard on the heels of his anguished cry 'who shall deliver me?' But here is the answer: 'God alone, through Jesus Christ our Lord! Thanks be to

[1] D. MacFarlane, in *The Free Presbyterian Pulpit* (1961), p. 20.

God!' (NEB). Just how this deliverance from indwelling sin may be appropriated is described more fully in chapter viii; for the moment, after his brief indication that the situation is not hopeless, Paul goes back to summarize the moral predicament of vii. 14–24.

So then with the mind I myself serve the law of God: but with the flesh the law of sin. It is unnecessary to treat this sentence as misplaced. Moffatt makes it stand as a parenthesis after verse 23, which, he says, 'seems its original and logical position before the climax of ver. 24'—a transposition which C. H. Dodd says is 'surely right'. G. Zuntz thinks that it 'may be an addition by Paul himself or a summing up by some early reader; in any case, its present position is unsuitable and suggests that a marginal gloss has been inserted into the text' (*The Text of the Epistles*, p. 16). It appears in its present position, however, in our earliest authorities; and it is a precarious procedure to rearrange the words of Paul in the interests of a smoother logical sequence.

'I myself' (*autos egō*) is emphatic: it is 'I by myself' who experience this defeat and frustration, but 'I', as a Christian, am not left to 'myself': 'the law of the Spirit of life in Christ Jesus' has come to dwell within me, and His presence and power make an almighty difference.

c. Freedom from death (viii. 1–39)

i. Life in the Spirit (viii. 1–17). 'The flesh lusteth against the Spirit, and the Spirit against the flesh: and these are contrary the one to the other: so that ye cannot do the things that ye would.' These words from Galatians v. 17 have already been quoted as a summary of the situation which Paul describes at greater length and in more vivid and personal terms in Romans vii. 14–25. But immediately before these words he had said: 'Walk in the Spirit, and ye shall not fulfil the lust of the flesh' (Gal. v. 16). The counterpart to this exhortation now lies before us in Romans viii. 1–17. There has been no mention of the Holy Spirit in chapter vii, but He pervades chapter viii, which describes the life of victory and hope lived by those 'who walk not after the flesh, but after the Spirit' (viii. 4), those who are 'in Christ Jesus' (viii. 1).

So long as they endeavour to go a-warring at their own charges, they fight a losing battle; when they avail themselves of the resources of life and power that are theirs 'in Christ Jesus' they are more than conquerors. There is therefore no more reason why those who are 'in Christ Jesus' should go on in a life of penal servitude, bound to carry out the dictates of the tyrannical law of sin and death. Christ dwells within them by His Spirit, and His Spirit infuses into them a new principle—the law of life—which is stronger than the strength of indwelling sin and sets them free from its tyranny.

Under the old order it was simply impossible to do the will of God, and if that old order still dominates men's lives, to do His will remains an impossibility. But those whose life is controlled by the Spirit, those who follow His promptings, do the will of God from the heart. Their own spirit, formerly dead and insensitive, is now instinct with the life which the Spirit of God imparts; their body may still for the time being be subject to the law of death which results from the entry of sin into the world; but the last word remains with the Spirit of life.

For not only does the Spirit maintain life and power in the spirit of believers here and now; His indwelling presence is a token that their body, still subject to mortality, will rise to new life as Christ's own body rose. The body is not excluded from the benefits of the redemption which Christ has procured. Paul had already used this fact in an appeal to the members of the Corinthian Church to regard their bodies and bodily actions in a spirit of Christian responsibility: 'ye are bought with a price: therefore glorify God in your body'[1] (1 Cor. vi. 20). So here he suggests that intimations of a coming immortality are conveyed by the Spirit even in this period of mortality:

[1] The words which follow in AV, 'and in your spirit, which are God's' are a later addition which blunts the point of Paul's appeal.

this is one of the many ways in which the presence of the Spirit in this very time is the first-fruits of a heritage of glory yet to be realized. If those who go on in conformity with the old order have the sentence of death within themselves, those who reckon the old order as belonging to the dead past and follow the guidance of the Spirit of God have the assurance that life immortal has already begun within them. Indeed, the fact that they respond to the leading of the Spirit of God is a clear proof that they are sons of God.

For Paul, the leading of the Spirit is not a matter of sporadic impulse, but the believer's habitual experience; it is the very principle of the freedom of the Christian life. 'If ye be led of the Spirit, ye are not under the law' (Gal. v. 18). The old legal bondage has been thrown off; the Spirit introduces believers into a new relationship as free-born sons of God. It is the prompting of the Spirit that causes Christians to address God spontaneously as their Father, using the very expression that Jesus Himself used when speaking to God as His Father—an expression proper to the intimate atmosphere of family affection. No wonder that in a similar passage in Galatians Paul says that God has sent 'the Spirit of his Son' into His people's hearts, crying 'Abba, Father' (Gal. iv. 6). They have, in other words, received the same Spirit who descended in power on Jesus at His baptism (Mk. i. 10), led Him in the wilderness (Mk. i. 12), supplied the energy for His mighty works (Mt. xii. 28), and animated His whole life and ministry (Mk. i. 8; Lk. iv. 14, 18).

Thus the Spirit of God and the Christian's own spirit bear consentient witness to the fact that he is a child of God. God's children, moreover, are His heirs—heirs to that glory which is Christ's by unique right, and which by grace He shares with His 'brethren', who are thus joint-heirs with Him. Those who in this present life experience the fellowship of His suffering can look forward to the fellowship of His glory. 'Suffering now, glory hereafter' is a recurring theme in the New Testament, and one that corresponded to the realities of early Christian life. 'We must through much tribulation enter into the kingdom of God', said Paul and Barnabas to their converts in South Galatia (Acts xiv. 22), and the same warning is repeated as each new community of Christians is formed, and it is speedily confirmed by experience. 'If we suffer, we shall also reign with him' (2 Tim. ii. 12) means the reproduction in the lives of Christians of the pattern perfectly exemplified in their Master, who by divine necessity passed through suffering, and so entered into His glory (Lk. xxiv. 26; 1 Pet. i. 11, v. 1).

1. *There is therefore now no condemnation to them which are in Christ Jesus.* If 'condemnation' were simply the opposite of 'justification', Paul would be saying that those who are in Christ Jesus are justified; but that stage in the argument was reached in iii. 21 ff. The word *katakrima* means 'probably not "condemnation", but the punishment following sentence' (Arndt-Gingrich)—in other words, 'penal servitude'. There is no reason why those who are 'in Christ Jesus' should go on doing penal servitude as though they had never been pardoned and never been liberated from the prison-house of sin.

'In Christ Jesus' (or 'in Christ' or 'in the Lord') is Paul's description of the new order into which men and women are introduced by faith in Christ. Christian baptism is a baptism 'into Christ'; by faith-union with Christ His people are reckoned to have died with Him, been buried with Him, been raised with Him. It is no longer they who live, but Christ who lives in them. The common life in the body of Christ is Christ's own resurrection life shared with His people; if from one point of view He lives in them, from another they live in Him. The Old Testament concept of 'corporate personality' was still alive and readily available for the thought and language of a man like Paul; in terms of this concept it was not difficult for his mind to move back and forth between Christ in His own Person and Christ as a corporate personality, comprising the Christ now exalted at God's right hand and all His people who share His life. 'To be "in Christ" is to be a member of the church; not, of course, to have your name on the books, but to be in real sense a limb or organ of Christ's body, dependent upon Him, subject to His will, dedicated to His ends.'[1]

The addition *who walk not after the flesh* and the still later addition *but after the Spirit* are not parts of the original text of verse 1 (cf. RV, RSV, NEB) but were introduced under the influence of verse 4b, where they properly belong.

2. *The law of the Spirit of life in Christ Jesus hath made me free.* . . . Compare 2 Corinthians iii. 17, 'where the Spirit of the Lord is, there is liberty'; also Galatians v. 13, 'ye have been called unto liberty.' 'Law' here probably means 'principle' (see pp. 52 f.). It is the 'law of the Spirit' by contrast with 'the law of sin which is in my members' (vii. 23); it is the 'law of life' by contrast with the 'law of death'. It is perhaps better to take the two genitives 'of the Spirit' and 'of life' as alike dependent on 'law'; the law of the Spirit is the law of life. The Spirit 'by His determining influences produces regulated action without any code'.[2]

Apart from the anticipatory mention of the Spirit in Romans v. 5, where His coming is said to flood the hearts of believers with the love of God (and the brief reference in i. 4 to the 'spirit of holiness' in connection with Christ's being raised from the dead), this is the first place in the Epistle where the Spirit of God enters the argument. It is no accident that with His entry there is no further talk of defeat. The warfare between the two natures still goes on, but where the Holy Spirit is in control the old nature is compelled to give way.

For 'me' in 'hath made me free' some weighty authorities (including the eastern witnesses *Aleph* and B and the western witness G), followed by the Nestle-Kilpatrick text, read 'thee' (cf. NEB: 'has set you free').

3. *In the likeness of sinful flesh.* Lit., 'in likeness of flesh of sin'.

---

[1] C. H. Dodd, *Gospel and Law* (1951), pp. 36 f.
[2] N. Q. Hamilton, *The Holy Spirit and Eschatology in Paul* (1957), p. 30.

The words are carefully chosen. 'In likeness of flesh' by itself would be docetic; the essence of the apostolic message is that the Son of God came 'in flesh' and not merely 'in likeness of flesh'. Paul might have said simply 'in flesh', but he wished to emphasize that human flesh was the realm in which sin gained a foothold and dominated the situation until the grace of God drew near. Hence he says not simply 'flesh', but 'sinful flesh' ('flesh of sin'). But to say that the Son of God came 'in sinful flesh' would imply that there was sin in Him, whereas (as Paul puts it elsewhere) He 'knew no sin' (2 Cor. v. 21). Hence He is described as being sent 'in the likeness of sinful flesh'.

And for sin. Gk. *peri hamartias* ('for sin') is the regular phrase used in the LXX to render Heb. *ḥaṭṭa'th*, 'sin-offering',[1] and that is its force here; hence RV, rightly, renders 'as an offering for sin' (cf. NEB, 'as a sacrifice for sin'). This is probably the force of 'sin' also in 2 Corinthians v. 21 where Christ is said to have been 'made . . . sin for us' (although it is the simple noun *hamartia*, and not the phrase *peri hamartias*, that is used there).

Condemned sin in the flesh. That is, in the flesh of Christ, in His human nature, sentence was passed and executed on sin. Therefore, for those who are united to Christ, the power of sin has been broken (cf. vi. 6 f.).

4. *That the righteousness of the law might be fulfilled in us.* The 'righteous requirement' of the law is summed up in xiii. 9 in the single commandment 'Thou shalt love thy neighbour as thyself.' The Greek word is *dikaiōma*, used here as in ii. 26 (for other meanings see p. 133, n. 1). Here we have the fulfilment of Jeremiah's prophecy of the new covenant (quoted in part in xi. 27), under which, said God, 'I will put my law in their inward parts, and write it in their hearts; and will be their God, and they shall be my people. And they shall teach no more every man his neighbour, and every man his brother, saying, Know the Lord: for they shall all know me, from the least of them unto the greatest of them' (Je. xxxi. 33 f.). Cf. the

---

[1] In Is. liii. 10 it is the LXX rendering of Heb. *'asham*, 'guilt-offering' (see p. 37).

parallel prophecy of Ezekiel xxxvi. 26 f., where God says: 'A new heart also will I give you, and a new spirit will I put within you: and I will take away the stony heart out of your flesh, and I will give you an heart of flesh. And I will put my spirit within you, and cause you to walk in my statutes, and ye shall keep my judgments, and do them.' The New Testament writers recognize in the gospel the fulfilment of these ancient prophecies.

Christian holiness is not a matter of painstaking conformity to the individual precepts of an external law-code; it is rather a question of the Holy Spirit's producing His fruit in the life, reproducing those graces which were seen in perfection in the life of Christ. The law prescribed a life of holiness, but it was powerless to produce such a life, because of the inadequacy of the human material that it had to work upon. But what the law was powerless to do has been done by God. Now that God's own Son, sent to earth 'in the likeness of sinful flesh', has given up His life as a sin-offering on His people's behalf, the death-sentence has been passed on indwelling sin. It found no foot-hold in the life of Jesus; it was effectively overcome in His death; and the fruits of that victory are now made good to all who are 'in Him'. All that the law required by way of conformity to the will of God is now realized in the lives of those who are controlled by the Holy Spirit and are released from their servitude to the old order. God's commands have now become God's enablings.

> 'To run and work the law commands,
> Yet gives me neither feet nor hands;
> But better news the gospel brings:
> It bids me fly, and gives me wings.'

'Grace was given', as Augustine puts it, 'that the law might be fulfilled.'[1]

'Not until, by the death and resurrection of Christ, the new creation had come into being, did it become possible for God to

[1] *'Gratia data est, ut lex impleretur.'*

send the Spirit of his Son into the hearts of lost and helpless men; and with the Spirit came life, freedom and power. Those who live by the Spirit, as Paul says, produce the fruits of the Spirit. A vine does not produce grapes by Act of Parliament; they are the fruit of the vine's own life; so the conduct which conforms to the standard of the Kingdom is not produced by any demand, not even God's, but it is the fruit of that divine nature which God gives as the result of what he has done in and by Christ.'[1]

Who walk not after the flesh, but after the Spirit. Cf. Galatians v. 25, 'If we live in the Spirit, let us also walk in the Spirit' (also Gal. v. 16, quoted on p. 156). It is at first sight difficult to decide whether 'spirit' (*pneuma*) should be spelt with an initial capital or not here. When 'spirit' is used in contrast to 'flesh', it might be natural to suppose that the human spirit is meant. Yet, so frequently in the following argument does the word clearly refer to the Spirit of God that it is better to take it as referring to Him throughout (even where it appears in antithesis with 'flesh' as here and in verse 9), except where the context rules this sense out. The human spirit is not excluded, however, where the divine Spirit is understood. For Paul, the human spirit is dormant or dead until it is aroused to life by the Spirit of God; hence to 'walk . . . after the *pneuma*' implies the action of the human spirit in response to the guidance of the divine Spirit.

5. *They that are after the flesh do mind the things of the flesh; but they that are after the Spirit, the things of the Spirit.* Cf. Galatians v. 17 (quoted on pp. 152, 156).

6. *To be carnally minded . . . to be spiritually minded.* Lit., 'the mind of the flesh . . . the mind of the spirit'. Compare the antithesis in Galatians v. 19 ff. between 'the works of the flesh' and 'the fruit of the Spirit'.

9. *If any man have not the Spirit of Christ, he is none of his.* 'If a man does not possess the Spirit of Christ, he is no Christian'

[1] S. H. Hooke, *The Siege Perilous* (1956), p. 264.

(NEB). Since it is the Spirit alone who brings men into living relation with Christ, there can be no such relation with Christ apart from the Spirit.

10. *If Christ be in you, the body is dead because of sin.* It is best to translate the clause beginning 'the body is dead' as a subordinate clause; the true apodosis to the conditional clause 'if Christ be in you' is 'the Spirit is life because of righteousness'. Cf. RSV, NEB; the latter version renders it: 'But if Christ is dwelling within you, then although the body is a dead thing because you sinned, yet the spirit is life itself because you have been justified.' 'The body is dead' in the sense that it is 'mortal', 'subject to death'.

But the Spirit is life because of righteousness. Is the 'Spirit' the Spirit of God (AV) or the human spirit of the believer (RV, RSV, NEB)? The statement is true whichever interpretation be preferred, but Paul meant the one or the other—which? In view of the sense of *pneuma* in the verses immediately preceding and following, he probably meant the Spirit of God; we may then paraphrase his statement thus: 'If Christ dwells within you, then, while your body is still subject to that temporal death which is the consequence of sin, the Spirit who has taken up His abode in you, the living and quickening Spirit, imparts to you that eternal life which is the consequence of justification' (cf. v. 18, 'justification of life').

11. *He that raised up Christ from the dead shall also quicken your mortal bodies by his Spirit that dwelleth in you.* Cf. 1 Corinthians vi. 14; 2 Corinthians iv. 14; 1 Thessalonians iv. 14, where the resurrection of believers is similarly made dependent on the resurrection of Christ (see note on i. 4, pp. 72 ff.). Here, however, the relation of the Spirit to resurrection is emphasized as it is not in those earlier passages; but cf. 2 Corinthians v. 5: 'he that hath wrought us for the selfsame thing (the putting on of the heavenly body) is God, who also hath given unto us the earnest of the Spirit.'

13. *If ye through the Spirit do mortify the deeds of the body.*
'Mortify' is equivalent to 'reckon . . . dead' (vi. 11); whereas
in vi. 11 believers are exhorted to reckon themselves dead in
relation to sin, here they are told to reckon their former sinful
practices dead in relation to themselves (so also in Col. iii. 5 f.).
We may compare Galatians v. 24, 'they that are Christ's have
crucified the flesh with the affections and lusts (thereof)', and
our Lord's more vivid language about plucking out the eye
and cutting off the hand or foot that leads one into sin (Mt.
v. 29 f.; Mk. ix. 43 ff.).

14. *As many as are led by the Spirit of God, they are the sons of
God.* Cf. Galatians v. 18: 'if ye be led of the Spirit, ye are not
under the law.' In Galatians iii. 23–iv. 7 Paul contrasts the
former bondage of slaves ('kept under the law') with the new
freedom of sons, into whose hearts 'God hath sent forth the
Spirit of his Son . . . crying, Abba, Father.'

15. *Ye have not received the spirit of bondage again to fear; but ye
have received the Spirit of adoption.* Compare 1 Corinthians ii. 12,
'we have received, not the spirit of the world, but the spirit
which is of God'; 2 Timothy i. 7, 'God hath not given us the
spirit of fear; but of power, and of love, and of a sound mind.'
'Here is a beautiful chain of experimental verses, all cast in
the same mould, all built upon the same pattern, with the
negative first and the positive second; on one side bondage,
worldliness, and fear; on the other sonship, spiritual gifts,
power, love, and sanctified common-sense.'[1]
The Spirit of adoption is so called because it is those who are
led by the Spirit of God that are sons of God (verse 14). 'The
Spirit of adoption' or sonship (*huiothesia*) is, in other words, the
Spirit who makes believers sons of God and enables them to
call God their Father. In Galatians iv. 6 they are enabled to
do this by 'the Spirit of his Son'; for when believers address
God by the same name as Jesus used, it is evident that His

[1] J. Rendel Harris, *Aaron's Breastplate* (1908), p. 92.

Spirit is now in them. The term 'adoption' may smack some-what of artificiality in our ears; but in the first century AD an adopted son was a son deliberately chosen by his adoptive father to perpetuate his name and inherit his estate; he was no whit inferior in status to a son born in the ordinary course of nature, and might well enjoy the father's affection more fully and reproduce the father's character more worthily.

Abba, Father. This phrase occurs in two other places in the New Testament—in Mark xiv. 36 and Galatians iv. 6 (see notes immediately above, pp. 158, 165). In Greek it is *Abba, ho patēr,* where *ho patēr* ('the Father') simply indicates the mean-ing of the non-Greek word *Abba. Abba* is an Aramaic word (in the 'emphatic state') which came to be used among the Jews (and is used to this day in Hebrew-speaking families) as the familiar term by which children address their father. In Mark xiv. 36 Jesus is represented as using it in His prayer in Gethse-mane. The significance of this lies in the fact that *Abba* was not, and is not, the term used by Jews when addressing *God* as their Father. But the fact that this Aramaic word found its way into the worshipping vocabulary of the Gentile churches strongly suggests that it was used in this way by Jesus, and Mark xiv. 36 confirms this. There is strong presumption, too, that when Jesus taught His disciples to begin their prayers with 'Father, Hallowed be thy name' (Lk. xi. 2, RV), the word He used for 'Father' was *Abba.* This sufficiently explains the passage of the Aramaic term into the usage of Greek-speaking Christians.

On *Abba, Father* Luther says: 'This is but a little word, and yet notwithstanding it comprehendeth all things. The mouth speaketh not, but the affection of the heart speaketh after this manner. Although I be oppressed with anguish and terror on every side, and seem to be forsaken and utterly cast away from thy presence, yet am I thy child, and thou art my Father for Christ's sake: I am beloved because of the Beloved. Wherefore this little word, Father, conceived effectually in the heart, passeth all the eloquence of Demosthenes, Cicero, and of the most eloquent rhetoricians that ever were in the world. This matter is not expressed with words, but with groanings, which groanings cannot be uttered with any words or eloquence, for no tongue can express them' (on Gal. iv. 6, Middleton's translation).

16. *The children of God.* The word here is *tekna*, 'children', and not *huioi*, 'sons', as in verse 14; but the course of the argument makes it perfectly plain that Paul is using the two substantives interchangeably. In Galatians iii. 23–iv. 7 he does indeed make a distinction between the period of infancy, when his readers were under the guardianship of the law, and the attainment of their responsible status as sons (*huioi*) of God, now that the gospel has been introduced. But their previous status is qualified by the term *nēpioi* ('infants'), not *tekna* ('children'). Nowhere in the New Testament can a valid distinction be made between being 'children (*tekna*) of God' and 'sons (*huioi*) of God'. In the Johannine writings this relationship is conveyed throughout by the word *tekna* (cf. Jn. i. 12; 1 Jn. iii. 1 f.), the word *huios* being reserved for Christ as the Son of God.

17. *And if children, then heirs.* Cf. Galatians iv. 7: 'Wherefore thou art no more a servant (Gk. *doulos*, 'slave'), but a son; and if a son, then an heir of God through Christ.' The crisis of what is called the conversion of John Wesley came when, in his own words, he "exchanged the faith of a servant for the faith of a son".[1]

Heirs of God, and joint-heirs with Christ. They are joint-heirs with Christ because the glory which they will inherit by grace is the glory which is His by right (cf. Jn. xvii. 22–24).

If so be that we suffer with him, that we may be also glorified together. The suffering is the necessary prelude to the glory. Thus when Paul says (2 Cor. iv. 16) that 'though our outward man perish, yet the inward man is renewed day by day', he means that the same afflictions and privations which destroy

[1] C. A. Anderson Scott, *Words* (1939), p. 15.

the 'outward man' are the means which the Spirit of God uses to renew the 'inward man' more and more, until at last the 'outward man' disappears altogether and the 'inward man' is fully formed after the image of Christ. Cf. 2 Corinthians iv. 10: 'always bearing about in the body the dying of the Lord Jesus, that the life also of Jesus might be made manifest in our body.'

ii. The glory to come (viii. 18–30). But the glory to come far outweighs the affliction of the present. The affliction is light and temporary when compared with the all-surpassing and everlasting glory. So Paul, writing against a background of recent and (even for him) unparalleled tribulation, had assured his friends in Corinth a year or two previously that 'our light affliction, which is but for a moment, worketh for us a far more exceeding and eternal weight[1] of glory' (2 Cor. iv. 17). It is not merely that the glory is a compensation for the suffering; it actually grows out of the suffering. There is an organic relation between the two for the believer as surely as there was for his Lord.

When the day of glory dawns, that glory will be manifested on a universal scale in the people of God, the glorified body of Christ. Something of the glory is already visible: Paul elsewhere sees a special splendour in the church as the fellowship of the reconciled, and thinks of it as being displayed even at this present time to celestial beings as God's masterpiece of reconciliation: 'that now unto the principalities and powers in heavenly places might be known by the church the manifold wisdom of God' (Eph. iii. 10). But what is now seen in a limited and all too distorted fashion will be seen in perfection when the people of God at last attain the goal which He has ever had in view for them—complete conformity to His glorified Son.

But it is not only Christians who have this hope of glory. All creation, says Paul, is waiting with earnest longing for the day

---

[1] The expression 'weight of glory' probably came the more naturally to Paul's mind because in Hebrew one root (*kbd*) does duty for both concepts—'weight' and 'glory'.

when the sons of God will be manifested in glory. At present, as old Qoheleth proclaimed, 'Vanity of vanity' is writ large over all things beneath the sun. But this vanity—this state of frustration and bondage—is only temporary; just as man at present falls short of the glory of God, so creation as a whole cannot attain the full end for which she was brought into being. Like man, creation must be redeemed because, like man, creation has been subject to a fall.

This doctrine of the cosmic fall is implicit in the biblical record from Genesis iii (where the ground is cursed for man's sake) to Revelation xxii (where 'there shall be no more curse') ; and is demanded by any world-outlook which endeavours to do justice to the biblical doctrine of creation and the facts of life as we know them. Man is part of nature, and the whole 'nature' of which he forms part was created good, has been subjected to frustration and futility by sin, and will ultimately be redeemed. It is no accident that the redemption of nature is here seen as coinciding with the redemption of man's body— that physical part of his being which links him with the material creation. Man was put in charge of the 'lower' creation and involved it with him when he fell; through the redemptive work of the 'second man' the entail of the fall is broken not only for man himself but for the creation which is dependent on him. Even now man, who by selfish exploitation can turn the good earth into a dust bowl, can by responsible trusteeship make the desert blossom like the rose; what then will the effect of a completely redeemed mankind be on the creation entrusted to his care? When Isaiah looked forward to the peaceful coexistence of wolf and lamb in the messianic age, he voiced his hope in the language of poetry, but his poetry enshrines no pathetic fallacy but something much more biblical and substantial:

'They shall not hurt or destroy
    in all my holy mountain;
for the earth shall be full of the knowledge of the Lord
    as the waters cover the sea' (Is. xi. 9, RSV).

The Christian will neither hold that at present 'all is for the best in the best of all possible worlds', nor will he write the world off as belonging to the devil.[1] The world is God's world, and God will yet be glorified by all His works. And when God is glorified, His creatures are blessed.

If words mean anything, these words of Paul denote not the annihilation of the present material universe on the day of revelation, to be replaced by a universe completely new, but the transformation of the present universe so that it will fulfil the purpose for which God created it. Here again we have an echo of an Old Testament hope—the creation of new heavens and a new earth 'wherein dwelleth righteousness' (2 Pet. iii. 13, quoting Is. lxv. 17, lxvi. 22; cf. Rev. xxi. 1).[2] But the transformation of the universe depends upon the completion of man's transformation by the working of God's grace.

The grace of God has already begun to work in the lives of the justified; its continued working is sufficiently attested by the indwelling of the Spirit, and it is that same grace which, on 'the day of Jesus Christ', will bring to completion the divine work so well begun.

> 'Grace all the work shall crown
> To everlasting days;
> It lays in heaven the topmost stone,
> And well deserves the praise.'

But the indwelling of the Spirit is not only the evidence that God's grace is continually at work with us now; it is the guarantee of the coming glory—and more than the guarantee, it is the first instalment of the coming glory. There is no discontinuity between here and hereafter, so far as God's working in and for His people is concerned.

If inanimate creation longs blindly for the day of its liberation, the community of the redeemed, who see the glory

[1] Cf. J. Wren-Lewis, 'Christian Morality and the Idea of a Cosmic Fall', *ExT*, LXXI (1959–60), pp. 204 ff.

[2] The apocalyptic language of Rev. xx. 11, xxi. 1, is to be understood in the light of more prosaic statements such as the present, and not *vice versa*.

shining before them, strain forward intelligently for that same consummation. For them it is 'the adoption'—that is to say, the day when they will be publicly and universally acknowledged as the sons of God; for them, too, it means 'the redemption of the body'—the day of resurrection when the present body of humiliation will be transformed into the likeness of Christ's glorified body, when the whole personality will finally experience the benefits of His redemptive work.

This is the hope of the people of God—'Christ in you, the hope of glory', as Paul puts it in another Epistle (Col. i. 27). This hope is an essential element in their salvation; this hope enables them to accept the trials of the present, so that by patient endurance they may win their lives; it is, along with faith and love, one of the crowning graces which are distinguishing marks of the Christian.

In all the trials of the present, too, the indwelling Spirit aids by His intercession. The aspirations after holiness and glory to which He gives rise in the lives of believers are too deep to be adequately expressed in words. At a certain stage of religious life the accurate form of words is regarded as essential to the efficacy of prayer; when the spirit of man is in closest harmony with the Spirit of God words may not only prove inadequate; they may even hinder prayer. But God, before whom the thoughts of all men are like an open book, recognizes in those unspoken 'groanings' deep in His people's hearts the voice of the Spirit interceding for them in tune with His own will, and answers them accordingly.

Indeed, God's overruling grace co-operates in all things for His people's good, even in those things which at the time are so distressing and perplexing and hard to bear. 'We know' that this is so, says Paul, speaking as one who had proved its truth in his own experience, finding, for example, that his hardships turned out for the furtherance of the gospel (Phil. i. 12) and that his sorest and most disagreeable trials were the means by which the power of Christ rested upon him (2 Cor. xii. 9 f.).

And now he lets his mind run back and forward to survey

the whole course of God's dealings with His people. Before the world's foundation God foreknew and foreordained them—foreordained them for the day of final redemption, when they would be fully conformed to the image of His Son. The Son of God is Himself 'the image of the invisible God' (Col. i. 15; cf. 2 Cor. iv. 4). God's creating man 'in his image' was an early step towards the accomplishment of His age-long purpose, to have creatures of His own sharing His glory as fully as created beings can share the glory of their Creator. When the image of God in the old creation was defaced by sin, so that man as he now is falls short of the glory for which he was made, the purpose of God was not frustrated. When the due time arrived, the divine image was displayed among men by the new Man, into whose image those who are united with Him by faith are progressively changed—from one degree of glory to another—until the day when, to quote another New Testament writer, they will be perfectly conformed to His likeness, because they will see Him 'as he is' (1 Jn. iii. 2).

18. *The sufferings of this present time are not worthy to be compared with the glory which shall be revealed in us.* Cf. Luke vi. 22 f.: 'Blessed are ye, when men shall hate you . . . Rejoice ye in that day, and leap for joy; for, behold, your reward is great in heaven.'

20. *The creature was made subject to vanity.* In addition to the idea of futility or frustration, 'vanity' (*mataiotēs*), as elsewhere in the Greek Bible (cf. Acts xiv. 15), may mean the worship of false gods; the creation has been enslaved to malignant powers (cf. 1 Cor. xii. 2).

By reason of him who hath subjected the same. This is most probably God. An early view is that Adam is intended, since his sin brought death into the world and involved the earth in the ensuing curse. More recently Karl Heim has argued that the subjecting agency is 'the revolutionary power of sin . . . the Satanic power' which existed before men and brought them 'under its spell by its tempting wiles'.[1] But this comes near to an unPauline dualism, and in any case such a sinister power could not be said to have subjected the world to frustration 'in hope'.

21. *Because the creature itself also shall be delivered from the bondage of corruption.* 'Because' (*hoti*) should probably be replaced by the conjunction 'that', and the clause which it introduces taken as directly dependent on 'in hope' at the end of verse 20: 'in hope that the creation itself also shall be delivered . . .' (RV).
Into the glorious liberty of the children of God. For the basic thought cf. James i. 18: 'Of his own will begat he us with the word of truth, that we should be a kind of firstfruits of his creatures.'

22. *The whole creation groaneth and travaileth in pain together until now.* Paul may have in mind the current Jewish expectation of 'the birth-pangs of the Messiah'—the time of distress which would usher in the messianic age (cf. Mk. xiii. 8, NEB: 'the birth-pangs of the new age begin'). If so, he regards all mankind, and indeed creation as a whole, as sharing in these birth-pangs and looking forward to the joy which will follow them.

23. *The firstfruits of the Spirit.* The indwelling of the Spirit here and now is the 'firstfruits' (*aparchē*), i.e. the 'first instalment' or 'down-payment' of the eternal heritage of glory which awaits believers. In 2 Corinthians i. 22, v. 5 and Ephesians i. 14 the same teaching about the Spirit is conveyed by the use of *arrhabōn*, 'pledge' or 'earnest' (the word employed in modern Greek for an engagement-ring, as the pledge or earnest of the coming marriage).
It has been suggested that some readers of the Epistle may have inferred from Paul's use of *aparchē* here that the possession

[1] *The World: its Creation and Consummation* (1962), pp. 125 f.

of the Spirit is the believer's 'identification-card', since there is papyrus evidence for this sense of the word. Although that is not precisely what Paul means here, they would not have been far astray if they did make this inference, as something of this sort is implied by the 'sealing' with the Spirit in Ephesians i. 13, iv. 30. For another use of the *aparchē* figure see Romans xi. 16 (pp. 216 f.).

We ourselves groan within ourselves. Cf. 2 Corinthians v. 2: 'in this (tabernacle, i.e. body) we groan, earnestly desiring to be clothed upon with our house which is from heaven.'

Waiting for the adoption, to wit, the redemption of our body. The 'adoption' here is the full manifestation of believers' status as sons of God (cf. verses 14, 15), their entry upon the inheritance which is theirs by virtue of that status. 'The redemption of our body', the resurrection, is a theme on which Paul had recently enlarged in 2 Corinthians iv. 7–v. 10. The same hoped-for occasion is called 'the day of redemption' in Ephesians iv. 30, where believers are said to be sealed with the Spirit in view of it.

24. *For what a man seeth, why doth he yet hope for?* We should probably prefer the shorter reading of P[46] and the first hand of B: 'for who hopes for what he sees?'

25. *We hope for that we see not.* Cf. 2 Corinthians iv. 18: 'we look not at the things which are seen, but at the things which are not seen: for the things which are seen are temporal; but the things which are not seen are eternal.'

26. *The Spirit also helpeth our infirmities.* Read the singular, 'infirmity' (RV) or 'weakness' (RSV, NEB).

The Spirit itself (better 'himself', RV, RSV, NEB) *maketh intercession for us.* Cf. Ephesians vi. 18, 'praying always with all prayer and supplication in the Spirit'. When believers pray 'in the Spirit', the Spirit Himself intercedes on their behalf. (See p. 50.)

With groanings which cannot be uttered. 'Through our inarticulate groans' (NEB). Speaking to God in the Spirit with 'tongues' (1 Cor. xiv. 2) may be included in this expression, but it covers those longings and aspirations which well up from the spiritual depths and cannot be imprisoned within the confines of everyday words. James Montgomery caught the apostle's meaning well when he wrote:

> 'Prayer is the soul's sincere desire,
> Uttered or unexpressed,
> The motion of a hidden fire
> That trembles in the breast.
>
> Prayer is the burden of a sigh,
> The falling of a tear,
> The upward glancing of an eye,
> When none but God is near.'

In such prayer it is the indwelling Spirit who prays, and His mind is immediately read by the Father to whom the prayer is addressed. Moreover, these 'inarticulate groans' cannot be dissociated from the groaning of verse 23, with which believers (together with all creation) long for the coming resurrection-glory, which will consummate the answer to all their prayers. (See p. 51 with n. 1.)

28. *And we know that all things work together for good to them that love God.* 'We know' expresses the knowledge of faith. Grammatically 'all things' may be either subject or object of the verb 'work together'; it is more probably the object. The subject will then be 'he', which some ancient texts (including P[46]) make more explicit by the addition of the nominative 'God' (an addition which makes the sentence excessively heavy). Thus RVmg. renders: 'to them that love God God worketh all things with them for good.' RSV construes 'all things' as an adverbial accusative, and translates: 'We know

that in everything God works for good with those who love
him.' NEB, however, revives an ancient and attractive interpretation which has in general received little attention from
translators and commentators, according to which the subject
of 'worketh together' is the subject of the previous verse—the
Spirit. Its rendering, then, is: '. . . he pleads for God's own
people in God's own way; and in everything, as we know, he
co-operates for good with those who love God . . .'[1] (cf. 1 Cor.
ii. 9 for the blessings prepared for those who love God).

To them who are the called according to his purpose. 'The called',
not in the general sense in which 'many are called, but few are
chosen'; but in the sense of that 'effectual calling' which is 'the
work of God's Spirit, whereby, convincing us of our sin and
misery, enlightening our minds in the knowledge of Christ,
and renewing our wills, he doth persuade and enable us to
embrace Jesus Christ, freely offered to us in the gospel'
(*Westminster Shorter Catechism*). Cf. i. 6 ('the called of Jesus
Christ'), i. 7 ('called to be saints'), ix. 11 ('him that calleth').

29. *For whom he did foreknow, he also did predestinate to be conformed to the image of his Son, that he might be the firstborn among
many brethren.* God's purpose of grace is set out in verses 29 and
30 by means of the construction called 'sorites', in which the
logical predicate of one clause becomes the logical subject of
the next. Here the new creation, a community of men and
women conformed to the image of Christ (who is Himself
'the image of God', 2 Cor. iv. 4; Col. i. 15), is seen to have been
from the beginning the object of God's foreknowledge and
foreordaining mercy. The fulfilment of this purpose is involved,
for the New Testament writers, in the creative words of
Genesis i. 26: 'Let us make man in our image, after our likeness.' The old creation in itself is insufficient for the realization
of this goal: it requires the redemptive work of Christ and His
consequent status as Head of the new creation, 'that he might

[1] Cf. M. Black, 'The Interpretation of Romans viii. 28', in *Neotestamentica
et Patristica* (Cullmann *Festschrift*, Leiden, 1962), pp. 166 ff.

be the firstborn among many brethren'. He who is 'the first-born of all creation' in the old order because 'all things were created through him and for him' is also by resurrection the head of a new order, 'the beginning, the first-born from the dead' (Col. i. 15–18, RSV).

As for the words 'whom he did foreknow', they have that connotation of electing grace which is frequently implied by the verb 'to know' in the Old Testament. When God takes knowledge of people in this special way, He sets His choice upon them. Cf. Amos iii. 2 ('you only have I known of all the families of the earth'); Hosea xiii. 5 ('I did know thee in the wilderness'). We may also compare Paul's own language in 1 Corinthians viii. 3 ('if any man love God, the same is known of him'); Galatians iv. 9 ('ye have known God, or rather are known of God'). This aspect of the divine knowledge is emphasized also in the Qumran *Rule of the Community*: 'From the God of Knowledge comes all that is and shall be. Before even they existed He established their whole design, and when, as ordained for them, they come into being, it is in accord with His glorious design that they fulfil their work.'[1]

30. *Whom he did predestinate, them he also called: and whom he called, them he also justified.* The people of God respond to His call in faith, and by faith they are justified.

And whom he justified, them he also glorified. The glorifying of the people of God is their ultimate and complete conformity 'to the image of his Son': 'when Christ, who is our life, shall appear, then shall ye also appear with him in glory' (Col. iii. 4; cf. 1 Jn. iii. 2).

This, then, is the purpose of God's predestinating grace—the creation of a new race displaying their Creator's glory. He advanced His purpose further by calling and justifying those on whom He had laid His choice. 'And whom he justified, them he also glorified.' The foreknowing and foreordaining belong to God's eternal counsel; the calling and justifying

[1] G. Vermes, *The Dead Sea Scrolls in English*, p. 75.

have taken place in His people's experience; but the glory, so far as their experience is concerned, lies in the future. Why then does Paul use the same past tense for this as he does for the other acts of God? Perhaps he is imitating the Hebrew use of the 'prophetic past', by which a predicted event is marked out as so certain of fulfilment that it is described as though it had already taken place.[1] As a matter of history, the people of God have not yet been glorified; so far as the divine decree is concerned, however, their glory has been determined from all eternity, hence—'them he also glorified'.

Why does Paul move directly here from justification to glory, without saying anything about the Christian's present experience of sanctification under the power of the Spirit? Partly, no doubt, because the coming glory has been in the forefront of his mind; but even more because the difference between sanctification and glory is one of degree only, not one of kind. Sanctification is progressive conformity to the image of Christ here and now (cf. 2 Cor. iii. 18; Col. iii. 10); glory is perfect conformity to the image of Christ there and then. Sanctification is glory begun; glory is sanctification completed. Paul looks forward to the completion of the work—a completion guaranteed by its inception: 'whom he justified, them he also glorified.'

iii. The triumph of faith (viii. 31–39). Could anything be a stronger encouragement to faith than the contemplation of God's saving purpose for His people, moving forward to its appointed consummation? Since God is their strong salvation, what force can prevail against them? Since His love was supremely manifested in the sacrifice of His own Son on their behalf, what good thing will He withhold from them? Paul for a moment envisages the situation in terms of a court of law, where the believer stands to be judged. But who will dare

---

[1] A similar use of the Greek aorist indicative to denote a future event is found in Jude 14, which literally runs, as in RV and RSV, 'Behold, the Lord came . . .'.

to come forward as prosecutor? God Himself, the Judge of all, has pronounced his acquittal and justification; who can call His sentence in question? The prosecutor may not venture to appear, but the counsel for the defence is present and active: 'it is Christ Jesus that died, yea rather, that is risen again, who is even at the right hand of God, who also maketh intercession for us.' And nothing can come between His love and His people—not all the trials and afflictions which they had experienced or might yet experience. In the spiritual warfare mighty forces—supernatural as well as natural—are arrayed against the people of Christ, but through Him they overcome them all and remain irrevocably encircled and empowered by His unchanging love.

32. *He that spared not his own Son.* An echo of Genesis xxii. 12, where God says to Abraham: 'thou hast not withheld (LXX 'spared', Gk. *pheidomai,* as here) thy son, thine only son from me.' The 'binding of Isaac' (the title traditionally given by Jews to the narrative of Gn. xxii) may play a greater part in Paul's thinking about the sacrifice of Christ than appears on the surface.[1] In Jewish interpretation it is treated as the classic example of the redemptive efficacy of martyrdom.

How shall he not with him also freely give us all things? Cf. Matthew vi. 33: 'all these things shall be added unto you.'

33, 34. *It is God that justifieth. Who is he that condemneth?* (RV, 'shall condemn?'). In the forensic language of this passage we catch an unmistakable echo of the similar challenge of the Servant of the Lord in Isaiah l. 8 f.: 'He is near that justifieth me; who will contend with me? let us stand together: who is mine adversary? let him come near to me. Behold, the Lord God will help me; who is he that shall condemn me?' A good Old Testament illustration of the text is the silence of Satan, chief prosecutor in the heavenly court, when God declares His acceptance of Joshua the high priest (Zc. iii. 1 ff.).

[1] Cf. H. J. Schoeps, *Paul* (1961), pp. 141 ff.

34. *Who is even at the right hand of God.* An echo of Psalm cx. 1, 'The Lord said unto my Lord, Sit thou at my right hand, until I make thine enemies thy footstool.' These words, whose messianic interpretation was axiomatic among the Jews of our Lord's time (cf. Mk xii. 35–37), were applied to Jesus from the earliest days of the Church, and form the biblical foundation of the doctrine of His exaltation and session at the Father's right hand—that is, in the place of supremacy over the universe.

'But one day, as I was passing in the field, and that too with some dashes on my conscience, fearing lest yet all was not right, suddenly this sentence fell upon my soul, Thy righteousness is in heaven; and methought withal, I saw, with the eyes of my soul, Jesus Christ at God's right hand; there, I say, is my righteousness; so that wherever I was, or whatever I was a-doing, God could not say of me, He wants my righteousness, for that was just before him. I also saw, moreover, that it was not my good frame of heart that made my righteousness better, nor yet my bad frame that made my righteousness worse; for my righteousness was Jesus Christ Himself, the same yesterday, and today, and for ever' (John Bunyan, *Grace Abounding*, § 229).

Who also maketh intercession for us. Another echo of the fourth Servant Song (Is. lii. 13–liii. 12): the Servant 'made intercession for the transgressors' (Is. liii. 12). (See note on Rom. iv. 25, pp. 118 f.) The Targum of Jonathan speaks of the Servant-Messiah as making entreaty for trespasses not only in Isaiah liii. 12 but also in verses 4 and 11. So believers have an intercessor at God's right hand as well as an intercessor here (verse 27)—that, however, is not the force of 'also', which simply serves to emphasize the relative 'who'.

36. *As it is written, For thy sake we are killed all the day long; we are accounted as sheep for the slaughter.* A quotation from Psalm xliv. 22, a plea to God for speedy aid in a time of sore distress for Israel.

37. *In all these things.* Perhaps a Hebraism, meaning 'despite all these things', 'for all that'.

We are more than conquerors. Gk. *hupernikōmen*, 'we are super-conquerors.'

38. *Nor powers.* The weight of the textual evidence favours a position for this phrase after 'nor things to come' at the end of the verse; intrinsic probability would otherwise point to the AV position after 'nor principalities' as being more appropriate. In any case, the principalities and powers are the forces of evil in the universe, the 'spiritual hosts of wickedness in the heavenly places' of Ephesians vi. 12 (RV). (Not all 'principalities and powers' are hostile; but those who are well-disposed would not attempt to separate believers from the love of Christ.) Nothing in the expanses of space ('nor height, nor depth'[1]) or in the course of time ('nor things present, nor things to come'[2]), nothing in the whole universe of God ('nor any other creature') can sever the children of God from their Father's love, secured to them in Christ.

V. HUMAN UNBELIEF AND DIVINE GRACE
(ix. 1–xi. 36)

a. The problem of Israel's unbelief (ix. 1–5)

To the modern reader chapters ix–xi form a parenthesis in the course of Paul's argument. Had he proceeded straight from viii. 39 to xii. 1 we should have been conscious of no hiatus in his reasoning. He has just pointed his readers forward to the culmination of God's purpose of grace, the glory that is going to be revealed in the sons of God. What more can he

[1] 'Height' and 'depth' were technical terms in astrology, and later in Gnosticism. Paul may not have had their technical significance in mind, but if he had, they would be closely associated with the 'principalities and powers' that were believed to control the movements of the heavenly bodies, especially the planets, and thus to control the destinies of mortals. But fate, whether real or imaginary, has no power over those whose lives are 'hid with Christ in God' (Col. iii. 3).

[2] Perhaps a reference to the two ages—this age and the coming one.

say but press home upon his readers their responsibility to live in this world as befits heirs of the glory to come? If 'I beseech you therefore' (xii. 1) came in at this point, we should be quite ready for it.

Not so Paul. The problem with which he proceeds to grapple was one of intense personal concern to him. He gloried in his ministry as apostle to the Gentiles, and rejoiced in their salvation. But his own kith and kin, the Jewish nation, had for the most part failed to accept the salvation proclaimed in the gospel, even though it was presented to them first. What then? Should they simply be written off as 'unworthy of everlasting life'? No indeed: they were his own people, and he neither would nor could dissociate himself from them. He too, like so many of them, had once opposed the gospel, but he had been arrested by the risen Jesus and set on the Christian way. How he longed that they too might have the scales removed from their eyes! Indeed, if their salvation could be purchased by his own damnation, right readily would he consent, if such a thing were possible, to be 'anathema from Christ' for their sakes. The ingathering of the Gentiles, no matter on how extensive a scale, could never compensate for the defection of his own nation, which caused him such unceasing mental anguish.

He takes up the subject too, we may infer, because the situation in the Roman church required it. The original believers in Rome appear to have been Jews, but by this time they were becoming outnumbered by Gentiles. There was perhaps a tendency on the part of some of the Gentile Christians to think of their Jewish brethren as poor relations, mercifully rescued from an apostate nation. The tendency for some at least of the Jewish Christians might be to resent any aspersion on their nation and to stress their continued solidarity with them, to a point where they were in danger of underestimating those distinctive features of Christian faith and life which forged a bond between them and their Gentile brethren in the Lord stronger than the bond which bound them to their Jewish brethren in the flesh. (It may well be that we meet a later stage of this tendency in the Epistle to the Hebrews.) Paul appreciated the wisdom of showing both sides something of the part played by both Jews and Gentiles in the saving purpose of God.

But, above all else, a real problem in theodicy was involved. The present situation called in question the whole exposition of the gospel set out in the foregoing chapters. It was of the essence of Paul's argument that the gospel which he (and his fellow-apostles) preached was no innovation. It was attested in the Hebrew Scriptures; it was the fulfilment of God's promise to the fathers; it proclaimed that God's way of righteousness through faith, by which Abraham had been blessed, was still open to all who believed in God as Abraham did. How came it, then, that it was pre-eminently Abraham's descendants who refused to believe the gospel? Surely, had Paul's claims been valid, the Jewish people would have been the first to acknowledge them? Such objections were no doubt voiced, and Paul could appreciate their force, although he was well aware of the fallacy which they involved. Yet it was a paradox, not to say a scandal, that the very nation which had been specially prepared by God for this time of fulfilment, the nation which could glory in so many unique privileges of divine grace (including above all the messianic hope), the nation into which in due course the Messiah had been born, should have failed to recognize Him when He came, while men and women of other nations which had never enjoyed such privileges embraced the gospel eagerly the first time they heard it. How could this be harmonized with God's choice of Israel and His declared purpose of blessing the world through Israel?

In these three chapters, then, Paul wrestles with this problem. This was not the first time that he had done so; the contents of these chapters are the fruit of many years of thought and prayer on his part, no doubt. It has indeed been suggested that the three chapters existed already as a separate treatise, but this is doubtful. It seems plain that, as Paul dictates to Tertius, he wrestles with the problem afresh, pressing towards a solution now along this road and now along that, until at last he emerges into the full light of the wisdom of God's overruling grace. He begins with one statement of God's ways in election and ends with another, but at the end he sees farther into the character and aim of God's election than he did at the outset. He begins with the particular problem of Jewish resistance to the gospel, and ends with an unfolding of 'the divine purpose in history'[1] which in some ways goes beyond any comparable passage in the whole Bible.

The first two answers that he gives to the problem are:

(i) This is how it has come about in the unchallengeable ordering of God's electing purpose (ix. 6–29).

(ii) In resisting the gospel Israel is following the precedent repeatedly set throughout her history: 'a gainsaying and disobedient people' she has always been in face of God's overtures to her (ix. 30–x. 21).

These are followed by two more, which are fraught with greater promise:

(iii) The fact that a 'remnant' of Israel has already believed the gospel is the token that Israel as a whole will yet do so (xi. 1–16).

(iv) If Israel's present rejection of the gospel has been the occasion of so much blessing for the Gentiles, Israel's future acceptance of the gospel will usher in the day of world-wide regeneration (xi. 17–32).

1. *My conscience also bearing me witness in the Holy Ghost.* Cf. note on ii. 15 (p. 91).

3. *I could wish that myself were accursed from Christ.* The prayer of Moses after the incident of the golden calf comes to mind

[1] The title given to chapters ix–xi in C. H. Dodd's commentary and in NEB. W. Manson entitles them 'The Righteousness of God in History' (*New Testament Essays in Memory of T. W. Manson*, p. 164)—which brings out even better their integrity with the main theme of the Epistle.

as a parallel: 'Yet now, if thou wilt forgive their sin—; and if not, blot me, I pray thee, out of thy book which thou hast written' (Ex. xxxii. 32). But whereas Moses refuses to survive if his people perish, Paul could almost welcome perdition for himself if it meant salvation for Israel.

4. *To whom pertaineth the adoption* ('sonship'). That is, the people of Israel are called collectively the 'son' of God (Ex. iv. 22 f.; Ho. xi. 1) or individually His 'sons' (Ho. i. 10).

And the glory. The *shekhinah* of God, the token of His dwelling among them, e.g. in the Mosaic tabernacle (Ex. xl. 34) and in Solomon's temple (1 Ki. viii. 10 f.).

And the covenants. There is very weighty evidence (P[46], B, D, etc.) for the singular reading 'the covenant', in which case the covenant at Sinai (Ex. xxiv. 8) would be meant. But the plural should probably be preferred (cf. Eph. ii. 12); 'the covenants' will then include those made by God with Abraham (Gn. xv. 18, xvii. 4 ff.), with Israel in the days of Moses (Ex. xxiv. 8, xxxiv. 10; Dt. xxix. 1 ff.) and Joshua (Dt. xxvii. 2 ff.; Jos. viii. 30 ff., xxiv. 25), and with David (2 Sa. xxiii. 5; Ps. lxxxix. 28); not to mention the new covenant, promised in the first instance to 'the house of Israel and . . . the house of Judah' (Je. xxxi. 31).

And the giving of the law. The Mosaic legislation (Ex. xx. 1 ff.).

And the service of God. The prescriptions for divine worship (*latreia*), especially those in the book of Leviticus, on which the temple ceremonial at Jerusalem was still based when Paul was dictating these words.

And the promises. Including the messianic promises, 'the sure mercies of David' (Is. lv. 3; Acts xiii. 23, 32–34); but a special place must be given to the promise to Abraham and his seed, which is basic to the receiving of God's righteousness through faith (iv. 13–21).

5. *Whose are the fathers.* That is, the patriarchs (Abraham, Isaac, Jacob and his twelve sons), the primary recipients of the promises just mentioned.

Of whom as concerning the flesh Christ came. Cf. the affirmation of Christ's Davidic descent in i. 3, and the later statement that Christ came as 'a minister of the circumcision for the truth of God, to confirm the promises made unto the fathers' (xv. 8). In Him all God's promises to Israel reach their consummation.

Who is over all, God blessed for ever. The relation of these words to those which precede is a disputed point. It is equally permissible to construe the Greek phrase (*ho ōn*[1] *epi pantōn theos eulogētos eis tous aiōnas*) as being in apposition to 'Christ' (so AV, RV, RSVmg., NEBmg.), or to take it as an independent ascription of praise to God, prompted by the mention of the Messiah as the One in whom God's many blessings to Israel have reached their climax—'Blessed for ever be God over all!' (cf. RVmg., RSV, NEB).

The former construction is more in keeping with the general structure of the sentence (cf. i. 25, where the words 'who is blessed for ever. Amen' are not an independent ascription of praise, but form the integral peroration of the sentence); it is further supported by the consideration that something is required to balance the phrase 'as concerning the flesh'. The Messiah, 'as concerning the flesh'—that is, with regard to His human descent—came of a long line of Israelite ancestors; but as regards His eternal being, He is 'God over all, blessed for ever'. A formal parallel to this antithesis appears in i. 3 f., where Christ is said to have been born a descendant of David 'according to the flesh', but installed as Son of God 'with power' by the dispensation of the Spirit (see pp. 72 f.).

It is true that Paul is not in the habit of calling Christ 'God' in this direct way; he reserves for Him the title 'Lord'. Thus, 'to us there is one God, the Father, of whom are all things, and we unto him; and one Lord, Jesus Christ, through whom are all things, and we through him' (1 Cor. viii. 6, RV; cf. 1 Cor. xii. 3–6; Eph. iv. 4–6). Yet for Paul Christ is the one 'in' whom, 'through' whom, and 'unto' whom all things were

---

[1] The conjectural emendation of *ho ōn* to *hōn ho*, as though the clause meant 'whose (finally) is God Himself . . .', has little to commend it.

created (Col. i. 16), in whom 'dwelleth all the fulness of the Godhead bodily' (Col. ii. 9). 'The judgement-seat of God' (Rom. xiv. 10, RV, etc.) is called in 2 Corinthians v. 10 'the judgment seat of Christ'. Moreover, when Paul gives Christ the title 'Lord', he does so because God the Father Himself has given Him that title as the 'name which is above every name' (Phil. ii. 9). This title 'Lord' is given to Jesus by Paul as the equivalent of the Hebrew *Yahweh* (Jehovah): the way in which he applies Isaiah xlv. 23 (cf. Rom. xiv. 11) to Jesus in Philippians ii. 10 f., indicates that, to him, the confession 'Jesus Christ is Lord' means 'Jesus Christ is Jehovah'. Besides, Paul would have been as alive as the writer of Hebrews was to the significance of Psalm xlv, where the king to whom it is said in verse 2, 'God hath blessed thee for ever', is in verse 6 himself addressed as God: 'Thy throne, O God, is for ever and ever' (cf. Heb. i. 8 f.); the wording of the psalm may well be echoed by Paul here.

On the other hand, the legitimacy of the alternative punctuation must be conceded, and it is outrageous to cast doubt on the orthodoxy of those translators or commentators who prefer it here, as though they were determined (in Dean Burgon's severe words about the revisers of 1881) to have 'a Socinian gloss gratuitously thrust into the margin of every Englishman's New Testament'[1]—or even into the text itself.

b. God's sovereign choice (ix. 6–29)

Has God's plan gone awry? No indeed, says Paul. The present situation reproduces a pattern of divine action which has been unfolded often enough in the past. Some have always opened their hearts to God's revelation, while others have hardened theirs; and by the variety of their response they have shown

[1] J. W. Burgon, *The Revision Revised* (1883), p. 214. For the view that Paul does here call Christ 'God', cf. the commentary by A. Nygren, *ad loc.*; also J. Munck, *Christus und Israel* (Copenhagen, 1956), pp. 29 f.; O. Cullmann, *The Christology of the New Testament* (1959), pp. 312 f. For the alternative view, cf. C. H. Dodd's commentary, *ad loc.*; V. Taylor, 'Does the New Testament call Jesus God?' *ExT*, LXXIII (1961–62), pp. 116 ff.

whether or not they were among those on whom God had set His sovereign choice.

Paul has already pointed out (ii. 28 f.) that the true Jew is the man whose life brings forth praise to God, that natural descent and physical circumcision are not the things that matter most. Now he points out in similar vein that not all the descendants of Israel are Israelites in the inward sense, that not all the descendants of Abraham are 'children of Abraham' in the spiritual sense which has been explained in chapter iv. Throughout Old Testament history God's purpose was handed down through an inner group, an elect minority, a saving remnant. Abraham had a number of sons, but only through one of them, Isaac, the child of promise, was the line of God's promise to be traced. Isaac in his turn had two sons, but only through one of them, Jacob, was the holy seed transmitted. And God's choice of Jacob and passing over of his brother Esau did not in the least depend on the behaviour or character of the twin brothers: He had declared it in advance before they were born.

So today, Paul implies, when some receive the light and others do not, the divine election may be discerned, operating antecedently to the will or activity of those who are its objects. If God does not reveal the principles on which He makes His choice, that is no reason why His justice should be called in question. He is merciful and compassionate because such is His will. 'The quality of mercy is not strained', and least of all so when it is God who shows mercy; for if He were compelled to be merciful by some cause outside Himself, not only would His mercy be so much the less mercy, but He Himself would be so much the less God.

Nor is it only in His dealings with the 'chosen seed of Israel's race' that this principle operates. It can be seen in the Exodus story of His dealings with the king of Egypt, who stubbornly and repeatedly refused to let Israel go. Why did God endure Pharaoh's obstinacy so long? He supplies the answer Himself: 'for this purpose have I let you live, to show you my power,

so that my name may be declared throughout all the earth'
(Ex. ix. 16, RSV). All the recalcitrance and rebellion of a man
like Pharaoh will never avail to thwart the purpose of God;
God's glory will triumph, whether man obeys or not.

Well, the retort comes, if God foreordains men's ways by
His own will, why should He blame them for their ways? They
don't oppose His will; they act in accordance with it.

'My good sir,' is Paul's reply, 'who are you to answer back
to God?' And he takes up the analogy of a potter and his pots,
which came as readily to Hebrew prophets as it did to Omar
Khayyám. Jeremiah learned a lesson about God's dealings
with His people the day he went down to the potter's house
and saw how the potter moulded the clay as he saw fit,
squeezing a vessel that had gone wrong into a shapeless lump
so as to make a new vessel out of it again (Je. xviii. 1–10).

'Woe to him who strives with his Maker,
 an earthen vessel with the potter!
Does the clay say to him who fashions it, "What are you
making"?
or "Your work has no handles"?' (Is. xlv. 9, RSV).

It may be granted that the analogy of a potter and his pots
covers only one aspect of the Creator's relation to those whom
He has created, especially to men, whom He created in His
own image. Pots are not made in the potter's image, and they
do not in any case answer him back or find fault with his
workmanship. Men, just because they are made in the image
of God, insist on answering back. But there are different ways
of answering Him back. There is the answering back of faith,
as when a Job or a Jeremiah calls out for an account of God's
mysterious ways with him. Even the Christ upon the cross
could cry: 'Why hast thou forsaken me?' But when the man
of faith cries out like this, it is precisely because the righteousness of God, as well as His power, is the major premiss of all
his thinking. There is, on the other hand, the answering back
of unbelief and disobedience, when man tries to put God in

the dock and sit in judgment upon Him. It is a man like this whom Paul rebukes so sternly and reminds of his creaturely status. Paul has been misunderstood and unfairly criticized through failure to recognize that it is the God-defying rebel and not the bewildered seeker after God whose mouth he so peremptorily shuts. God, in His grace, does abide His people's question; but He will not be cross-examined at the judgment-bar of a hard and impenitent heart.

Suppose that God wishes to display His righteous judgment and His power, says Paul, why should He not bear patiently with people like Pharaoh—pots (to carry on the metaphor) made to be object-lessons of His wrath, fashioned to be destroyed? And why should He not display the greatness of His glory by means of other 'pots' which are to be the object-lessons of His mercy, prepared in advance for this glorious purpose? Paul, more cautious than some of his systematizers, does not say outright that God does this, but says, 'What if He does so? Who will bring Him to book?'

While Paul will allow no questioning of God's right to do what He will with His own, he lets his emphasis fall, not on God's wrath towards the reprobate, but rather the postponement of His wrath against men who have long since become ripe for destruction. As has been pointed out earlier (ii. 4), the mercy and forbearance of God are intended to afford men time for repentance; if, instead, they harden their hearts yet more, as Pharaoh did after repeated respites, they are simply storing up an increasing weight of retribution for themselves against the day of requital.

It is a pity that in some schools of theological thought the doctrine of election has been formulated to an excessive degree on the basis of this preliminary stage in Paul's present argument, without adequate account being taken of his further exposition of God's purpose in election at the conclusion of the argument (xi. 25–32). Yet this stage of his argument is undeniably in line with well-known facts of life which present a problem for any theodicy. Some people do have better spiritual opportunities than others; and of those who have equal opportunities some profit by them and others do not. Some nations have received much more gospel light than others—and are correspondingly accountable to God. The man who has experienced the forgiving grace of God will always wonder why his eyes should have been opened while the eyes of others remain closed.

The point on which Paul insists here is that all mankind is guilty in God's sight; no-one has a claim upon His grace. If He chooses to extend His grace to some, the others have no ground for arguing that He is unjust because He does not extend it to them. If it is justice they demand, they can have it, but:

> 'Though justice be thy plea, consider this,
> That, in the course of justice, none of us
> Should see salvation.'

In point of fact, as appears with blessed clarity later in the present argument, God's grace is far wider than anyone could have dared to hope, but just because it *is* grace, no-one is entitled to it, and no-one can demand that God should give an account of the principles on which He bestows His grace, or that He should bestow it otherwise than in fact He does. Grace in its sovereignty may impose conditions, but it cannot be made subject to them.

But God delights to show mercy, and He has lavished it upon men and women beyond counting—from Gentiles and Jews alike. The fact that Gentiles as well as Jews are among those whom He has called and marked out for glory is illustrated by two quotations from Hosea (see pp. 195 f.).

For centuries the Gentiles had been looked upon by the chosen people, with but few exceptions, as 'vessels of wrath fitted for destruction'; and certainly God had 'endured' them 'with much longsuffering'; but now the purpose of His patience was made plain; what He desired was not their doom but their salvation.

And if Israel at present had to such a large extent turned away from God, yet the same pattern of divine action would be reproduced among them too. Here Paul calls upon Isaiah as witness to his hope.

In a day of widespread national apostasy Isaiah saw that judgment would fall upon Israel and Judah on such a scale that only a handful—the merest 'remnant'—would survive. Yet in this remnant he saw the hope of the future embodied; God's purposes and promises to His people Israel, and through them to the other nations, would not be frustrated, provided that a remnant emerged from the crucible of invasion, defeat and exile, to become the nucleus of a new and purified Israel. The 'saved' remnant would thus be also a 'saving' remnant.

This remnant Paul sees embodied anew in that minority of Jews who, like himself, had acknowledged Jesus as Lord; a minority they might be, but their existence was a guarantee of a wholesale turning to the Lord on the part of Israel on a day to come. This hope is developed more fully later (in chapter xi); for the present, he turns his attention to another reason why the blessings of the gospel had for the present fallen upon Gentiles rather than Jews.

7. *In Isaac shall thy seed be called.* A quotation from Genesis xxi. 12, where God tells Abraham not to oppose Sarah's demand for the expulsion of Hagar and Ishmael, because his descendants are to be reckoned through Isaac, and not through Ishmael (although Ishmael too will be the ancestor of a nation, 'because he is thy seed').

8. *They which are the children of the flesh, these are not the children of God: but the children of the promise are counted for the seed.* 'The children of the promise' in Paul's exegesis are those who, like Abraham, believe the promise of God, and are therefore Abraham's spiritual offspring. Compare iv. 11 ff., and also the 'allegory' which Paul draws out of the Isaac-Ishmael incident in Galatians iv. 22–31.

9. *At this time will I come, and Sara shall have a son.* A quotation from Genesis xviii. 10: 'I will surely return to you in the spring, and Sarah your wife shall have a son' (RSV). This was the 'promise' in accordance with which Isaac was born—the promise which provoked Sarah to laughter (Gn. xviii. 12; cf. xxi. 6).

11. *Not of works, but of him that calleth.* Cf. viii. 28 for the 'calling'.

12. *The elder shall serve the younger.* From the birth oracle to Rebekah (Gn. xxv. 23). This prophecy relates not to the individuals Esau and Jacob (for Esau did not render service to Jacob) but to their descendants; it relates to the long periods during which the Edomites were in bondage to Israel or Judah (cf. 2 Sa. viii. 14; 1 Ki. xxii. 47; 2 Ki. xiv. 7, etc.).

13. *Jacob have I loved, but Esau have I hated.* From Malachi i. 2 f., where again the context indicates it is the nations of Israel and Edom, rather than their individual ancestors Jacob and Esau, that are in view. The way in which communities can so freely be spoken of in terms of their ancestors is an example of the common oscillation in biblical (and especially Old Testament) thought and speech between individual and corporate personality (cf. v. 12 ff.). Israel was the elect nation, and Edom had incurred the wrath of God because of their unbrotherly conduct towards Israel in the day of Israel's calamity (cf. Ps. cxxxvii. 7; Is. xxxiv. 5 ff.; Je. xlix. 7 ff.; Ezk. xxv. 12 ff., xxxv. 1 ff.; Ob. 10 ff.).

15. *I will have mercy on whom I will have mercy, and I will have compassion on whom I will have compassion.* Quoted from Exodus xxxiii. 19, where God replies to Moses' request to let him see His glory, after Moses' intercession for the Israelites because of their worship of the golden calf.[1] The force of the words is that the mercy and compassion of God cannot be subject to any cause outside His own free grace.

16. *It is not of him that willeth, nor of him that runneth, but of God that sheweth mercy.* Again it is emphasized that God's mercy has its cause in Himself, and not in the will or activity of men. 'Running' stands for vigorous human activity here, as in Galatians ii. 2; Philippians ii. 16.

17. *The scripture saith unto Pharaoh.* 'The scripture' (here Ex. ix. 16) is practically personified here as a surrogate for the name of God, who is the actual speaker. The Pharaoh is the Pharaoh of the Exodus (successor to the 'Pharaoh of the oppression' whose death is noted in Ex. ii. 23).

Even for this same purpose have I raised thee up, or 'caused thee to stand'. The Hebrew uses the causative conjugation of the verb *'amad,* 'stand', which Paul renders by Gk. *exegeirō* (raise up). (He translates here direct from the Hebrew; LXX says 'thou wast preserved'.) The reference may be not merely to God's raising up Pharaoh to be king, but to His patience in preserving him alive, in spite of his disobedience.

That I might shew my power in thee, and that my name might be declared throughout all the earth. Cf. Exodus xv. 14 f.; Joshua ii. 10 f., ix. 9; 1 Samuel iv. 8, for the effect produced on other nations by the news of the Exodus and attendant events.

18. *Therefore hath he mercy on whom he will have mercy, and whom he will he hardeneth.* The first part of this verse is a further echo of Exodus xxxiii. 19 (cf. verse 15); the second part refers to the occasions on which God is said to 'harden' the hearts of Pharaoh and the Egyptians (Ex. vii. 3, ix. 12, xiv. 4, 17).

[1] Cf. note on verse 3 (pp. 184 f.).

20. *Shall the thing formed say to him that formed it, Why hast thou made me thus?* See, in addition to Isaiah xlv. 9, quoted above (p. 189), Isaiah xxix. 16:

'Shall the potter be regarded as the clay;
that the thing made should say of its maker,
"He did not make me";
or the thing formed say of him who formed it,
"He has no understanding"?' (RSV).

God is not answerable to man for what He does. Yet He can be relied upon to act in consistency with His character, which has been disclosed supremely in Christ. With such a God to trust, why should any of His people question His ways?

21. *One vessel unto honour, and another unto dishonour.* Cf. 2 Timothy ii. 20, where, however, the vessels are made of various materials, and those which are 'to dishonour' are simply designed for less noble or ornamental (but not necessarily less useful) purposes than those which are 'to honour'.

22. *The vessels of wrath fitted to destruction.* Not the instruments of His wrath by which He works destruction (cf. Is. xiii. 5, liv. 16; Je. l. 25) but objects of His wrath, designed to be destroyed.

25. *Osee.* Greek form of Hosea.
I will call them my people, which were not my people; and her beloved, which was not beloved. Paul's paraphrase of Hosea ii. 23: 'I will have mercy on her that had not obtained mercy; and I will say to them which were not my people, Thou art my people.' The Hosea prophecy was probably in general use in the early Church as a *testimonium* in this sense; its exegesis in Romans ix. 25 is not peculiarly Pauline. Compare the similar application of Hosea ii. 23 to Gentile Christians in 1 Peter ii. 10.

Hosea was taught to see in his own tragic domestic life a

parable of the relation between God and Israel. When he took Gomer the daughter of Diblaim as his wife and she in due course gave birth to a son, he acknowledged the child as his and named him Jezreel. But her second and third children, he was convinced, were not his, and the names he gave them expressed his disillusionment—Lo-ruhamah ('one for whom no natural affection is felt') and Lo-ammi ('no kin of mine'). These names betokened God's attitude to His people Israel, who had broken their covenant-loyalty to Him—Lo-ruhamah ('not the object of my affection, or mercy') and Lo-ammi ('not my people'). But, for old time's sake, God will not allow this broken relation to remain so for ever; He looks forward to a day when those who at present are not His people will once more be His people, and when those who at present have no claim on His kindly feelings will once more be the objects of His mercy.

What Paul does here is to take this promise, which referred to a situation within the frontiers of the chosen people, and extract from it a principle of divine action which in his day was reproducing itself on a world-wide scale. In large measure through Paul's own apostolic ministry, great numbers of Gentiles, who had never been 'the people of God' and had no claim on His covenant mercy, were coming to be enrolled among His people and to be the recipients of His mercy. The scale of the divine action was far wider than in Hosea's day, but the same pattern and principle were recognizable. Through the Gentile mission, in those lands where the people of God had once been unrepresented, there were now many believers who were acknowledged as 'sons of the living God'.

26. *It shall come to pass, that in the place where it was said unto them, Ye are not my people; there shall they be called the children* ('sons', RV, RSV, NEB) *of the living God.* Quoted from Hosea i. 10.

27. *Esaias.* Greek form of Isaiah.
Though the number of the children of Israel be as the sand of the

sea, a remnant shall be saved. Quoted from Isaiah x. 22a. The obvious meaning of these words is that, numerous as Israel may be, only a remnant, a small minority, will survive the impending judgment (in which God will use the Assyrians as His agents) and return from exile. But if *only* a remnant will survive, *at least* a remnant will survive and constitute the hope of restoration; not only will the remnant return from exile but 'the remnant shall return, even the remnant of Jacob, unto the mighty God' (Is. x. 21). This recurring theme of Isaiah's prophecy was given as a name to his elder son Shear-jashub ('Remnant will return'), who was thus a living 'sign' to the people of the message of God through his father (Is. vii. 3, viii. 18). Paul applies Isaiah's 'remnant doctrine' to the religious situation of his own day here, and again in xi. 5.

28. *For he will finish the work, and cut it short in righteousness: because a short work will the Lord make upon the earth.* In AV (following the 'Received Text') this quotation has been expanded into conformity with Isaiah x. 23 (LXX) by the addition of 'in righteousness: because a short work'; read with RV: 'the Lord will execute his word upon the earth, finishing it and cutting it short' (cf. RSV: 'the Lord will execute his sentence upon the earth with rigour and dispatch').

29. *Except the Lord of Sabaoth had left us a seed, we had been as Sodoma, and been made like unto Gomorrha.* In a time of acute peril for Judah and Jerusalem under the invading Assyrians, Isaiah uses this language (Is. i. 9), meaning in effect: 'If God had not spared a remnant among us ("the mere germ of a nation", NEB), we should have been wiped out as completely as Sodom and Gomorrah' (cf. Gn. xix. 24). 'Sabaoth' is a Greek transliteration of Heb. *ṣeba'oth*, 'hosts', 'armies'; 'the Lord of Sabaoth' is simply 'the Lord of hosts' (cf. Jas. v. 4). 'Sodoma' is a Greek form of 'Sodom', and 'Gomorrha' is the Greek spelling of 'Gomorrah'. The quotation is from LXX.

c. Man's responsibility (ix. 30-x. 21)

i. The stumbling-stone (ix. 30-33). Having considered the problem from the standpoint of divine election, Paul now considers it from the standpoint of human responsibility. What, in fact, has happened? The gospel, with its proclamation of the 'righteousness' bestowed by God upon believers, came to the Jew first, and also to the Gentile; but it was accepted by the Gentile first. The Gentiles responded gratefully to the message which assured them of their acceptance by God on the ground of their faith, and it was 'counted to them for righteousness'. The Jews as a whole continued to pursue the path of legal righteousness, seeking acceptance with God on the basis of their law-keeping, and yet never attained their goal. The reason was simple: they were following the wrong path. Acceptance by God was assured to faith and not to the works enjoined by the law. It was indeed a hard lesson for them to learn that, in spite of all the privileges which were theirs as Israelites, the divine righteousness could be attained by them only in the same way as it was open to those complete outsiders of Gentiles who had been for ages past shut out from the knowledge of God and His ways. No wonder that the gospel was a stumbling-block to them.

But the very fact of its being a stumbling-block had been foreseen. And here Paul quotes from Isaiah again, and gives a conflated version of two oracles—Isaiah viii. 14 f. and xxviii. 16 f.—whose common term is a 'stone' divinely laid in a time of disaster and judgment.

31. *Followed after the law of righteousness.* That is, a law by conformity to which they hoped to be justified before God.

Hath not attained to the law of righteousness. The best-attested text omits 'of righteousness'. The meaning is that the requirements of the law were not met by those who followed the way of legal righteousness, as they are met by those 'who walk not after the flesh, but after the Spirit' (viii. 4).

32. *By the works of the law.* Read simply 'by works' (RV).

They stumbled at that stumblingstone. In Isaiah viii. 13–15 the prophet foretells how the Assyrian invasion will sweep over the land of Israel like the waters of a great flood. But there will be one place of refuge from the overwhelming water: God Himself will prove 'a sanctuary' to all who put their trust in Him, a rock on which they will stand secure. But those who do not entrust themselves to Him but put their confidence in other powers or other resources will be swept by the flood against this rock and come to grief upon it; to them, far from being a place of refuge, it will prove a dangerous obstacle— 'a stone of stumbling' and 'a rock of offence'. The passage is quoted to the same effect in 1 Peter ii. 8, where Christ is described as 'a stone of stumbling, and a rock of offence, even to them which stumble at the word, being disobedient: whereunto also they were appointed' (appointed, that is, by the word of God spoken through Isaiah).

33. *As it is written, Behold, I lay in Sion a stumblingstone and rock of offence.* In Isaiah xxviii. 16, in the course of a warning about the impending deluge from Assyria which will sweep away 'the refuge of lies' in which king and people are putting their trust, the word of God comes to the prophet: 'Behold, I lay in Zion for a foundation a stone, a tried stone, a precious corner stone,[1] a sure foundation; he that believeth shall not make haste' (or better, 'shall not panic'). This foundation-stone appears to be the righteous remnant,[2] the hope of the future, which is embodied personally in the promised Prince of the house of David. This prophecy is here conflated with Isaiah viii. 14 (referred to in the note on verse 32 above). The combination of the two passages as a prophecy of Christ and His salvation is a commonplace of early Christian apolo-

---

[1] Cf. Eph. ii. 20. See 'The Corner-Stone of Scripture' in S. H. Hooke, *The Siege Perilous*, pp. 235 ff.

[2] In the Qumran literature the Qumran community is identified with this precious corner-stone (cf. G. Vermes, *The Dead Sea Scrolls in English*, p. 38).

getic, and is in fact pre-Pauline. We find them similarly combined in 1 Peter ii. 6–8, where they are linked with a third 'stone' *testimonium*—the rejected stone of Psalm cxviii. 22. (In Luke xx. 17 f. the rejected stone of the psalm and the stone of stumbling of Isaiah viii. 14 are brought into association with yet another 'stone' *testimonium*—the stone 'cut out without hands' which smashed Nebuchadnezzar's dream-image in Daniel ii. 34 f.)

Whosoever believeth on him shall not be ashamed. Cf. x. 11. Isaiah xxviii. 16 is here quoted according to LXX; the meaning is that those who trust in God need never fear that their trust in Him will prove to be ill-founded. God vindicates His people's faith, so that they need not feel embarrassed on His account, even when men say, 'He committed his cause to the Lord; let him deliver him, let him rescue him, for he delights in him!' (Ps. xxii. 8, RSV). The Hebrew text, however, reads 'He who believes will not be in haste' (RSV); that is, the man who stands on God's foundation will 'keep his head when all about him are losing theirs and blaming it on him'; he will not fuss and rush around but trust in God, confident that His purpose will be accomplished in His own time. It is possible that the LXX translators read in the Hebrew text before them *lo' yebosh* ('will not be ashamed') instead of *lo' yaḥish* ('will not haste'), but this is not a necessary supposition.

ii. The two ways of righteousness (x. 1–13). For all that, Paul will not cease praying for Israel's salvation. He understands their state of mind better than most: 'a zeal of God, but not according to knowledge' exactly describes his own attitude before he met the risen Christ. Of that zeal of his he speaks elsewhere: his zeal for the ancestral traditions of his people impelled him to forge ahead of his contemporaries in his devotion to the study and practice of the Jewish religion, and supplied the motive power in his energetic harrying of the infant church of Jerusalem (cf. Gal. i. 13 f.; Phil. iii. 6). He too had kicked against the stone of stumbling until the scales

fell from his eyes and his life was reorientated; now his con-
suming ambition was that Christ might be magnified in all
his life and work (cf. Phil. i. 20).

And if this had happened to him, why could it not happen
to his people? True, for the present they did not know God's
way of righteousness, but endeavoured to establish their own.
Yet, as he himself had found that Christ put an end to the law,
conceived as a means of acquiring favour in God's sight, so
might his fellow-Jews when they too found the way of faith.

The two ways—the way of law and the way of faith—are
illustrated by quotations from the Pentateuch. The first one
comes from Leviticus xviii. 5: 'Ye shall therefore keep my
statutes, and my judgments: which if a man do, he shall live
in them.' There, says Paul, the principle of righteousness by
law is clearly expressed: the man who *does* these things will
attain life by so doing. 'What is wrong with that?' it might be
asked. Just this, Paul would reply, that no-one has succeeded
in doing them perfectly, and therefore no-one has succeeded
in gaining life this way. Even if he could describe his own earlier career as 'touching the righteousness which is in the law,
blameless' (Phil. iii. 6), he knew that it was blameless only in
the sight of men, but not before God.

To illustrate the righteousness which comes by faith, he goes
to another place in the Pentateuch—Moses' farewell exhortation to Israel in Deuteronomy xxx—and he quotes verses
11–14: 'For this commandment which I command thee this
day, it is not hidden from thee, neither is it far off. It is not in
heaven, that thou shouldest say, Who shall go up for us to
heaven, and bring it unto us, that we may hear it, and do it?
Neither is it beyond the sea, that thou shouldest say, Who shall
go over the sea for us, and bring it unto us, that we may hear it,
and do it? But the word is very nigh unto thee, in thy mouth,
and in thy heart, that thou mayest do it.' These words he
finds admirably suited to the language of 'the righteousness
which is of faith', and gives a brief running commentary on
them in this sense.

This is the gist of his commentary: God has brought His salvation near to us, in Christ. We do not have to 'climb the heavenly steeps' to procure it, for Christ has come down with it; we do not need to 'plumb the lowest deeps' for it, for Christ has risen from the dead to make it secure to us. It is here, present and available; what we are called upon to do is to accept it by inward faith—believing in our hearts that God raised Him from the dead—and to acknowledge Him aloud as Lord. The saving faith is resurrection faith: 'if Christ be not raised, your faith is vain' (1 Cor. xv. 17). And the confession of Christ is public confession: 'Jesus is Lord' is the earliest, as it remains the sufficient, Christian creed.

Those who thus put their faith in Christ for salvation have as their encouragement the assurance of Isaiah xxviii. 16 (already quoted in ix. 33): those who commit themselves to Christ will never be 'let down'.

This righteousness which God imparts is open without distinction to all men and women of faith, whether they are Jews or Gentiles. His saving mercy is lavished without discrimination or restriction: all who call on Him will receive it. At an earlier stage in Paul's argument the words 'There is no difference' had a grim sound, because they convicted Jew and Gentile together of sin against God and incapacity to win His acceptance by personal effort or desert; now the same words have a joyful sound, because they proclaim to Jew and Gentile together that the gates of God's mercy stand wide open for their entrance, that His free pardon is assured in Christ to all who claim it by faith.

1. *For Israel.* Read 'for them' (RV, RSV).

2. *I bear them record.* That is, 'I testify on their behalf.'

3. *Going about to establish their own righteousness.* 'Going about' is an archaic English expression for 'endeavouring'; cf. Acts xxi. 31, AV: 'as they went about to kill him' (RV, 'as they were seeking to kill him').

4. *Christ is the end of the law for righteousness to every one that believeth.* 'Christ ends the law and brings righteousness for everyone who has faith' (NEB). The word 'end' (*telos*) has a double sense; it may mean 'goal' or 'termination'. On the one hand, Christ is the goal at which the law aimed in that He is the embodiment of perfect righteousness, having 'magnified the law and made it honourable' (cf. Is. xlii. 21); His own words in Matthew v. 17 ran: 'Think not that I am come to destroy the law, or the prophets: I am not come to destroy, but to fulfil.' And the law is fulfilled in the lives of those who are 'in Christ Jesus' (cf. viii. 3 f.). On the other hand (and this is the primary force of Paul's words), Christ is the termination of the law in the sense that with Him the old order, of which the law formed part, has been done away, to be replaced by the new order of the Spirit. In this new order, life and righteousness are available through faith in Christ; therefore no-one need attempt any more to win these blessings by means of the law. (See p. 56.)

5. *The man which doeth those things shall live by them.* Paul had already quoted Leviticus xviii. 5 to similar effect in Galatians iii. 12, showing that 'the law is not of faith'; there the contrasting scripture is Habakkuk ii. 4: 'The just shall live by faith.'

6–8. *But the righteousness which is of faith speaketh on this wise.* . . . Here the contrasting scripture to Leviticus xviii. 5 is Deuteronomy xxx. 11–14. But in its primary setting the meaning of the latter is almost precisely that of the earlier quotation from Leviticus xviii. 5. There the statutes and judgments of God were enjoined upon the people that they might do them and live. Here, similarly, it is God's commandment that is presented to each one of them, 'that thou mayest *do* it' (Paul significantly omits this last clause). And that the doing of the commandment was the way of life is evident from the words of Moses which follow immediately upon those that have just been quoted: 'See, I have set before thee this day life and

good, and death and evil; in that I command thee this day
to love the Lord thy God, to walk in his ways, and to keep
his commandments and his statutes and his judgments, that
thou mayest *live* and multiply' (Dt. xxx. 15 f.). Granted
that Deuteronomy is suffused with a prophetic, and at times
almost evangelical, fervour which is not prominent in Leviticus
—granted, too, that there is an inwardness in the wording of
Deuteronomy xxx. 11–14 ('in thy mouth, and in thy heart')
which anticipates the 'new covenant' oracle of Jeremiah
xxxi. 33—yet it is not so easy for us as it was for Paul to draw
a distinction between the meaning of Leviticus xviii. 5 and
that of Deuteronomy xxx. 11 ff. It may be that Paul was
already familiar with an interpretation of the Deuteronomy
passage which facilitated his application of it to the gospel.
If he had been accustomed to see in this passage a reference to
wisdom (it is referred to wisdom in Baruch iii. 29 f.), then
Paul, for whom Christ was the wisdom of God (cf. 1 Cor. i.
24, 30), could readily have given it a Christian interpretation.

Here, then, is his exposition of the language appropriate
to the righteousness which is received by faith (rather in the
pesher style now familiar to us from the Qumran texts):

Do not say to yourself, 'Who will go up to heaven?'—that is, to
bring Christ down (as though He had never become in-
carnate and lived on earth).
Do not say, 'Who will go down to the nethermost deep?'—that is,
to bring Him back from the abode of the dead (as though
He had not already been raised up to newness of life).
What does it say, then? This!
The message is close beside you, on your tongue, in your heart—
that is, the message of faith which we proclaim, that if you
confess Jesus as Lord with *your tongue*, and believe in *your
heart* that God raised Him from the dead, salvation will be
yours. It is with the *heart* that men exercise the faith by
which God accepts them as righteous; it is with the *tongue*
that they make confession and so receive His salvation.

9. *If thou shalt confess with thy mouth the Lord Jesus.* The last three words should be placed within quotation marks; cf. NEB: 'If on your lips is the confession, "Jesus is Lord".' This is the confession (*kurios Iēsous*) which, as Paul says in 1 Corinthians xii. 3, no-one can make except 'in the Holy Spirit' (RV). Cf. Philippians ii. 11, where the confession 'Jesus Christ is Lord' is man's acknowledgment of the supreme honour to which God has exalted Him (see p. 187). Some commentators have thought particularly of the confession of His name before magistrates (cf. Lk. xxi. 12–15; 1 Pet. iii. 13–16); but if we are to think of one outstanding occasion for such a confession to be made, we should more probably think of that first confession—'the answer of a good conscience' (1 Pet. iii. 21)—made in Christian baptism.

13. *Whosoever shall call upon the name of the Lord shall be saved.* Quoted from Joel ii. 32, where it relates to the period on the eve of 'the great and the terrible day of the Lord' when God's Spirit is to be poured out on all flesh; compare Peter's use of the same Scripture to explain the events of the day of Pentecost: 'This is that which was spoken by the prophet' (Acts ii. 16).

iii. The world-wide proclamation (x. 14–21). Hence arises the necessity of proclaiming the gospel world-wide. Men are urged to call on the name of the Lord and be saved; but they will not call on His name unless they have been moved to believe in Him, they cannot believe in Him unless they hear about Him, they cannot hear about Him unless someone brings them the news, and no-one can bring them the news unless he is sent to do so. The preacher is an 'apostle' in the primary sense of the word; he is a herald or ambassador conveying a message from someone who has authorized him to deliver it. Here Paul magnifies the office of the apostle or evangelist; it is God's good pleasure by their proclamation of

His amnesty to bring His mercy home to those who believe the message. Of those who bring this joyful news the prophet spoke centuries before: 'How beautiful upon the mountains are the feet of him that bringeth good tidings, that publisheth peace; that bringeth good tidings of good, that publisheth salvation; that saith unto Zion, Thy God reigneth!' (Is. lii. 7; see note on Rom. i. 1, pp. 71 f.).

But how does all this apply to the problem of Jewish unbelief? The message came to the Jews as well as to the Gentiles; indeed, it came to the Jews first. But the Jews (for the most part) did not pay heed to it. Well, even this was not unforeseen, as may be gathered from the question of Isaiah liii. 1, 'Who has believed our message?' The relevance of these words to the gospel arises not only from the general context of Isaiah xl–lxvi, but even more so from the particular context of the fourth Servant-Song (Is. lii. 13–liii. 12), which has contributed so greatly to the New Testament interpretation of the passion and triumph of Jesus. This verse, however, is quoted elsewhere in the New Testament as one of a number of Isaianic quotations used to account for Israel's unbelief.

But if the disappointed messenger asks 'Who has believed our message?' it is evident that the message was designed to produce faith. And the message itself rests for its authority on the direct command and commission of Christ.

Perhaps, however (an interested inquirer suggests), the people of Israel did not all *hear* the message? Indeed they did, Paul replies; to every place where there is a Jewish community the gospel has been carried. He says this by quoting in relation to the gospel the words of Psalm xix about the message of the heavenly bodies. The language of the quotation as thus used has often seemed to be an exaggeration; after all, the gospel had not been carried throughout all the earth, not even to all the lands that were then known to inhabitants of the Graeco-Roman world. Paul was well aware of that; at this very time he was planning the evangelization of Spain, a province where the name of Christ was not yet known. All that he means is that, wherever there were Jews, there the gospel had been preached.

Well, says our inquirer again, they have heard, it seems, but perhaps they did not understand? No, says Paul, it was not that. They understood well enough, but they refused to obey. They have shown their envy and indignation when the Gentiles accepted the message, but they would not believe it themselves. But this too has fulfilled the word of prophecy. In the Song of Moses (Dt. xxxii) the disobedience and ungratefulness of Israel are described. God charges them with idolatry (verse 21):

'They have moved me to jealousy with that which is not God; they have provoked me to anger with their vanities.'

Then He pronounces sentence:

'I will move them to jealousy with those which are not a people;
I will provoke them to anger with a foolish nation.'

By Paul—and in all probability not by him only—the language of this sentence, 'I will provoke them to jealousy with a no-people', is interpreted of the Gentile world. How does God provoke Israel to jealousy by means of the Gentile 'no-people'? By letting Israel see the blessings which fall upon the Gentiles when they embrace Christ by faith: God no longer speaks of them as 'not-my-people' but calls them His people. Israel, provoked to jealousy by the sight, asks why these same blessings should not even more rightfully be hers, and is assured that they will indeed be hers on the same basis—faith in Christ. This hope is elaborated by Paul in chapter xi, but he sums up this phase of his argument by two contrasted passages which stand in juxtaposition in Isaiah lxv. The first verse of that chapter is applied to the Gentiles, who after long centuries of living without the knowledge of the true God, had turned to seek Him. Isaiah, says Paul, goes to the very limit of daring in the language he uses of them, representing God as saying:

'I was found by those who did not seek me;
I appeared to those who did not ask for me.'

But the next verse is applied to Israel:

'All the day long I stretched out my hands
to a people that disobeyed and contradicted me.'

14. *How then shall they call . . .?* The subject is indefinite; cf. RSV: 'But how are men to call . . .?'

15. *How beautiful are the feet of them that preach the gospel of peace, and bring glad tidings of good things!* The clause 'that preach the gospel of peace' has been added to Paul's text in later MSS (beginning with some western witnesses) to bring the quotation into greater conformity with Isaiah lii. 7 (cf. RV, RSV, NEB). Paul here gives his own Greek rendering of the gist of the Hebrew instead of reproducing the LXX, which obscures the sense in this verse.

These words were spoken in the first instance of those who carried the good news home to Jerusalem from Babylon that the days of exile were past and restoration was at hand. But in the New Testament this whole section of the book of Isaiah, from chapter xl onwards, is interpreted of the gospel age. The deliverance from Babylon under Cyrus, like the deliverance from Egypt in the days of Moses, is treated as the foreshadowing of the greater and perfect deliverance wrought by Christ. The voice of Isaiah xl. 3 which calls for the preparation of a way through the desert by which God may lead His liberated people home to Zion becomes the voice of John the Baptist, calling together in the wilderness of Judaea a people prepared for the Lord; the 'acceptable year of the Lord' (Is. lxi. 2) is proclaimed by Jesus at the outset of His Galilaean ministry; and further examples of the Christian fulfilment of these chapters appear in the verses that follow.

16. *Lord, who hath believed our report?* The vocative 'Lord' is an addition of the LXX. In Isaiah liii. 1 the question is asked by those who hear the announcement of the Suffering Servant's exaltation (cf. the verse immediately preceding, Is. lii. 15, quoted below in xv. 21). 'Who would have believed the announcement which we have heard?' they ask in surprise, as they recall the Servant's humiliation. The announcement, now embodied in the gospel message, is still received with incredulity, says Paul—not now by the kings and nations of Isaiah lii. 15 so much as by the bulk of the Jewish people. Isaiah liii. 1 is quoted in John xii. 38 to account for the failure of the people to believe in Jesus as the Messiah during His ministry in Jerusalem; it is coupled there with the quotation of Isaiah vi. 9 f., also widely current in primitive Christian times as a *testimonium* predicting Jewish unbelief (cf. xi. 8).

17. *Faith cometh by hearing, and hearing by the word of God.* 'Hearing' is the same word as 'report' in the quotation from Isaiah liii. 1 in the previous verse (Gk. *akoē*); here it denotes the message that is heard. For 'the word of God' the best attested reading is 'the word of Christ' (RV, NEB), i.e. 'the preaching of Christ' (RSV), the gospel message, which awakens faith in its hearers.

18. *Their sound went into all the earth, and their words unto the end of the world.* It is unnecessary to suppose that Paul regarded Psalm xix. 4 as a *prediction* of the world-wide dissemination of the gospel; he means that the dissemination of the gospel is becoming as world-wide as the light of the heavenly bodies. 'Their sound' follows LXX as against Hebrew 'their line'; possibly the LXX translators read *qolam* ('their voice') in the Hebrew copy before them, instead of *qawwam* ('their line'). For the 'representative universalism'[1] implied in the quotation cf. Colossians i. 5 f. ('the gospel; which is come unto you, as it is in all the world'), 23 ('the gospel, which . . . was preached to every creature which is under heaven').

[1] See p. 223, n. 1.

19. *Moses saith.* The quotation is taken from the Song of Moses (Dt. xxxii. 21). But here Moses represents God as speaking. The Song of Moses furnished the early Christians with a remarkable number of *testimonia*—largely, but not exclusively, on the subject of Jewish unbelief (cf. 1 Cor. x. 20, 22, echoing Dt. xxxii. 16 f.; Phil. ii. 15, echoing Dt. xxxii. 5; Heb. i. 6, quoting Dt. xxxii. 43, LXX).[1] The later writers of anti-Judaic apologies regarded it as a strong point in their argument that in this Song Moses himself testifies against the Jews (cf. Justin, *Dialogue with Trypho* 20, 119, 130). The Song also appears to have played an important part in the theological thinking of the Qumran community.[2]

I will provoke you to jealousy by them that are no people. Because they had provoked God to jealousy by their worship of a 'no-god' (Heb. *lo'-'el*), He would provoke *them* to jealousy by means of a 'no-people' (Heb. *lo'-'am*). That is to say, in the course of history He used as the instruments of His judgment on Israel this or that Gentile nation—those whom they regarded as being a 'no-people' in the sense that they did not enter into God's electing purpose as a people in the way that Israel did. But in the light of the passages he has already quoted from Hosea (cf. ix. 25 f.) Paul reinterprets these words with reference to the new gospel situation. To one acquainted with the Hebrew Bible, as Paul was, the comparison between Moses' *lo'-'am* and Hosea's *lo'-'ammi* (see pp. 195 f.) suggested itself readily (more so than to one who depended exclusively on LXX). Just how Paul understood the Gentiles' provocation of Israel to jealousy is seen below in xi. 11.

By a foolish nation I will anger you. The Gentiles were 'foolish' from the Jewish viewpoint in that they were cut off from the knowledge of God.

---

[1] Cf. J. R. Harris, 'A factor of Old Testament Influence in the New Testament', *ExT*, XXXVII (1925–26), pp. 6 ff.; B. Lindars, *New Testament Apologetic* (1961), pp. 244 f., 258, 274.

[2] For a Qumran quotation of Dt. xxxii. 28 against Israel see G. Vermes, *The Dead Sea Scrolls in English*, p. 102.

20. *But Esaias is very bold.* That is, he goes to the very limit of daring, even beyond the point reached by Moses, in his affirmation of the paradox of God's bestowing His covenant mercies on those who were not His people, and had no claim on these mercies.

I was found of them that sought me not. . . . In their original context, these words from Isaiah lxv. 1 perhaps refer to rebellious Israel (cf. RSV: 'I was ready to be sought by those who did not ask for me. . . .'); but, as in his application of the Hosea prophecy, Paul recognizes here a principle which in the situation of his day is applicable to Gentiles.

21. *But to Israel he saith.* If Paul finds Isaiah lxv. 1 applicable to the Gentiles' eager acceptance of the gospel, he finds Isaiah lxv. 2 equally applicable to the Jews' general refusal of it.

d. God's purpose for Israel (xi. 1–29)

i. Israel's alienation not final (xi. 1–16). A 'disobedient and gainsaying people' Israel might be, but God had no more written them off now than in earlier days when they rejected His word through Moses and the prophets. 'Whom he did foreknow, he also did predestinate' is a principle not set aside in their case. As in Old Testament times, so in apostolic times God's purpose in choosing His people was safeguarded by His reservation of a faithful remnant. In Elijah's day, in a period when national apostasy had assumed the dimensions of a landslide, there was a faithful minority of seven thousand who refused to worship Baal; and so in Paul's day there was a faithful minority who had not rejected the gospel. Paul ought to know; he was one of them. His descent from Abraham through one of the sons of Israel was well established, and yet he was a believer in Jesus, as were many more of his kinsmen 'according to the flesh'. They constituted a faithful remnant, chosen by God's grace, and their existence was in itself proof that God had not abandoned Israel or given up His purpose for them. Even if Israel as a whole had failed to attain His purpose, the elect remnant had attained it. The blindness which affected the majority had been foreseen by God (here three more *testimonia* are adduced, in addition to the composite 'stone' *testimonium* of ix. 33—one from Isaiah, one from Deuteronomy and one from the Psalter). But it was not to be a permanent condition.

Israel had stumbled, but had not fallen so as to rise no more. Through her stumbling the blessings of the gospel had been extended more immediately to the Gentiles. Repeatedly in the Acts of the Apostles it is the refusal of the Jewish community in one place or another to accept the proffered salvation that is the occasion for the apostles' presenting it directly to the Gentiles. 'It was necessary,' said Paul and Barnabas to the Jews of Pisidian Antioch, 'that the word of God should first have been spoken to you: but seeing ye put it from you, and judge yourselves unworthy of everlasting life, lo, we turn to the Gentiles' (Acts xiii. 46; cf. xxviii. 28). Had the Jews accepted the gospel, it would have been their privilege to make it known to the Gentiles; as it was, the Gentiles heard it without their mediation. But if the *stumbling* of Israel had been the occasion of so much blessing to the Gentiles, what would Israel's revival and restoration mean but a veritable resurrection!

Paul then addresses himself more personally to the Gentiles among his readers, who might be inclined to think lightly of their Jewish brethren, and think nothing at all of those Jews who had not received the gospel. 'Jew as I am by birth,' he says, 'I am the Gentiles' apostle, and I esteem the honour of my commission very highly. This I do not only for the sake of the Gentiles to whom I carry the gospel, but for the sake of my Jewish brethren as well. I want to stir them to jealousy, as they see the Gentiles entering into the full enjoyment of gospel blessings. I want to make them say: "Why should the Gentiles have all these blessings? Why should we not have a share in them?" Well may they say so, for these blessings are the fulfilment of their own ancestral hope; they are bound up with faith in their own Messiah. And when at last Israel as a whole is stimulated to claim the Messiah with all the blessings He brings, words cannot describe the blessing which their conversion will mean to the world.'

This consummation is not an idle dream, Paul maintains; it is guaranteed by the indefectible purpose of God. The first cake of the batch has already been presented to God, and its consecration means that the whole batch is holy to Him. 'The root of the tree is holy, and the branches inevitably share its holiness.'

1. *Hath God cast away his people?* This question (so framed in Greek as to require the answer 'No') and the statement in verse 2, 'God hath not cast away his people . . .', echo the LXX wording of Psalm xciv. 14: 'the Lord will not cast off his people' (cf. 1 Sa. xii. 22).

Of the seed of Abraham. Here the phrase is used in the natural as well as in the spiritual sense (cf. 2 Cor. xi. 22).

Of the tribe of Benjamin. (Cf. Phil. iii. 5.) It is an 'undesigned coincidence' between the Pauline Epistles and Acts that, while it is only from the former that we learn that Paul belonged to the tribe of Benjamin, it is only the latter that tells us that his Jewish name was Saul. It is not surprising that parents who traced their descent from the tribe of Benjamin and cherished high ambitions for their new-born son should give him the name borne by the most illustrious member of that tribe in the history of Israel—'Saul the son of Kish, a man of the tribe of Benjamin' (to quote Paul's own reference to Israel's first king in Acts xiii. 21, RV).

2, 3. *Wot ye not . . .?* 'Do you not know . . .?' (RSV). 'Wot' is the archaic present tense of the verb 'to wit' (cf. viii. 23); it is amazing that it was retained here by the RV of 1881.

What the scripture saith. (Cf. ix. 17.) The reference here is to 1 Kings xix. 10, 14 where Elijah is the actual speaker.

Of Elias. Elias is the Greek form of Elijah. Read '*in* Elijah' (*en Ēleia*), where 'Elijah' appears to be the title of that section of the books of Kings (perhaps 1 Ki. xvii. 1–2 Ki. ii. 18) from which the quotation is taken (cf. Mk. xii. 26, where 'in the bush' means 'in the section of the book of Exodus entitled "The Bush" ').

4. *The answer of God*. Gk. *chrēmatismos*, used of a divine response, like the transitive verb *chrēmatizō* (cf. Mt. ii. 12, 22; Lk. ii. 26; Acts x. 22; Heb. viii. 5, xi. 7, xii. 25).

I have reserved to myself seven thousand men, who have not bowed the knee. . . . Quoted from 1 Kings xix. 18, in a form closer to the Hebrew text than LXX (which reads '*thou* wilt reserve . . .') —although there is nothing in the Hebrew (or LXX) corresponding to 'to myself'. The Hebrew text is best rendered by the future tense: 'Yet will I leave. . . .' (RV, cf. RSV)—the reference being to the remnant of seven thousand who alone will survive the slaughter to be wrought by the swords of Hazael, Jehu and Elisha (1 Ki. xix. 17).

To the image of Baal. As AV shows by means of italics, there is no word in the Greek text (or in the underlying Hebrew) corresponding to 'image'. The translators introduced it in an attempt to do justice to the odd phenomenon of the masculine substantive *Baal* being preceded by a feminine form of the definite article (*tē*). This reading is not found at 1 Kings xix. 18 in our extant LXX MSS, but it apparently reflects a Hebrew text in which the idolatrous name Baal was marked for replacement (in public reading, at least) by the feminine noun *bosheth*, 'shame'.

6. *But if it be of works, then it is no more grace: otherwise work is no more work.* This intrusion into Paul's argument is no part of the original text (cf. RV, RSV, NEB); it was probably written as a marginal note by some scribe or reader who thought he could state the converse to the principle stated in the first half of the verse, and was later incorporated by error into the text.

7. *The rest were blinded* ('hardened', RV, RSV). The Greek verb *pōroō* means 'to harden' or 'render insensitive' rather than 'to blind' (cf. the substantive *pōrōsis* in verse 25, rendered 'blindness' by AV, NEB; 'hardening' by RV, RSV). In modern English idiom 'blindness' is freely used to denote this moral insensitiveness; hence NEB: 'The rest were made blind to the truth.' If it be asked by whom they were hardened or blinded, verse 8 makes the answer plain. Not for the first time in this Epistle (cf. i. 21b, ix. 17 f.)[1] such moral insensitiveness is divinely inflicted as a judicial penalty for refusal to heed the word of God.

8. *God hath given them the spirit of slumber, eyes that they should not see, and ears that they should not hear; unto this day.* Quoted from Isaiah xxix. 10 ('the Lord hath poured out upon you the spirit of deep sleep, and hath closed your eyes') and Deuteronomy xxix. 4 ('the Lord hath not given you an heart to perceive, and eyes to see, and ears to hear, unto this day'). The reference to unseeing eyes and unhearing ears is reminiscent also of Isaiah vi. 9 f. ('Hear ye indeed, but understand not; and see ye indeed, but perceive not . . .'), used by all four Evangelists as a *testimonium* of Jewish failure to recognize Jesus as the Messiah (Mt. xiii. 14 f.; Mk. iv. 12; Lk. viii. 10; Jn. xii. 40; cf. also Acts xxviii. 26 f.). (See note on x. 16, pp. 208 f.)

The word translated 'slumber' in AV (RV and RSV 'stupor') is *katanuxis* (so Is. xxix. 10, LXX), which literally means 'pricking' or 'stinging', and hence comes to be used also of the numbness which results from certain kinds of sting (NEB accordingly renders 'a numbness of spirit').

There is no good reason for AV's printing all of this verse except the last three words as a parenthesis; 'unto this day' is part of the quotation from Deuteronomy xxix. 4.

9. *And David saith, Let their table be made a snare. . . .* Verses 9 and 10 are taken from Psalm lxix. 22 f. (LXX). This psalm

---

[1] A different word (*sklērunō*) is used of the hardening of Pharaoh's heart in ix. 18, but the meaning is not greatly different from that of *pōroō* here.

was widely current in the Church from earliest days as a
testimonium of the ministry, and especially the passion, of Christ
(cf. the allusion to verse 4 in Jn. xv. 25; to verse 9 in Jn. ii. 17
and Rom. xv. 3; to verse 21 in Mt. xxvii. 48). If the speaker
in the psalm is Christ, those against whom complaints are
voiced are interpreted as His enemies (cf. the application of
verse 25 to Judas Iscariot in Acts i. 20). We should note the
recurrence of the motif of the unseeing eyes (verse 10, quoting
Ps. lxix. 23); here lies the principal relevance of the quotation
for Paul's present argument—the temporary 'blindness' that
has overtaken all Israel with the exception of the believing
remnant.

11. *Through their fall salvation is come unto the Gentiles, for to provoke them to jealousy.* This is Paul's interpretation of the words
from the Song of Moses (Dt. xxxii. 21) already quoted in x. 19.
It is by the blessing He bestows on those who were formerly a
'no-people' in relation to Him, by the salvation which 'a
foolish nation' has received through readily embracing the
gospel, that God will provoke Israel to jealousy.

12. *How much more their fulness?* The 'fulness' (*plērōma*) of the
Jews is to be understood in the same sense as the 'fulness' of the
Gentiles (verse 25); the large-scale conversion of the Gentile
world is to be followed by the large-scale conversion of Israel
(cf. verse 26).

15. *Life from the dead.* The meaning may be that Israel's
conversion will be the immediate precursor of the resurrection,
to coincide with Christ's parousia (see note on xi. 26, p. 222).

16. *If the firstfruit be holy, the lump is also holy.* The allusion is
probably to Numbers xv. 17–21, where the Israelites are commanded to offer to God a cake from the dough of the first-
ground flour, newly come from the threshing-floor. The
presentation of this cake to God hallows the whole baking.

In 1 Corinthians xv. 23, 'Christ the firstfruits', while the word (Gk. *aparchē*) is the same, the allusion is rather to the sheaf of the firstfruits of barley harvest which was to be 'waved' before the Lord on the Sunday following Passover, thus consecrating the whole harvest (Lv. xxiii. 10 f.). Here the 'firstfruit' most probably comprises those people of Jewish birth who had, like Paul, accepted Jesus as Messiah and Lord.

And if the root be holy, so are the branches. Changing the metaphor, Paul now says that since the whole of a tree is of one character throughout, the holiness of the root sanctifies the branches. It is natural to give the 'root' the same significance as the 'firstfruit', but if the 'root and branch' figure stood by itself, we should think of the patriarchs as constituting the root of the tree whose branches are the Israelites of the Christian era. This would be in line with Paul's later description of Israel as 'beloved for the fathers' sakes' (verse 28). Perhaps there is a transition of thought here as Paul passes from the one metaphor to the other.[1]

ii. The parable of the olive-tree (xi. 17–24). The reference to the root and the branches leads Paul on to develop his parable of the olive-tree—a parable which has often been quoted against him as showing that he was a typical town-dweller, unfamiliar with the most ordinary phenomena of the countryside. For a gardener does not graft a slip from a wild fruit-tree on to a cultivated fruit-tree; it is a shoot or 'scion' from a cultivated tree that must be grafted on to a stock of the same or an allied species. Sir William Ramsay does, indeed, quote Theobald Fischer as saying that it was customary in Palestine sixty years ago 'to reinvigorate an Olive-tree which is ceasing to bear fruit, by grafting it with a shoot of the Wild-Olive, so that the sap of the tree ennobles this wild shoot and the tree now again begins to bear fruit.'[2] That a similar

---

[1] It is, of course, possible to interpret the 'firstfruit' of verse 16 of the patriarchs, but this is a less likely interpretation.

[2] *Pauline and Other Studies* (1906), p. 223.

process was familiar in Roman times is evident from Paul's contemporary Columella, according to whom, when an olive-tree produces badly, a slip of a wild-olive is grafted on to it, and this gives new vigour to the tree.[1]

At any rate, Paul's parable is clear. Here are two olive-trees —a cultivated olive and a wild-olive. The latter produced poor fruit which contained little oil; the former normally produced good fruit. The olive is Israel, the people of God; the wild-olive is the Gentile world. But the olive began to grow weak and unproductive; old branches were therefore cut away and a graft was made from the wild-olive. 'The cutting away of the old branches was required to admit air and light to the graft, as well as to prevent the vitality of the tree from being too widely diffused over a large number of branches' (W. M. Ramsay, *op. cit.*, p. 224). The graft from the wild-olive is the sum-total of Gentile believers, now incorporated into the people of God; the old branches which were cut away are those Jews who refused to accept the gospel.

In such an unusual grafting, we are told, both the graft and the stock on which it is grafted are affected; the old stock is reinvigorated by the new graft, and the new graft in turn, fed by the sap of the olive stock, is able to bear such fruit as the wild-olive could never produce.

The Gentile believers must not yield to the temptation to look down upon the Jews. But for the grace of God which ingrafted them among His people and made them 'fellow-citizens with the saints' (Eph. ii. 19) they would have remained for ever lifeless and fruitless. The new life which enables them to produce fruit for God is the life of the old stock of Israel on which they have been grafted. Israel owes no debt to them; they are indebted to Israel. And if they reply that at least they are better than the *unbelieving* Jews, the branches which were cut off, they are exhorted to learn a salutary lesson from the removal of those old branches. Why were they cut off? Because of unbelief. And if a spirit of pride leads the new graft

[1] Columella, *De re rustica*, v. 9.

—the Gentile church—to forget its reliance on divine grace and exchange faith in God for self-confidence, it will suffer the same fate as the old branches; it, too, will be cut off. It is by faith that membership in the true people of God is acquired and maintained; it is by unbelief that it is forfeited. This principle, says Paul, is applied without partiality, to Gentiles as much as to Jews. On the other hand—and here the practical processes of grafting are certainly left behind, for the sake of the spiritual facts which the parable is intended to illustrate— if those Jews who through unbelief lost their status as members of the true Israel come at length to faith in Christ, they will be incorporated afresh in the people of God. If old branches which had been cut away from an olive were grafted on to the parent tree once more and began to produce fruit again, that would be an unprecedented miracle in the natural realm. Equally, the reincorporation of the Jewish nation among the people of God when unbelief is replaced by faith would be a miracle in the spiritual realm; but, says Paul, it is a miracle which God is going to perform.

17. *Thou . . . wert graffed in among them.* 'Graffed' is modern English 'grafted' (so in verses 23, 24; and 'graff' in verse 23 is modern English 'graft').

20. *Thou standest by faith.* 'By faith' is emphatic: 'by faith you hold your place' (NEB). Cf. Romans v. 2 (p. 123).

22. *But toward thee, goodness.* Read with RV: 'but toward thee, God's goodness' ('God's kindness', RSV; 'divine kindness', NEB). (Cf. ii. 4.)

If thou continue in his goodness: otherwise thou also shalt be cut off. Throughout the New Testament continuance is the test of reality. The perseverance of the saints is a doctrine firmly grounded in New Testament (and not least in Pauline) teaching; but the corollary to it is that it is the saints who persevere. Since 'thou standest by faith' (verse 20), it is a healthy exercise to heed Paul's injunction to the Corinthian Christians: 'Examine yourselves, whether ye be in the faith' (2 Cor. xiii. 5).

24. *Contrary to nature.* Paul may be thought to disarm criticism in advance by showing that he is aware of the unnaturalness of the particular kind of grafting here described. But he need mean no more than that the process of grafting is itself 'contrary to nature'—a view which was commonly taken by the ancients.

iii. The restoration of Israel (xi. 25–29). Here is the mystery of God's purpose for Israel—a purpose formerly concealed but now made known. Israel's blindness is only partial (for some Israelites have already been enlightened), and only temporary, with a view to the blessing of the Gentiles. So far as the proclamation of the gospel is concerned, the order is 'To the Jew first'; so far as the reception of the gospel is concerned, the order is 'By the Gentile first, and then by the Jew'. When the full tale of believing Gentiles was achieved—a consummation which Paul's own apostleship was bringing nearer—then *all* Israel, not a faithful remnant but the nation as a whole, would see the salvation of God. If their temporary stumbling was prophetically foretold, so was their ultimate and permanent restoration (Is. lix. 20 f. and Je. xxxi. 33 are quoted to this effect). The new covenant will not be complete until it embraces the people of the old covenant. Temporarily alienated for the advantage of the Gentiles, they are eternally the objects of God's electing love because His promises, once made to the patriarchs, can never be revoked.

It has been objected that Paul here lets his patriotism override his logic.[1] He has emphasized more than once in the Epistle that natural descent from the patriarchs is not what matters in God's sight, and now he says that because of God's

---

[1] So A. Harnack, *The Date of the Acts and of the Synoptic Gospels* (1911), pp. 40–66; 'the Jew in himself', says Harnack, 'was still too strong' (p. 61).

promises to the patriarchs, their natural descendants must be restored to covenant relation with Him. It might suffice to say 'The heart has its reasons . . .'; but there is more than that to be said. Paul had a deeper and clearer insight into God's grace than his critics; if God's grace operated in accordance with strict logic, the outlook would be dismal for Jews and Gentiles alike.

One further point: in all that Paul says about the restoration of Israel to God, he says nothing about the restoration of an earthly Davidic kingdom, nothing about national reinstatement in the land of Israel. What he envisaged for his people was something infinitely better.

25. *I would not . . . that ye should be ignorant of this mystery.* By the word 'mystery' Paul probably means (cf. 1 Cor. xv. 51; Col. i. 26 f.) that what follows is a new revelation which he has received. The remnant principle of verses 1–7 was a subject of ancient prophetic revelation; that 'all Israel' would yet be saved was a new revelation, conveyed through Paul. He has been accused of trying to eat his cake and have it—of consoling himself with the thought of 'a remnant according to the election of grace' and at the same time insisting on a wholesale restoration of Israel—but if his claim to have received a new revelation be taken seriously, he cannot fairly be blamed. Moreover, even in Old Testament prophecy, the remnant of the old Israel was at the same time the nucleus of the new Israel. So it is here: the existence of the believing remnant was the earnest of the ultimate salvation of 'all Israel'.

Until the fulness of the Gentiles be come in. Cf. the practically synonymous 'offering up of the Gentiles' (xv. 16) and 'obedience of the Gentiles' (xv. 18, RV). The bringing in of the 'fulness' or full complement (*plērōma*) of the Gentiles is to be followed by the bringing in of the 'fulness' of the Jews (verse 12).

26. *And so all Israel shall be saved.* It is impossible to entertain an exegesis which takes 'Israel' here in a different sense from

'Israel' in verse 25 ('blindness in part is happened to Israel'). To the argument that Paul does not say 'and *then* all Israel shall be saved' but 'and *so* all Israel shall be saved' (as though the ingathering of the full tale of Gentiles were in itself the salvation of all Israel), it should suffice to point out the well attested use of Gk. *houtōs* ('so', 'thus') in a temporal sense. 'All Israel' is a recurring expression in Jewish literature, where it need not mean 'every Jew without a single exception' but 'Israel as a whole'. Thus 'all Israel has a portion in the age to come', says the Mishnah tractate *Sanhedrin* (x. 1), and proceeds immediately to name those Israelites who have no portion therein.

There shall come out of Sion the Deliverer, and shall turn away ungodliness from Jacob. Quoted from Isaiah lix. 20: 'And he will come to Zion as Redeemer, to those in Jacob who turn from transgression' (RSV). Paul's text conforms with LXX, except that LXX reads 'for Zion's sake' and not 'out of Zion'. Whichever form of text be followed, the reference is to a manifestation to Israel of her divine Redeemer—a manifestation which Paul may well identify in his mind with the parousia of Christ. See note on verse 15 (p. 216). A similar interpretation has sometimes been put on Acts iii. 19–21 and 2 Cor. iii. 16.

27. *For this is my covenant unto them, when I shall take away their sins.* For the first few words Paul continues the quotation of Isaiah lix (verse 21 goes on: 'As for me, this is my covenant with them, saith the Lord'), but then passes into the promise of the new covenant in Jeremiah xxxi. 33 f.: 'But this shall be the covenant that I will make with the house of Israel . . . I will forgive their iniquity, and I will remember their sin no more' (see notes on vii. 6, p. 147, and viii. 4, p. 161).

28. *As concerning the gospel, they are enemies for your sakes.* Their present estrangement from God has been the occasion for you Gentiles to embrace the blessings of the gospel and be reconciled to Him.

As touching the election, they are beloved for the fathers' sakes.
These words have been interpreted in terms of the 'merits of
the fathers' (Heb. *zekhuth ha'aboth*)—the Jewish doctrine that
the righteousness of the patriarchs constitutes a store of merit
which is credited to their descendants. But this is not Paul's
meaning here: the whole argument of this Epistle is contrary
to such a conception of merit (cf. iv. 2). He means that the
promises which God made to the patriarchs when He called
them are secured to their descendants, not on the ground of
merit, but on the ground of God's fidelity to His word.

e. God's purpose for mankind (xi. 30–36)

God's ultimate purpose for the world is now revealed; it is
mercy for Jew and Gentile alike. The faithful remnant has not
been chosen by grace so that the rest might be consigned to
perdition; its election is a token that the divine mercy is to be
extended to all without distinction (cf. viii. 19–21). There is an
unmistakable universalism in Paul's language here, even if it
be an eschatological universalism and not a present one, or a
representative rather than an individual universalism.[1]

'All have sinned, and come short of the glory of God', Paul
has already announced (iii. 23). All have been convicted before
the tribunal of God; none, whether Jew or Gentile, can lay any
claim to His mercy. If there is to be hope for any, it must
depend solely on God's grace; but hope is held out in unstinted
measure. God's purpose in shutting Jews and Gentiles together
in a place where their disobedience to His law must be acknowledged and brought to light was that He might bestow His
unmerited mercy on Jews and Gentiles alike.

---

[1] By an eschatological universalism is meant the hope that ultimately
'the elect will be all the world' (C. H. Spurgeon, quoted in A. C. Benson,
The Life of Edward White Benson, ii, 1900, p. 276), that 'in the age-long
development of the race of men, it will attain at last a complete salvation,
and our eyes will be greeted with the glorious spectacle of a saved world'
(B. B. Warfield, *Biblical and Theological Studies*, Philadelphia, 1952, p. xxx).
By a representative universalism is meant that 'there has been a representative acceptance of the Gospel by the various nations' (J. Munck, *Paul and the
Salvation of Mankind*, 1959, p. 278). See pp. 168 ff., 209, 261.

Here then is the height of Paul's great argument: here is matter for unending praise to God. The doxology of verses 33–36 rounds off not merely chapters ix–xi; it concludes the whole argument of chapters i–xi: 'O the unfathomable wealth of God's wisdom and knowledge! How unsearchable are His decrees! How inscrutable His ways! Well has the prophet said:

> "Who has grasped the Lord's purpose?
> Who has shared His counsel?
> Who has first given to Him,
> That he should be repaid his gift?"

From Him all things proceed; through Him all things exist; to Him all things return: to Him be the glory throughout all ages. Amen.'

32. *That he might have mercy upon all.* That is, upon all without distinction rather than all without exception. Paul is not here thinking of those who, like Pharaoh in ix. 17, persistently refuse the divine mercy. He 'does not intend to make a definite pronouncement about the ultimate destiny of each individual man. But the hope of mankind is more, not less, secure because it is rooted in the truth about God, rather than in a truth about man himself' (C. K. Barrett, *ad loc.*).

34. *For who hath known the mind of the Lord? or who hath been his counsellor?* An echo of Isaiah xl. 13: 'who hath directed the Spirit of the Lord, or being his counsellor hath taught him?'

35. *Or who hath first given to him, and it shall be recompensed unto him again?* An echo of Job xli. 11: 'who hath first given unto me, that I should repay him?' (RV).

B. The Christian Way of Life (xii. 1–xv. 13)

I. THE LIVING SACRIFICE (xii. 1, 2)

In view of all that God has accomplished for His people in Christ, how should His people live? They should present themselves to God as a 'living sacrifice', consecrated to Him. The animal sacrifices of an earlier day have been rendered for ever obsolete by Christ's self-offering, but there is always room for the worship rendered by obedient hearts. Instead of living by the standards of a world at discord with God, believers are exhorted to let the renewing of their minds by the power of the Spirit transform their lives into conformity with God's will.

Doctrine is never taught in the Bible simply that it may be known; it is taught in order that it may be translated into practice. 'If ye know these things, happy are ye if ye do them' (Jn. xiii. 17). Hence Paul repeatedly follows up an exposition of doctrine with an ethical exhortation, the two being linked together, as here, by 'therefore' (cf. Eph. iv. 1; Col. iii. 5).

It is worthy to note, moreover, that the ethical admonitions of this and other New Testament Epistles, whether Paul's or not, bear a close resemblance to the ethical teaching of Christ recorded in the Gospels. They are based, in fact, on 'the law of Christ', as Paul calls it (Gal. vi. 2; cf. 1 Cor. ix. 21). In particular, an impressive list of parallels can be drawn up between Romans xii. 3–xiii. 14 and the Sermon on the Mount. While none of our canonical Gospels existed at this time, the teaching of Christ recorded in them was current among the churches—certainly in oral form, and perhaps also in the form of written summaries.

1. *Present your bodies.* Cf. vi. 13, 19; the Greek verb here is the same as that rendered 'yield' there. Paul now brings out in greater detail what is involved in their presenting themselves to God to be used in His service.

A living sacrifice. The new order has its sacrifices, which do not consist in the lives of others, like the ancient animal sacrifices (cf. Heb. xiii. 15 f.; 1 Pet. ii. 5).

Your reasonable service. So RV text; RVmg. and RSV render 'your spiritual worship'; NEB, 'the worship offered by mind and heart' (mg.: 'the worship which you, as rational creatures, should offer'). The substantive is *latreia*, used already in ix. 4 of 'the service of God' (AV, RV) or the 'worship' (RSV; cf. NEB, 'the temple worship') ordained for the Israelites. The adjective is *logikos* (derived from *logos*), which may mean either 'reasonable' (the service of obedient lives is the only reasonable or logical response to the grace of God)[1] or 'spiritual', as in 1 Peter ii. 2, where the 'milk of the word' (AV) is more appropriately rendered 'spiritual milk' in RV, RSV and NEB. Here 'spiritual worship' is probably to be preferred, in contrast to the externalities of Israel's temple worship.

2. *And be not conformed to this world* ('this age', RVmg.). 'This age' (*aiōn*), as in 1 Corinthians i. 20, ii. 6, iii. 18; 2 Corinthians iv. 4; Galatians i. 4, is distinguished from 'the age to come' (as in Eph. i. 21, 'not only in this age, but also in that which is to come', RVmg.). While it is called 'this present evil age' (Gal. i. 4, RVmg.), and is dominated by 'the god of this age' who blinds the minds of unbelievers (2 Cor. iv. 4, RVmg.), yet it is possible for people belonging temporally to 'this age' to live as heirs of the age to come, the age of renewal and resurrection. Those are the people upon whom 'the ends of the ages are come' (1 Cor. x. 11, RV), for whom, because they are a 'new creation' in Christ, 'the old has passed away, behold, the new has come' (2 Cor. v. 17, RSV). It is by the power of the indwelling Spirit, the pledge of their inheritance in the coming age, that they can resist the tendency to live on the level of 'this age'.

Be ye transformed. The Greek verb is *metamorphoō*, which is translated 'transfigure' in the transfiguration narratives of

---

[1] It has been well said that in Christianity theology is grace and ethics is gratitude; and it is not by accident that both 'grace' and 'gratitude' are expressed by one and the same Greek word, *charis* (see note on i. 7, p. 76).

Matthew xvii. 2; Mark ix. 2. The only other place where it appears in the New Testament is 2 Corinthians iii. 18, of believers being 'changed' into the likeness of Christ 'from one degree of glory to another' by the operation of 'the Lord who is the Spirit' (RSV)—a passage which is a helpful commentary on the present one.

II. THE COMMON LIFE OF CHRISTIANS
(xii. 3-8)

Diversity, not uniformity, is the mark of God's handiwork. It is so in nature; it is so in grace, too, and nowhere more so than in the Christian community. Here are many men and women with the most diverse kinds of parentage, environment, temperament, and capacity. Not only so, but since they became Christians they have been endowed by God with a great variety of spiritual gifts as well. Yet because and by means of that diversity, all can co-operate for the good of the whole. Whatever kind of service is to be rendered in the church, let it be rendered heartily and faithfully by those divinely qualified, whether it be prophesying, teaching, admonishing, administering, making material gifts, sick-visiting, or performing any other kind of ministry.

To illustrate what he means, Paul uses the figure of a human body, as he had already done in 1 Corinthians xii. 12-27. Each part of the body has its own distinctive work to do, yet in a healthy body all the parts function harmoniously and inter-dependently for the good of the whole body. So should it be in the church, which is the body of Christ.

3. *Through the grace given unto me.* That is, the 'grace' or spiritual gift of apostleship (cf. i. 5, xv. 15). According to verse 6, each member of the church has received a special 'grace' in this sense, which is to be exercised for the good of all.

The measure of faith. 'Faith' here has a rather different sense from that which it has in the earlier part of the Epistle; here it denotes the spiritual power given to each Christian for the discharge of his special responsibility; cf. 'according to the proportion of faith' in verse 6 (NEB, 'in proportion to a man's faith').

5. *One body in Christ.* Compare 1 Corinthians xii. 27: 'ye are the body of Christ.' In 1 Corinthians and Romans the human body is used simply as an illustration of the corporate life of Christians, but the idea is carried much farther in Colossians and Ephesians. In these later Epistles emphasis is laid on the relation which the church, as the body, bears to Christ as the Head. In them there is no possibility of an ordinary member of the church being compared to the head, or to part of the head (as is done in 1 Cor. xii. 16 f., 21); in them, too, the body ceases to be used as a mere simile and becomes rather the most effective term which the apostle can find to express the vital bond which unites the life of believers with the risen life of Christ.[1]

8. *With simplicity.* NEB, 'with all your heart.'
He that ruleth. The exercise of leadership in the church is as truly a spiritual gift as any of the others mentioned.
He that sheweth mercy. NEB, 'if you are helping others in distress.'

III. THE LAW OF CHRIST (xii. 9–21)

The injunctions in this section to deep, unaffected and practical love are particularly reminiscent of the Sermon on the Mount. Mutual love, sympathy and honour within the brotherhood of believers are to be expected, but something more is enjoined here—love and forgiveness to those outside the fellowship, and not least to those who persecute them and wish them ill.

9. *Without dissimulation.* Gk. *anupokritos*, lit., 'without hypocrisy' (NEB, 'in all sincerity').

10. *In honour preferring one another.* Cf. Philippians ii. 3: 'each counting other better than himself' (RV).

[1] Cf. E. Best, *One Body in Christ* (1955).

11. *Fervent in spirit.* The same expression is used of Apollos in Acts xviii. 25. Whether or not it has the same force in both places is debatable; here RSV is probably right in taking the reference to be to the Holy Spirit: 'be aglow with the Spirit.'

Serving the Lord. RVmg., 'serving the opportunity', represents a western reading which replaced the dative *kuriō* ('Lord') by *kairō* ('time', 'opportunity').

14. *Bless them which persecute you: bless, and curse not.* Cf. Luke vi. 28: 'Bless them that curse you, and pray for them which despitefully use you.' But there is good ancient evidence (including that of P⁴⁶) for the omission of 'you' after 'persecute'; in that case Christians are exhorted to call down blessings on persecutors, whether they themselves are the victims of the persecution or not. For Paul's own practice in this regard cf. 1 Corinthians iv. 12b–13a; Acts xxviii. 19b.

15. *Rejoice with them that do rejoice, and weep with them that weep.* This is no Stoic teaching, according to which an impassive detachment was essential to the good life; it is consistent, however, with the way of Christ.

16. *Be of the same mind one toward another.* (Cf. xv. 5 f.) See also Philippians ii. 2 ff., where the injunction to 'be likeminded' (not the same thing as 'seeing eye to eye') is followed by a statement of the only way in which this is possible in a Christian sense: 'Let this mind be in you, which was also in Christ Jesus.'

Mind not high things. Cf. verse 3; also xi. 20: 'Be not highminded.'

Condescend to men of low estate. NEB, 'go about with humble folk.'

Be not wise in your own conceits. A quotation from Proverbs iii. 7a.

17. *Recompense to no man evil for evil.* Cf. Matthew v. 44: 'Love your enemies' (see also 1 Pet. iii. 9).

Provide things honest in the sight of all men. 'Let your aims be such as all men count honourable' (NEB). A quotation from Proverbs iii. 4 (LXX).

19. *Give place unto wrath.* Make room for the law of divine retribution to operate whether now or on 'the day of wrath' (ii. 5).

Vengeance is mine; I will repay. A quotation from Deuteronomy xxxii. 35: 'Vengeance is mine and recompense' (so MT; LXX has 'in the day of vengeance I will repay'). This form of the text, found also in Hebrews x. 30, appears in the Aramaic Targums and was probably current in a Greek version not now extant. The point of the quotation in the present context is that, since vengeance and requital are God's prerogative, they should be left to Him. So in the Qumran community private vengeance was forbidden on the ground that, according to Nahum i. 2, it is God alone who 'takes vengeance on his adversaries and keeps wrath for his enemies'.[1]

20. *If thine enemy hunger, feed him; if he thirst, give him drink: for in so doing thou shalt heap coals of fire on his head.* A quotation from Proverbs xxv. 21 f. Paul omits the concluding clause: 'and the Lord shall reward thee.' The original force of the admonition may have been 'Treat your enemy kindly, for that will increase his guilt; you will thus ensure for him a more terrible judgment, and for yourself a better reward—from God.' An alternative view is that the proverb refers to an Egyptian ritual in which a man gave public evidence of his penitence by carrying a pan of burning charcoal on his head. In any case, by placing the proverb in this context and omitting the last clause, Paul gives it a nobler meaning: 'Treat your enemy kindly, for this may make him ashamed and lead to his repentance.' In other words, the best way to get rid of an enemy is to turn him into a friend, and so 'overcome evil with good' (verse 21).

[1] Cf. G. Vermes, *The Dead Sea Scrolls in English*, p. 110.

IV. THE CHRISTIAN AND THE STATE
(xiii. 1–7)

The relation of Christians, whether as individual subjects or corporately united in church life, to the ruling powers, was one which was destined to be specially acute within the decade that followed the writing of this Epistle.

So long as the church was mainly Jewish in composition, problems of this kind were not lacking, but they were not so acute as they were later to become. The position of Jews within the Roman Empire was regulated by a succession of imperial edicts. The Jews, indeed, as a subject nation within the Empire, enjoyed quite exceptional privileges. Their religion was legally registered as a *religio licita*, and their various religious practices which marked them off from Gentiles were confirmed to them. These practices might seem absurd and superstitious to the Romans, but they were safeguarded none the less by imperial law. They included the sabbath law and food-laws, and the prohibition of 'graven images'. Imperial policy forbade successive governors of Judaea to bring the military standards, with imperial images attached to them, within the walls of the holy city of Jerusalem, as that was an affront to the Jews' religious susceptibilities. If by Jewish law the trespassing of a Gentile upon the inner courts of the Jerusalem temple was a sacrilege deserving the death penalty, Rome confirmed Jewish law in this respect to the point of ratifying the death-sentence for such a trespass even when the offender was a Roman citizen.

For the first generation after the death of Christ Roman law, when it took cognizance of Christians at all, tended to regard them as a variety of Jews. When the Corinthian Jews in AD 51 accused Paul before Gallio, the new proconsul of Achaia, with propagating an illegal religion, Gallio paid little attention to the charge (Acts xviii. 12 ff.). To him Paul was as self-evidently a Jew as his accusers were, and the dispute between him and them was in Gallio's eyes a difference of interpretation on points of Jewish law, and he had not come to Achaia as proconsul in order to adjudicate on matters of that kind.

Gallio's decision constituted an important precedent; for some ten years thereafter Paul availed himself of the protection which it gave him in his apostolic service, as he continued to propagate the Christian message not only in the provinces of the Roman Empire, but in Rome itself (Acts xxviii. 30 f.).

His happy experience of Roman justice is no doubt reflected in his insistence here that the magistrates, whom he calls 'God's ministers' (verse 6), 'are not a terror to good works, but to the evil' (verse 3). Yet the principles laid down here were valid even when the 'higher powers' were not so benevolent towards Christians as Gallio had been towards Paul.

There is another side to the picture of Christianity's relation to the state. Christianity started out with a tremendous handicap in the eyes of Roman law, for the sufficient reason that its Founder had been convicted and executed by the sentence of a Roman magistrate. The charge against Him was summed up in the inscription attached to the cross: 'The king of the Jews.' Whatever Jesus may have said to Pilate about the nature of His Kingship, the one record of Him known to Roman law was that He had led a movement which challenged the sovereign claims of Caesar. When Tacitus, many years later, wishes his readers to know what kind of people Christians were, he deems it sufficient to say that 'they got their name from Christ, who was executed under the procurator Pontius Pilate when Tiberius was emperor.'[1] That was sufficient to indicate their character. When Paul's opponents at Thessalonica wished to stir up as much trouble for him and his companions locally as they could, they went to the civic magistrates and laid information before them: 'These men who have fomented subversion throughout the world have come here too . . . they all act contrary to Caesar's decrees and claim that there is another emperor, Jesus' (see Acts xvii. 6, 7). This was a subtle misrepresentation of the truth, but one which was

[1] Tacitus, *Annals* xv. 44.

rendered the more colourable by the fact that Jesus Himself had been arraigned before Pilate on the charge of being an agitator and leader of sedition, and of claiming Kingship for Himself.

Nor was Thessalonica the only place where trouble of this kind broke out about the same time. Rome had its riots, stirred up 'at the instigation of Chrestus';[1] and Alexandria perhaps was the scene of similar disturbances, if all the facts were known. Even Paul's best friends could not but admit that his arrival in a city was as often as not a signal for breaches of the peace. Granted that Paul was not responsible for this, the custodians of law and order would naturally take notice of it, and draw their own conclusions. It was all the more necessary, therefore, that Christians should be specially careful of their public behaviour, and give their traducers no handle against them, but rather pay all due honour and obedience to the authorities. Indeed, Jesus had set them a precedent in this matter, as in so much else, for although His words, 'Render to Caesar the things that are Caesar's, and to God the things that are God's' (Mk. xii. 17), were spoken with reference to the payment of tribute, they express a principle of more general application.

Paul places the whole question on a very high plane. God Himself is the fount of all authority, and those who exercise authority on earth do so by delegation from Him; therefore, to disobey them is to disobey God. Human government is a divine ordinance, and the powers of coercion and commendation which it exercises have been entrusted to it by God, for the repression of crime and the encouragement of righteousness. Christians of all people, then, ought to obey the laws, pay their taxes, respect the authorities—not because it will be the worse for them if they don't, but because this is one way of serving God.

But what if the authorities themselves are unrighteous? What if Caesar claims not only the things that are his, but the

[1] See p. 14.

things that are God's? Paul does not deal with this question here, but it was to be a burning question in Rome for generations to come. Caesar could so far exceed the limits of his divinely-given jurisdiction as to claim divine honours for himself and wage war against the saints. Can we recognize Paul's magistrate, 'the minister of God', for reward or retribution, in John's 'beast from the abyss', who receives his authority from the great red dragon and uses it to enforce universal worship of himself and to exterminate those who withhold worship from him? We can indeed, for Paul himself foresaw precisely such a development when the restraint of law was withdrawn (2 Thes. ii. 6 ff.). 'Without justice,' said Augustine, 'what are kingdoms but great gangs of robbers?'

Yet the evidence shows how, in face of gross provocation, Christians maintained their proper loyalty to the state, not least in Rome itself. 'The patience and faith of the saints' wore down the fury of persecution. When the decrees of the civil magistrate conflict with the commandments of God, then, say Christians, 'we ought to obey God rather than men' (Acts v. 29); when Caesar claims divine honours, the Christians' answer must be 'No'. For then Caesar (whether he takes the form of a dictator or a democracy) is going beyond the authority delegated to him by God, and trespassing on territory which is not his. But Christians will voice their 'No' to Caesar's unauthorized demands the more effectively if they have shown themselves ready to say 'Yes' to all his authorized demands.

So, some years later, in a document written from Rome on the eve of a fiery persecution we hear an echo of these words of Paul: 'Be subject for the Lord's sake to every human institution, whether it be to the emperor as supreme, or to governors as sent by him to punish those who do wrong and to praise those who do right. . . . Let none of you suffer as a murderer, or a thief, or a wrongdoer, or a mischief-maker; yet if one suffers as a Christian, let him not be ashamed, but under that name let him glorify God' (1 Pet. ii. 13 f., iv. 15 f., RSV).

And later still, towards the end of the first century, a leader in the Roman church who could remember the outrageous ferocity of the Neronian persecution thirty years before, and had very recent experience of Domitian's malevolence, could pray in these terms:

'Guide our steps to walk in holiness and righteousness and single-ness of heart, and to do those things that are good and acceptable in Thy sight, and in the sight of our rulers. Yes, Lord, cause Thy face to shine upon us in peace for our good, that we may be shel-tered by Thy mighty hand and delivered from every sin by Thine outstretched arm. Deliver us from those who hate us wrongfully. Give concord and peace to us and to all who dwell on earth, as Thou didst to our fathers, when they called on Thee in faith and truth with holiness, while we render obedience to Thine almighty and most excellent name, and to our earthly rulers and governors.

'Thou, O Lord and Master, hast given them the power of sovereignty through Thine excellent and unspeakable might, that we, knowing the glory and honour which Thou hast given them, may submit ourselves to them, in nothing resisting Thy will. Grant them therefore, O Lord, health, peace, concord and stability, that they may without failure administer the government which Thou hast committed to them. For Thou, O heavenly Master, King of the ages, dost give to the sons of men glory and honour and power over all things that are in the earth. Do Thou, O Lord, direct their counsel according to what is good and acceptable in Thy sight, that they, administering in peace and gentleness with godliness the power which Thou hast committed to them, may obtain Thy favour' (1 *Clement* lx. 2–lxi. 2).

Whether the prayer from which these petitions are taken was Clement's own composition or a prayer in general use in the Roman church, it shows how effectively that church took to heart Paul's injunctions about the duty of Christians to the powers that be.

1. *Let every soul be subject unto the higher powers.* 'The thirteenth chapter of the Epistle to the Romans', according to J. W. Allen,[1] 'contains what are perhaps the most important words ever

[1] *A History of Political Thought in the Sixteenth Century* (1928), p. 132.

written for the history of political thought. Yet (he continues) it would be a gross mistake to suppose that men, at any time, took their political opinions from St. Paul.' Some, however, have made a more deliberate effort to do so than others.

'Every soul' (*psuchē*) means simply 'every person'. And what of the 'higher powers'? Are they angelic powers, or human powers, or both angelic powers and human powers, as has been argued by Oscar Cullmann?[1] The general biblical view is that secular power is wielded by 'the host of the high ones that are on high' as well as by 'the kings of the earth upon the earth' (Is. xxiv. 21). It is likewise true that the plural of *exousia* ('power') is used freely by Paul in the sense of angelic rulers, whether benevolent or malignant (cf. Rom. viii. 38; Col. i. 16, ii. 10, 15; Eph. i. 21, iii. 10, vi. 12). We may compare what he has to say in 1 Corinthians ii. 8 about the 'princes (*archontes*) of this world', who in all probability include hostile angel-princes as well as human rulers. Yet in the present context the 'powers' appear to be human rulers, who wield 'the sword' for the punishment of wickedness and the protection of the good, who therefore command and should receive obedience, and who are to be paid appropriate taxes and other dues, together with fitting reverence and honour. Paul's references elsewhere to the angelic powers are very far from suggesting that Christians should be subject to them in any sense; on the contrary, Christians are liberated from their jurisdiction, being united to Him who is the creator and head of all those powers (Col. i. 16, ii. 10), and conqueror of those that set themselves in hostility to Him and His people (Col. ii. 15).

The powers that be are ordained of God. There is no contradiction between this principle and the argument of 1 Corinthians vi.

---

[1] *Christ and Time* (1951), pp. 191 ff., *The State in the New Testament* (1955), pp. 95 ff., *The Early Church* (1956), pp. 134 ff. The view that the reference is to angelic powers was held earlier by M. Dibelius (*Die Geisterwelt im Glauben des Paulus*, Göttingen, 1909), but he later retracted it. Cf. C. D. Morrison, *The Powers that Be* (1960), for an exhaustive survey of the exegesis of Rom. xiii. 1–7, and, on the more general issues involved, P. Meinhold, *Caesar's or God's?* (Minneapolis, 1962).

1 ff., where Christians are dissuaded from suing or prosecuting one another in the secular law-courts. Recognition of the civil authorities makes no difference to the principle that it is unbecoming for Christians to wash their dirty linen in public. And while the civil magistrates are divinely ordained, their civil authority carries with it no status in the church, not even if they are Christians (see note on verse 4 below).

2. *Whosoever therefore resisteth the power, resisteth the ordinance of God.* 'Few sayings in the New Testament have suffered as much misuse as this one', says O. Cullmann (*The State in the New Testament*, pp. 55 f.). He thinks especially of its misuse in justifying uncritical submission to the dictates of totalitarian governments. It is plain from the immediate context, as from the general context of the apostolic writings, that the state can rightly command obedience only within the limits of the purposes for which it has been divinely instituted—in particular, the state not only may but must be resisted when it demands the allegiance due to God alone. 'The obedience which the Christian man owes to the State is never absolute but, at the most, partial and contingent. It follows that the Christian lives always in a tension between two competing claims; that in certain circumstances disobedience to the command of the State may be not only a right but also a duty. This has been classical Christian doctrine ever since the apostles declared that they ought to obey God rather than men.'[1]

Shall receive to themselves damnation. 'Damnation' (cf. iii. 8; see also xiv. 23), is a word whose force has been intensified in English usage with the passing of time; here it means 'judgment' (RV, RSV) or 'punishment' (NEB).

3. *For rulers are not a terror to good works, but to the evil.* For the plural 'good works' the weight of the evidence favours the singular (RV 'the good work'; RSV 'good conduct'; NEB 'good behaviour'). Moffatt's rendering, 'magistrates are no terror to

[1] Sir T. M. Taylor, *The Heritage of the Reformation* (1961), pp. 8 f.

an honest man', is based on the slenderly supported but attractive reading *agathoergō* for *agathō ergō*.

Do that which is good, and thou shalt have praise of the same. Cf. 1 Peter iii. 13: 'who is he that will harm you, if ye be followers of that which is good?'

4. *A revenger to execute wrath upon him that doeth evil.* The state thus is charged with a function which has been explicitly forbidden to the Christian (xii. 17a, 19). The Christian state of later days lay, of course, outside the range of Paul's admonition, and no express direction is given by which the Christian ruler may reconcile his duty as a Christian to 'give place unto wrath' and his duty as a ruler to 'execute wrath'. This is not to say that from this and similar passages he may not extract principles to guide him. But it is plain that Paul envisages two quite distinct spheres of 'service' to God. 'The sanction that the Bible, here and elsewhere, gives to the forcible restraint of evil puzzles many modern Christians, because of its apparent contradiction to Christ's way of love and His precept of non-resistance to evil. But this comes from failing to distinguish the preservation of the world from the salvation of the world. The truth is that the Bible affirms both the Law "which worketh wrath" (Rom. iv. 15) and the "faith which worketh by love" (Gal. v. 6): both Christ's strange work and His proper work.'[1]

6. *For this cause pay ye tribute also.* In AV, as in Greek, this may be understood either as a statement or as a command; it is probably to be construed as the former. 'This is your justification for paying taxes to pagan rulers (a matter of conscience for many Jews, and perhaps for some Christians too), because they are God's servants . . .'

Irenaeus (*Against Heresies* v. 24.1) quotes this verse to prove that Paul in this paragraph refers 'not to angelic powers, or invisible rulers, as some (probably Gnostics) venture to expound the passage, but to actual human authorities'.

[1] A. R. Vidler, *Christ's Strange Work* (1944), p. 28.

They are God's ministers. Gk. *leitourgos,* a word which in New Testament and early Christian literature is used particularly of religious service. See p. 260, n. 1.

7. *Render therefore to all their dues.* Possibly an echo of the words of Jesus: 'Render (*apodote,* the same form as here) to Caesar the things that are Caesar's' (Mk. xii. 17). But the following verses make it plain that the duty of obedience to secular authorities is a temporary one, for the present period of 'night' (verse 12); in that 'day' which is 'at hand' a new order of government will be introduced, when 'the saints shall judge the world' (1 Cor. vi. 2). The state is to 'wither away' (on this Paul and Karl Marx agree); 'the city of God remaineth'.

Tribute. RSV, 'taxes'.

Custom. RSV, 'revenue'; NEB, 'toll'.

Fear. RSV, 'respect'; NEB, 'reverence'.

V. LOVE AND DUTY (xiii. 8–10)

Let the only debt you owe anyone be the debt of love; the man who has discharged this debt has fulfilled the law. The quotation of Leviticus xix. 18, 'Thou shalt love thy neighbour as thyself', as a summary of the commandments, places Paul right within the tradition of Jesus, who set these words as the second great commandment alongside 'Thou shalt love the Lord thy God . . .' (Dt. vi. 5), 'the first and great commandment', adding: 'On these two commandments hang all the law and the prophets' (Mt. xxii. 37–40; cf. Mk. xii. 28–34). Paul mentions the second here and not the first because the immediate question concerns a Christian's duty to his neighbour—the subject-matter of the commandments in the second table of the Decalogue. These commandments forbid us to harm our neighbour in any way; since love never harms another, love fulfils the law.

8. *He that loveth another hath fulfilled the law.* 'Another' is literally 'the other' (i.e. one's neighbour). It is just possible to translate this sentence 'he who loves has fulfilled the other law' —the 'other law' being in that case the 'second' of Matthew xxii. 39 and Mark xii. 31: 'Thou shalt love thy neighbour as thyself.' The translation in the text, however, is the preferable one, and the reference in any case is to the commandment which Jesus quoted as 'the second', which was 'like unto' the first.

9. *Thou shalt not commit adultery, Thou shalt not kill, Thou shalt not steal, Thou shalt not bear false witness, Thou shalt not covet.* The seventh, sixth, eighth, ninth and tenth commandments of the Decalogue (Ex. xx. 13–17; Dt. v. 17–21). The ninth, however ('Thou shalt not bear false witness'), is absent from the best authorities for the text here (cf. RV, RSV, NEB).

Thou shalt love thy neighbour as thyself. Compare Galatians v. 14: 'For all the law is fulfilled in one word, even in this; Thou shalt love thy neighbour as thyself.' In James ii. 8 this commandment is called 'the royal law' ('the sovereign law laid down in Scripture', NEB).

10. *Love is the fulfilling of the law.* 'Fulfilling' is Gk. *plērōma*, a word with a wide range of meaning (elsewhere in this Epistle translated 'fulness'; cf. xi. 12, 25; xv. 29).

VI. CHRISTIAN LIFE IN DAYS OF CRISIS
(xiii. 11–14)

Paul recognized the critical nature of the times. He was under no illusions about the permanence of his present opportunity of preaching the gospel without let or hindrance, but he was determined to exploit it to the full while it lasted. While he no longer uses the apocalyptic imagery of 2 Thessalonians ii. 1–12, he knows that the restraint upon the submerged forces of darkness and disorder may at any time be removed; Christians must therefore be on the alert. But the prospect should fill them with encouragement, not with despair: 'when these things begin to come to pass,' Jesus had said, 'then look up, and lift up your heads; for your redemption draweth nigh' (Lk. xxi. 28). And Paul echoes his Master: 'Now is our salvation nearer than when we believed.' The events of AD 64 and 66 —the beginning of imperial persecution of Christians and the outbreak of the Jewish revolt, which was to end with the collapse of the Second Jewish Commonwealth—were already casting their shadows before. That these events would not be the immediate precursor of the second advent and the final salvation of all believers was something which Paul could not foresee; if knowledge of that day and hour was withheld even from the Son of Man, how much more from one of His servants! But the words of Jesus, 'he that shall endure unto the end, the same shall be saved' (Mk. xiii. 13), verified themselves in the experience of His people who passed through these crises as they have done in other crises since then. With the affliction comes the way of deliverance: 'here is the patience and faith of the saints.'

Meanwhile the sons of light must live in readiness for the day of visitation, abjuring all the 'works of darkness'. Elsewhere Paul speaks of putting on 'the new man' (Eph. iv. 24; Col. iii. 10); here, more directly, he bids his readers 'put on the Lord Jesus Christ'. The Christian graces, the 'armour of light', which he exhorts them to display instead of gratifying the desires of the lower nature—what are they but those graces which were displayed in harmonious perfection in Jesus Christ? Paul's knowledge of the historic Jesus and his interest in Him were much greater than is allowed by those who misinterpret his words about not knowing Christ 'after the flesh'[1] to deny such knowledge or interest on Paul's part. For when he comes to enumerate in detail the graces which he desires his friends at Rome and elsewhere to 'put on', they are the graces which characterized Christ on earth.

[1] See p. 44, n. 2.

11. *It is high time to awake out of sleep.* The duty of spiritual vigilance was constantly enjoined in apostolic teaching; cf. I Thessalonians v. 4 ff.

Now is our salvation nearer than when we believed. The 'salvation' here is viewed in its future completeness; it is the 'adoption, to wit, the redemption of our body' for which believers wait according to viii. 23; cf. the 'salvation ready to be revealed in the last time' for which they are kept according to I Peter i. 5. The accomplishment of this salvation coincides with the manifestation of Christ in glory (cf. Heb. ix. 28).

12. *The works of darkness . . . the armour of light.* Cf. NEB: 'Let us therefore throw off the deeds of darkness and put on our armour as soldiers of the light.' The antithesis between light and darkness is found repeatedly in Paul's writings (cf. 2 Cor. vi. 14; Eph. v. 8; Col. i. 12 f.; I Thes. v. 4 f.), as well as in John's. It is one of the most obvious points of contact between the New Testament and the Qumran texts, where all men are governed either by the Prince of Light or by the Angel of Darkness, and the great conflict of the end-time is called 'the war of the sons of light against the sons of darkness'.[1] The 'armour of light' is described in greater detail in I Thessalonians v. 8 and Ephesians vi. 13–17.

13. *Not in chambering and wantonness.* NEB, 'no debauchery or vice.'

14. *Put ye on the Lord Jesus Christ.* The practical teaching given to Christian converts in primitive times (see pp. 141 f.) appears to have been arranged, for easy memorization, under various catchwords, of which 'Put on' was one. They were exhorted to 'put on' Christian virtues as they would put on clothes (cf. Col. iii. 12); and as these virtues were all aspects of the new Christian character which they received at conversion, they might be told to 'put on the new man' (Eph.

[1] Cf. G. Vermes, *The Dead Sea Scrolls in English*, pp. 75 f., 122 ff.

iv. 24), or to live as befitted those who had put him on once for all (Col. iii. 10). Since this 'new man' was the character of Christ reproduced in His people, it was a simple transition to say 'as many of you as have been baptized into Christ have put on Christ' (Gal. iii. 27), or, as here, to urge believers to 'put on' Christ in the sense of manifesting outwardly what they had already experienced inwardly. While Paul did not know the written Gospels which we have in the New Testament, it is noteworthy that when he commends to his readers those qualities which the Evangelists ascribe to our Lord, he does so by telling them to 'put on' the Lord Jesus Christ.

And make not provision for the flesh, to fulfil the lusts thereof. (Cf. vi. 12.) It was the words of verses 13 and 14 that kindled a flame of heavenly love in the heart of Augustine (see p. 58).

VII. CHRISTIAN LIBERTY AND CHRISTIAN CHARITY (xiv. 1-xv. 6)

a. Christian liberty (xiv. 1-12)

Paul enjoyed his Christian liberty to the full. Never was there a Christian more thoroughly emancipated from un-Christian inhibitions and taboos. So completely emancipated was he from spiritual bondage that he was not even in bondage to his emancipation. He conformed to the Jewish way of life when he was in Jewish society as cheerfully as he accommodated himself to Gentile ways when he was living with Gentiles. The interests of the gospel and the highest well-being of men and women were paramount considerations with him, and to these he subordinated everything else.

But he knew very well that many other Christians were not so completely emancipated as he was, and he insisted that these must be treated gently. A Christian's 'faith' in many respects might be weak, immature and uninstructed; but he must be welcomed warmly as a Christian and not challenged forthwith to a debate about those areas of life in which he is still unemancipated.

Paul mentions two areas of life in which this was liable to happen, and then enlarges on one of them. One was food; the other was the religious observance of certain days. Some Christians (like Paul himself) had no qualms of conscience about taking any kind of food; others had scruples about certain kinds. Some (again like Paul) made no distinction between more and less sacred days, regarding every day as 'holy to the Lord'; others felt that some days were holier than others. What is to be done when Christians of such different convictions find themselves in the same fellowship? Must they start to thrash the matter out, one side determined to convert the other? No, says Paul, let each one be satisfied in his own mind and conscience. The man who enjoys greater liberty must not despise the other as being spiritually immature; the man who has conscientious scruples must not criticize his fellow-Christian for doing what he himself would not do. Each Christian is the servant of Christ, and it is to Christ that he is accountable, both here and hereafter. Christ died, and is Lord of the dead; Christ lives, and is Lord of the living.

It is not for one Christian to judge another—can we hear an echo of our Lord's 'Judge not, that ye be not judged'?—for it is at God's tribunal that we must all appear to render an account and receive due assessment.

With these words Paul insists uncompromisingly on the principle of Christian liberty. 'A Christian man is a most free lord of all, subject to none' (Luther).[1]

1. *Not to doubtful disputations.* NEB, 'without attempting to settle doubtful points.'

2. *Another, who is weak, eateth herbs.* Either because of vegetarian principles or, more probably, in order to avoid eating the flesh of animals that had been consecrated to pagan gods or not properly slaughtered according to Jewish standards (cf. Dn. i. 8, 12). See pp. 247 ff.

[1] *'Christianus homo omnium dominus est liberrimus, nulli subiectus.'*

4. *Who art thou that judgest another man's servant? to his own master he standeth or falleth.* Cf. Matthew vii. 1; Luke vi. 37; and Paul's own words in 1 Corinthians iv. 3 ff.: 'with me it is a very small thing that I should be judged of you, or of man's judgment: yea, I judge not mine own self . . . he that judgeth me is the Lord. Therefore judge nothing before the time, until the Lord come. . . .' The word rendered 'servant' here is *oiketēs,* 'domestic servant', not *doulos,* 'slave'.

5. *Another (man) esteemeth every day alike.* There is no word in the Greek corresponding to 'alike', although it is added here in RV, RSV, NEB as well as in AV to complete the sense. It need not mean that 'another man' treats every day as secular; it may mean that he treats every day as equally to be dedicated to the service of God, and this was certainly Paul's attitude.

6. *He that regardeth the day, regardeth it unto the Lord . . . He that eateth, eateth to the Lord.* Therefore, 'let no man . . . judge you in meat, or in drink, or in respect of a feast day or a new moon or a sabbath day' (Col. ii. 16, RV).

He that regardeth not the day, to the Lord he doth not regard it. These words, although they are in the spirit of their context, are not part of the original text. They found their way into the later MSS and the 'Received Text' in order to balance the passage which comes later in the verse: 'he that eateth not, to the Lord he eateth not. . . .'

7. *None of us liveth to himself.* What Paul means, as verse 8 shows, is that each Christian lives out his life in Christ's sight, and as His servant; but the usual meaning given to the words, when they are quoted apart from their context, follows as a corollary: that each Christian's life affects his fellow-Christians and his fellow-men, and therefore he should consider his responsibility to them, and not consult his own interests only.

9. *Christ both died, and rose, and revived.* The best-attested reading is simply 'Christ died and lived' (i.e. lived again); cf. RV, RSV, NEB. By virtue of His death He is Lord of the dead; by virtue of His resurrection He is Lord of the living.

10. *Why dost thou judge thy brother?* There is no sin to which Christians—especially 'keen' Christians—are more prone than that of criticizing others. The apostle's words are seriously intended. 'Should a man not lay his hand upon his mouth before he criticizes his brethren? When we pass swift, uninformed, unloving, and ungenerous judgments, surely we have forgotten that if we speak evil of them, at the same time we speak evil of the Lord whose name they bear' (H. St. John). 'Let us not therefore judge one another any more' (verse 13).

We shall all stand before the judgment seat of Christ. The better attested reading is '. . . the judgment seat (or "tribunal", *bēma*) of God' (cf. RV, RSV, NEB). But the AV reading (which evidently arose under the influence of 2 Cor. v. 10) goes back to the first half of the second century, being attested by Polycarp and Marcion.

11. *As I live, saith the Lord, every knee shall bow to me, and every tongue shall confess* ('give praise', RSV) *to God.* A quotation from Isaiah xlv. 23: 'By myself have I sworn, . . . "To me every knee shall bow, every tongue shall swear" ' (RSV). Paul applies the same passage to Christ in Philippians ii. 10 f.

b. Christian charity (xiv. 13–23)

Martin Luther, who begins his treatise *On the Freedom of a Christian Man* with the words quoted above ('A Christian man is a most free lord of all, subject to none'), goes on in the next sentence to say: 'A Christian man is a most dutiful servant of all, subject to all.'[1] He was never a more faithful follower of Paul—and of Paul's Master and his—than in the juxtaposition of these two affirmations.

---

[1] *'Christianus homo omnium servus est officiosissimus, omnibus subiectus.'*

Paul, having asserted uncompromisingly the freedom of a Christian, now goes on to show how voluntary limits may, and should, be placed on this freedom. In doing so he enlarges on one of the subjects he has already used to illustrate his assertion of Christian freedom—the subject of food.

The question of what kinds of food might and might not be taken agitated the early Church in various ways. One of these ways affected Jewish Christians more particularly. The Jewish food-laws, which had been observed by the nation from its earliest days, were one of the principal features distinguishing the Jews from their Gentile neighbours. Not only was the flesh of certain animals absolutely prohibited; the blood of *all* animals was absolutely prohibited, and 'clean' animals slaughtered for food had to be killed in such a way that their blood was completely drained away. Since one could never be sure that meat eaten by non-Jews was free from every suspicion of illegality in one respect or another, it was impossible for an orthodox Jew to share a meal with a Gentile. Indeed, it was difficult enough for a strict Jew to share a meal with a fellow-Jew whom he suspected of laxity in these matters.

Jesus, on one memorable occasion, abrogated the food-laws by pronouncing all kinds of food to be 'clean' (Mk. vii. 19). Peter, in his vision on the roof of Simon the tanner's house in Joppa, learned not to count as unclean anything or anyone that God had pronounced clean, and thanks to that lesson he consented almost immediately to visit the Gentile Cornelius at Caesarea and accept his hospitality. But it was long before the majority of Jewish Christians could think of following his example. On one occasion, while Peter was resident in Antioch and enjoying unrestricted fellowship with the Gentile Christians there, one or more visitors from the Church of Jerusalem called on him and persuaded him to withdraw from table-fellowship with Gentiles and eat with Jews only. His example began to have devastating effect; even so liberal a man as Barnabas was disposed to follow it. Paul publicly accused Peter of 'play-acting'—acting a part which did not correspond to his inner convictions (Gal. ii. 11–14). When, shortly afterwards, the Council of Jerusalem agreed that Gentiles should be admitted to church fellowship, like Jews, on the ground of faith in Christ, a proviso was added to the effect that Gentile converts should abstain from food which was abhorrent to their Jewish brethren and conform to the Jewish marriage-laws (Acts xv. 20, 29). It has been widely held that Paul could never have been a party to this agreement (as the narrative of Acts declares he was), because it conflicted with his principles of Christian freedom, and in particular of the freedom of Gentile converts from obligations to the Jewish law. But that is not so certain. Where principles which he counted basic were at stake, Paul was uncompromising; but where these were safeguarded, Paul was the most conciliatory of men. In this case, when once the principle had been established that Gentiles were eligible for church membership on the one sufficient basis of faith in Christ, he himself would have been foremost in reminding his Gentile converts of the wisdom of placing a voluntary limit on their freedom for the sake of maintaining fellowship with their brethren of Jewish birth, not all of whom could be expected to be as completely emancipated in mind as Paul himself was. If Gentile Christians, especially those who lived alongside Jewish Christians, charitably refrained from food which their Jewish brethren would find obnoxious, fellowship between the two groups would be promoted. And in fact the food-provisions of the Council of Jerusalem retained their validity in some sections of the Church for many generations.[1]

One of the food-provisions of the Council of Jerusalem enjoined abstention from the flesh of animals which had been offered in sacrifice to idols. This was a question which arose in pagan surroundings; Paul had dealt with it in some detail in his correspondence with the Corinthian church, some

[1] In Asia Minor *c.* AD 69–96 (Rev. ii. 14 f., 20); in the Rhone valley in AD 177 (Eusebius, *Hist. Eccl.* v. 1. 26); and in North Africa *c.* AD 200 (Tertullian, *Apology* 9). In England Alfred the Great included them in his law-code at the end of the ninth century.

members of which had sought a ruling from him on the subject (1 Cor. viii. 1–13, x. 19–33).

The buying of butcher-meat in pagan cities such as Corinth and Rome presented some Christians with a conscientious problem. Much of the flesh exposed for sale in the market came from animals which had originally been sacrificed to a pagan deity. The pagan deity received his token portion; the rest of the flesh might be sold by the temple authorities to the retail merchants, and many pagan purchasers might be willing to pay a little more for their meat because it had been 'consecrated' to some deity. Among the Christians there were some with a robust conscience who knew that the meat was neither better nor worse for its association with the pagan deity, and were quite happy to eat it; others were not so happy about it, and felt that somehow the meat had become 'infected' by its idolatrous association.

In giving his judgment to the Corinthians on this question, Paul ranges himself on the one hand with those who knew that there was no substance in the pagan deities, and that a Christian was at perfect liberty to eat meat of this kind. But knowledge was not everything; the claims of love were to be considered. He himself was prepared to forgo his liberty if by insisting on it he would set a harmful example to a fellow-Christian with a weaker conscience. If a Christian who thought the eating of idol meat was wrong was encouraged by the example of his robuster brother to eat some, the resultant damage to his conscience would be debited to the other's lack of charity and consideration.

But a more serious aspect of the question appears to have arisen in Corinth than the mere buying and eating of the flesh of animals which had been consecrated to idols. It appears from 1 Corinthians viii. 10 that some members of the Corinthian church were quite happy to accept invitations from pagan friends to attend banquets in pagan temples. At such banquets not only was the meat dedicated to a false god; the whole occasion was expressly organized under the patronage of that god. Could a Christian, who sat at the Lord's table, feel equally at home at the table of an idol which, if it represented anything at all, represented a demon? The ultra-libertarians might argue that all things were lawful; but Paul reminded them that all things were not helpful, nor did all things build up a sound Christian character either in oneself or in those whose lives might be influenced by one's example. If, on the other hand, the invitation was to a meal in a private house, the case was different: a Christian was free to go and to eat whatever was set before him without asking questions. But if he saw that his attitude to meat which had been dedicated to idols was being made the test of the genuineness of his Christianity, he would do well to refrain from eating it. The glory of God and the spiritual welfare of others should be a Christian's chief consideration in eating and drinking, or in anything else.

Conscientious questions in relation to these matters were bound to arise at Rome as they had arisen at Corinth. The Roman church, including as it did both Jewish and Gentile Christians, could speedily disintegrate if some sections insisted on exercising their Christian liberty to the full in complete disregard of the scruples of others. If, on the other hand, those whose consciences were thoroughly emancipated in this regard voluntarily restricted their liberty in the interests of others who had not reached the same stage of spiritual maturity, the church would become a perfect school of charity. This is what Paul urged upon the Christians of Rome, and the testimony of history shows that they learned the lesson well.

Paul's own well-known example must have added great weight to his exhortation. 'Though I be free from all men,' he said elsewhere, 'yet have I made myself servant unto all, that I might gain the more' (1 Cor. ix. 19). For all his emancipation in such matters, he was prepared to restrict his liberty without limit if his weaker fellow-Christians might be helped in this way. He regarded all kinds of food as *kosher* for himself, but if his example in eating certain kinds of food was going to harm someone else, he would avoid them. Food is a means to an end, not an end in itself; one kind will serve as well as another, and it would be a pity to stunt the growth of a soul, the development of a work of God, for the sake of anything so unimportant in itself as some particular kind of food. It is not with food and drink that the kingdom of God is concerned, but with righteousness, peace and joy in the Holy Spirit; food and drink must be made subservient to these really important things.

It is good to be strong in faith, it is good to be emancipated in conscience; but Christians are not isolated individuals, each living to himself, but members of a fellowship, and it is the responsibility of all, and especially the stronger and more mature members, to promote the well-being of the fellowship.

13. *Let us not therefore judge one another any more: but judge this rather.* In the former clause 'judge' means 'criticize'; in the latter it means 'decide'. In Greek, as in English, the same word (*krinō*) does duty for both senses.

That no man put a stumblingblock or an occasion to fall in his brother's way. The kind of stumbling-block or hindrance which Paul has in mind is the setting of an example which might lead another into sin. A Christian 'stumbles' (cf. verse 21) if, following the example of a more emancipated Christian, he does something of which his own conscience does not really approve. In consequence his spiritual life will suffer grave injury. It would be better for the emancipated Christian to help his 'weaker' brother to have a more enlightened conscience; but this is a process which cannot be rushed.

14. *I know, and am persuaded by the Lord Jesus, that there is nothing unclean of itself.* Paul probably knew of our Lord's pronouncement on this subject, recorded for us in Mark vii. 14–19.

But to him that esteemeth any thing to be unclean, to him it is unclean. This insight, completely in accord with the teaching of Christ (cf. Mk. vii. 20–23), has far-reaching implications. Sin, moral defilement, worldliness, and so forth, are located in people's minds, not in material objects. Cf. Titus i. 15.

15. *If thy brother be grieved with thy meat.* 'Meat' in earlier English was a general term for 'food'.

Destroy not him with thy meat. RSV, 'Do not let what you eat cause the ruin of one . . .'; NEB, 'Do not by your eating bring disaster to a man . . .'

For whom Christ died. The divine measure of the worth of a human being.

16. *Let not then your good be evil spoken of.* NEB, 'What for you is a good thing must not become an occasion for slanderous talk.'

17. *The kingdom of God is not meat and drink; but righteousness, and peace, and joy.* Cf. Matthew vi. 31 ('take no thought, saying, What shall we eat? or, What shall we drink?'); Matthew v. 6, 9, 10, 12 ('Blessed are they which do hunger and thirst after righteousness. . . . Blessed are the peacemakers. . . . Blessed are they which are persecuted for righteousness' sake; for theirs is the kingdom of heaven. . . . Rejoice, and be exceeding glad . . .'). An interesting parallel to the construction of the verse is provided by 1 Corinthians iv. 20; 'the kingdom of God is not in word, but in power' (the 'power' being, of course, the Holy Spirit's).

In the Holy Ghost. As in chapter viii, the Holy Spirit brings believers here and now into the good of their coming inheritance. For Paul, 'the kingdom of God' (as distinct from the present kingdom of Christ) is the future inheritance of the people of God (cf. 1 Cor. vi. 9 f., xv. 50; Gal. v. 21; Eph. v. 5; 1 Thes. ii. 12; 2 Thes. i. 5); but 'in the Holy Ghost' its blessings can be enjoyed already.

19. *Things wherewith one may edify another.* To 'edify another' is to build up a stable Christian character for him, and thus (when all are engaged in this activity) to 'build up the common life' (NEB).

20. *It is evil for that man who eateth with offence.* NEB, 'anything is bad for the man who by his eating causes another to fall.' This is something quite different from 'giving offence' in the modern sense.

21. *Or is offended, or is made weak.* These words are absent from the best-attested text; in origin they were probably marginal glosses on the preceding verb 'stumbleth'.

22. *Hast thou faith?* 'Faith' in this sense is a firm and intelligent conviction before God that one is doing what is right, the antithesis of feeling self-condemned in what one permits oneself to do.

23. *He that doubteth is damned if he eat.* A good example of the weaker force which the English verb 'to damn' once had, by contrast with its present meaning of ultimate and irrevocable perdition. Here it means that the man who does something about which his conscience is uneasy is condemned at heart and contracts a sense of guilt; the man who does it knowing it to be permissible and right does it 'of faith'. There is sound sense in the apocryphal incident inserted in *Codex Bezae* after Luke vi. 4, which tells how our Lord, 'seeing a man working on the sabbath, said to him, "Man, if indeed thou knowest what thou art doing, blessed art thou; but if thou knowest not, accursed art thou and a transgressor of the law".'

For whatsoever is not of faith is sin. NEB, 'because his action does not arise from his conviction.' For evidence that one early edition of the Epistle came to an end here, see Introduction, pp. 26–29.

c. The example of Christ (xv. 1–6)

Paul concludes his words on Christian liberty and Christian charity by adducing the example of Christ. Who was more free from taboos and inhibitions than He? Yet who was more careful to bear with the weaknesses of others? It is so easy for a man whose own conscience is quite clear about some course of action to snap his fingers at his critics and say 'I'll please myself'. He has every right to do so, but that is not the way of Christ. His way is to consider others first, to consult their interests and help them in every possible way. 'Even Christ pleased not himself'; if He had done so we might wonder in what respect His life and ministry would have taken a different course from the course they did take. But the sense is that Christ did not put His own interests or welfare first (cf. Phil. ii. 5 ff.). Christ put the interests of others before His own, but perhaps Paul's meaning here is that He put the will of God first of all; this is suggested by his quotation of Psalm lxix. 9.

The words that follow the quotation embody a principle which can be traced throughout the New Testament, wherever the Old Testament is cited or referred to. The lessons of endurance which the Old Testament writings inculcate, and the encouragement which they supply to faithfulness, are a strong incentive to the maintenance of Christian hope. Paul presents them also as a strong incentive to the fostering of brotherly unity, and he prays that the God who teaches His people endurance and provides encouragement for them through these writings may grant them oneness of mind, so that He may be glorified by their united witness.

1. *We then that are strong ought to bear the infirmities of the weak.* Cf. Galatians vi. 1 f.: 'If a man be overtaken in a fault, ye which are spiritual, restore such an one. . . . Bear ye one another's burdens, and so fulfil the law of Christ.'

2. *For his good to edification.* NEB, 'think what is for his good and will build up the common life.' (Cf. xiv. 19; Phil. ii. 3 f.)

3. *The reproaches of them that reproached thee fell on me.* Quotation of Psalm lxix. 9. This psalm of affliction, as we have seen (cf. note on xi. 9 f., pp. 215 f.), was early interpreted in the church as a prophecy of Christ's passion and of the retribution to overtake His persecutors; since it is addressed to God, these words imply that Jesus endured reproach and insult for His faithfulness to God which He might have avoided by choosing an easier path.

4. *Whatsoever things were written aforetime were written for our learning.* Compare the statement of the same principle in 1 Corinthians x. 6, 11. The Scriptures (here, of course, the Old Testament Scriptures) provide ample evidence of God's fidelity, especially when they are read in the light of Christ's fulfilment of them; therefore their readers are encouraged to place their trust in the Lord and wait patiently for Him.

5. *To be likeminded one toward another according to Christ Jesus.* See note on xii. 16 (p. 229).

VIII. CHRIST AND THE GENTILES
(xv. 7–13)

So then, says Paul, follow the example of Christ, who welcomed us without discrimination, and make room for one another without discrimination.

This is what I mean, he continues: Christ came not to receive service but to give it—first to the Jews, in order to fulfil the promises which God had made to their ancestors, and then to the Gentiles, that they too might glorify God for His mercy. But if the bringing of the gospel to the Jews fulfilled Old Testament promises, so did the evangelization and conversion of the Gentiles; and Paul adduces a catena of Old Testament *testimonia* in which the Gentiles are presented as praising the God of Israel and placing their hope in Israel's Messiah.

The manner and extent of the blessing into which God would bring believing Gentiles—their incorporation along

with believing Jews in the community of the people of God—
might be a mystery concealed from earlier generations until
it became a reality through Paul's ministry (Col. i. 25 ff.;
Eph. iii. 2 ff.); but the fact that Gentiles would be blessed
by the gospel Paul sees as something clearly predicted in Old
Testament times. This meant that he viewed his own ministry
as God's means towards the fulfilment of His promises to the
Gentiles.

A prayer that they may abound in joy and peace, faith and
hope, concludes this division of the Epistle which has presented
the Christian way of life.

7. *Wherefore receive ye one another.* 'Welcome one another'
(RSV); take your fellow-Christians to your hearts as well as to
your homes. If Christ's example is followed, as Paul enjoins,
the welcome will be unreserved, and God will be glorified by
the mutual love and kindness of His people. Paul may have
especially, though by no means exclusively, in mind the
practice of unreserved fellowship between Jewish and Gentile
believers.

As Christ also received us. There is strong textual evidence in
favour of 'you' (*humas*) as against 'us' (*hēmas*); cf. RV, RSV.
(NEB, following the Nestle-Kilpatrick text, reads 'us'.) 'This
is why it is right that they should remain united together,
and not despise one another, because Christ despised neither
of them'[1] (Calvin).

8. *Jesus Christ.* Read simply 'Christ', with RV, RSV, NEB.
Was a minister of the circumcision. Cf. NEB: 'became a servant of
the Jewish people'; on His own testimony, during His earthly
ministry He was 'not sent but unto the lost sheep of the house
of Israel' (Mt. xv. 24). The noun translated 'minister' is
diakonos; we may compare Christ's own words, 'The Son of
man came not to be ministered unto (*diakonēthēnai*), but to

[1] That is, neither Jews nor Gentiles.

minister (*diakonēsai*)' (Mk. x. 45), and 'I am among you as he that serveth (*diakonōn*)' (Lk. xxii. 27).

For the truth of God. That is, 'to maintain the truth of God by making good his promises to the patriarchs' (NEB).

9. *For this cause I will confess to thee* (RV, 'give praise unto thee') *among the Gentiles, and sing unto thy name.* A quotation from Psalm xviii. 49, where David, having included non-Israelite nations in his empire, counts them as now belonging to the heritage of the God of Israel. For the Christian application of this idea cf. James's quotation of Amos ix. 11 f. (LXX) at the Council of Jerusalem (Acts xv. 16 f.).

10. *Rejoice, ye Gentiles, with his people.* A quotation from the Song of Moses, Deuteronomy xxxii. 43. (Compare earlier quotations from this Song in x. 19, xi. 11, xii. 19.)

11. *Praise the Lord, all ye Gentiles; and laud him, all ye peoples* (note that the last word is plural, Gk. *laoi*). A quotation from Psalm cxvii. 1, where the whole world is called upon to praise the God of Israel for His steadfast love and faithfulness.

12. *There shall be a root of Jesse, and he that shall rise to reign over the Gentiles; in him shall the Gentiles trust* (RV 'hope'). A quotation from Isaiah xi. 10, where the 'shoot from the stump of Jesse' (Is. xi. 1, RSV), i.e. the coming Messiah of David's line, 'shall stand as an ensign to the peoples; him shall the nations seek' (RSV).

13. *Now the God of hope fill you with all joy and peace in believing.* The title 'God of hope' is perhaps suggested by the words of Isaiah xi. 10 quoted immediately before (see RV). Cf. xiv. 17, where peace and joy are blessings of the kingdom of God. Because God is 'the God of hope'—the God who gives us hope in Himself—believers may enjoy these blessings now.

That ye may abound in hope, through the power of the Holy Ghost.

Once more, it is the Spirit who enables believers to experience in this life the blessings of the life to come. The grand object of their hope is the glory of God (Rom. v. 2).

EPILOGUE (xv. 14–xvi. 27)

a. Personal narrative (xv. 14–33)

Paul assures the Roman Christians that the teaching in his letter had not been given because he imagined they were incapable of teaching one another. He is well aware of their moral and intellectual quality, and what he has written is more by way of a reminder of what they already know than instruction in the elements of Christianity. Moreover, although he is not the founder of their church, he is the apostle to the Gentiles, and it is in that capacity that he has written to them. He views his apostleship as a priestly service, and his Gentile converts as the acceptable offering which he presents to God.

For well over twenty years now Paul had exercised his apostleship, and although his task was not yet complete, he had no reason, as he looked back over those years, to be dissatisfied with the work that Christ had accomplished through him. From Jerusalem to the frontiers of Illyricum he had preached the gospel: in the principal cities along the main roads of the provinces of Syria–Cilicia, Cyprus, Galatia, Asia, Macedonia and Achaia there were communities of believers in Christ to bear witness to Paul's apostolic activity. His aim had been throughout to preach the gospel where it had not been preached before, and now that he had completed his work in the east, he looked to the west and proposed to evangelize Spain. His journey to Spain would afford him an opportunity to realize his long-cherished desire of seeing Rome, and he looked forward to meeting the Christians in the capital and being refreshed by their fellowship.

First, however, he had to pay a visit to Jerusalem. The collection for the Jerusalem church which, for some years now, he had organized in his Gentile churches, was now ready to be handed over to its recipients, and Paul proposed to accompany the delegates appointed by the churches to deliver their gifts.

Only when his Aegean ministry had been thus 'sealed' would he take his journey to Spain and visit Rome on the way. He has already told the Romans of his eager desire to preach the gospel in their city and see some fruit for his apostolic work there, and now he speaks of his confidence that his visit to them will be attended by great blessing on his preaching of the gospel. For the present, he asks for their prayers. He was under no illusions about the trouble which he might have to face in Jerusalem; and how much he needed their prayers that he might 'be delivered from them that do not believe in Judaea' is clear from the narrative of Acts xxi. 27 ff. He may even have had misgivings about the welcome which he and his Gentile companions might receive from the Jerusalem church, and the way in which their gift would be accepted; at any rate he asks the Romans to pray that the gift might be acceptable. Here the narrative of Acts (xxi. 17 ff.) makes it quite plain— the more so because we are dealing with a 'we' section— that Paul and the delegates did meet with a cordial welcome when they visited James and his fellow-elders. But it is equally plain that James and his fellow-elders were anxious about the reaction of the ordinary members of their church—many thousands strong, and all zealots for the law—in view of reports that had reached them about Paul's teaching and practice in the lands of the Dispersion. In their anxiety to appease the rank-and-file they suggested to Paul a course of action which, as it turned out, led to his arrest, prosecution, appeal to Caesar, and eventual coming to Rome in circumstances quite different from those he envisaged when he wrote this Epistle.

15. *Nevertheless, brethren.* Omit 'brethren' (cf. RV, RSV, NEB). *I have written the more boldly unto you in some sort, as putting you* *in mind.* NEB, 'I have written to refresh your memory, and written somewhat boldly at times'—in view of the fact that the Roman church was not of his planting.

16. *That I should be the minister of Jesus Christ to the Gentiles, ministering the gospel of God, that the offering up of the Gentiles might be acceptable.* These clauses are full of the language of worship: Paul is a *leitourgos*;[1] his proclamation of the gospel is a 'priestly service' (*hierourgeō*); his Gentile converts are the offering which he presents to God.

Being sanctified by the Holy Ghost. There were some, no doubt, who maintained that Paul's Gentile converts were 'unclean', because they were not circumcised. To such cavillers Paul's reply is that his converts were 'clean', because they were sanctified by the Holy Spirit who had come to dwell within them (cf. verse 19, 'by the power of the Spirit of God'). 'We are the (true) circumcision,' he said in another place, 'who worship by the Spirit of God, and glory in Christ Jesus, and have no confidence in the flesh' (Phil. iii. 3, RV). The Judaizers, who did glory in the flesh (i.e. in the privileges bound up with Jewish birth and the law), were less sanctified than Gentiles who had learned to make their boast in Christ alone (cf. Rom. viii. 8). Similarly, Peter at the Council of Jerusalem reminds his fellow-Jewish believers how, when the Gentiles heard the gospel, God gave them the Holy Spirit 'even as he did unto us; and put no difference between us and them, purifying their hearts by faith' (Acts xv. 8 f.).

19. *From Jerusalem.* Paul began his career as a Christian preacher in Damascus and the surrounding territory of Nabataean Arabia (Acts ix. 19 ff.; Gal. i. 17). His more extended ministry as apostle to the Gentiles was based on Antioch (Acts xi. 25 ff., xiii. 1 ff.). Why then should he men-

---

[1] Cf. xiii. 6. In the New Testament the word always denotes religious service, and sometimes priestly service, as when Christ is described in Heb. viii. 2 as 'a *leitourgos* of the sanctuary, and of the true tabernacle'. (Cf. xv. 27.)

tion Jerusalem here as the starting-point of his ministry? He may conceivably have some particular occasion in mind, such as the vision described by him in Acts xxii. 17–21 or (less probably) the recognition-interview with the Jerusalem leaders which he relates in Galatians ii. 1–10; but it is more likely that he mentions Jerusalem as the starting-point and metropolis of the Christian movement as a whole (cf. Lk. xxiv. 47; Acts i. 4, 8, viii. 14, xi. 22, xv. 2).

And round about unto Illyricum. There is no mention of Illyricum (the Roman province bordering the eastern shore of the Adriatic Sea) in Acts or in any of the Pauline Epistles up to this time. But the interval between the end of Paul's Ephesian ministry and his setting out on his last journey to Jerusalem was probably greater than might be inferred from a casual reading of Acts, where it is compressed into half a dozen verses (Acts xx. 1–6). There is reason to think that Paul crossed to Macedonia in the summer or autumn of AD 55 (cf. 2 Cor. ii. 12 f.) and spent the next fifteen to eighteen months in Macedonia and Achaia. It must have been within this period that he traversed Macedonia from east to west along the Egnatian Road, to the frontier of Illyricum, possibly crossing into Illyricum and preaching the gospel there, for such a journey cannot well be fitted into his itinerary at any earlier point.

I have fully preached the gospel of Christ, lit., 'I have fulfilled the gospel of Christ' (cf. NEB, 'I have completed the preaching of the gospel of Christ'). He had done this by preaching it in every province between the limits named (not to every individual), and had thus discharged his apostolic commission in that part of the Gentile world.

20. *Lest I should build upon another man's foundation.* His practice was rather, as he states in 1 Corinthians iii. 10: 'as a wise masterbuilder, I have laid the foundation, and another buildeth thereon.' See p. 12.

21. *To whom he was not spoken of, they shall see: and they that have not heard shall understand.* Quoted from Isaiah lii. 15 (LXX). The Hebrew text (rendered in RSV, 'for that which has not been told them they shall see, and that which they have not heard they shall understand') refers to the surprise of the nations and their kings when they see the exaltation of the Suffering Servant whom formerly they had despised. The Greek version, however, lends itself well to Paul's present statement of his pioneer policy in preaching the gospel. We have already had ample evidence of the way in which this whole section of the book of Isaiah served as a source of gospel *testimonia* (see pp. 37, 208 f.).

24. *I will come to you.* This clause is a later addition, designed no doubt to ease the abrupt break in construction of the original text (cf. RV; the English of RSV and NEB here is smoother than Paul's Greek).

25. *To minister unto the saints.* The members of the church of Jerusalem are 'the saints' *par excellence* (cf. verse 31; 1 Cor. xvi. 1; 2 Cor. viii. 4, ix. 1, 12). But Paul's converts and other Gentile Christians have become their 'fellow-citizens' (Eph. ii. 19), so he makes a point of regularly referring to them also as 'saints', the holy people of God. The verb 'to minister' here is Gk. *diakoneō* (cf. xii. 7, xv. 8, xvi. 1).

Further details about this collection are provided elsewhere in Paul's extant correspondence, especially in 1 Corinthians xvi. 1–4 and 2 Corinthians viii, ix. It was evidently an undertaking to which Paul attached high importance.

For one thing, as he tells the Romans, it was a means of bringing home to the Gentile Christians their indebtedness to Jerusalem. It was from Jerusalem that the gospel had spread, first into the provinces adjoining Judaea (such as Syria, with its capital Antioch on the Orontes) and then to more distant territories (such as those which Paul had been evangelizing for the past ten years). It was a small return which the

Gentile churches were invited to make in recognition of their indebtedness if they were asked to contribute to the material needs of the mother-church of Christendom.

For another thing, Paul envisaged it as a means of cementing the fellowship that ought to be maintained between Jerusalem and the Gentile churches. He was well aware that many of the stricter brethren in Jerusalem looked with grave suspicion on his own Gentile mission, while some went so far as to think it their duty to win his converts from their allegiance to him over to a conception of Christian faith and life more in keeping with that which obtained among the rank and file of Jerusalem believers. Even when matters were not pushed to such an extreme, the cleavage between Jerusalem and the Gentile churches could do no good to the cause of Christ, and nothing could overcome it but a generous gesture of brotherly love.

The collection for Jerusalem marked no innovation in policy on Paul's part. Eleven years previously Barnabas and he had brought a similar gift from the Christians in Syrian Antioch to the Jerusalem church in time of famine,[1] and when the two of them had a meeting on that occasion with 'pillars' of the Jerusalem church, the latter freely recognized that Barnabas and Paul had been called to the work of Gentile evangelization, but requested them even so to go on remembering 'the poor' (see note on verse 26, p. 264); and in fact, says Paul when he relates this incident, 'I myself had made a point of doing this very thing'.[2]

Here indeed the question suggests itself whether the contribution was understood by Paul and by the Jerusalem leaders in the same sense. For Paul it was a spontaneous gesture of brotherly love, a token of grateful response on his converts' part to the grace of God which had brought them salvation. But in the eyes of the Jerusalem leaders it perhaps was a form of tribute, a duty owed by the daughter-churches to their mother, comparable to the half-shekel paid annually by Jews

[1] Acts xi. 30, xii. 25.   [2] Gal. ii. 10.

throughout the word for the maintenance of the Jerusalem temple and its services.

In Paul's eyes, however, it was all that has been said, and more. It was not only the Gentile Christians' recognition of their spiritual indebtedness to Jerusalem; it was not only a bond of fellowship and brotherly love; it was the climax of Paul's Aegean ministry and an act of worship and dedication to God before he set out for the west. It was, indeed, the outward and visible sign of that 'offering up of the Gentiles' which crowned his priestly service as apostle of Jesus Christ. That is why he had come to attach so much importance to his personally accompanying the Gentile delegates to Jerusalem, there to present this offering to God, perhaps by an act of worship at that very place in the temple where once Christ had appeared to him and sent him 'far hence unto the Gentiles' (Acts xxii. 21).

26. *It hath pleased them of Macedonia and Achaia.* Paul mentions the Christians in these two provinces here probably because he had been for several months past in close touch with them. But we have his own testimony in 1 Corinthians xvi. 1 that he had organized a similar collection in the churches of Galatia, and the presence of Tychicus and Trophimus with him at this time (Acts xx. 4; cf. xxi. 29) indicates that the churches of Ephesus and other cities in the province of Asia also had a share in this ministry.

The poor saints which are at Jerusalem. Lit., 'the poor of the saints'. In fact, the Jerusalem believers apparently referred to themselves as 'the poor'—cf. Galatians ii. 10, 'they would that we should remember the poor' (*ptōchoi*, as here)—and the designation, in its Hebrew form *'ebyonim*, survived among those Jewish Christians of later times who were known as the Ebionites. It is unnecessary to suppose, with K. Holl,[1] that Paul uses this expression to conceal his embarrassment over the fact that the collection was destined for the Jerusalem church as a

---

[1] *Gesammelte Aufsätze*, ii (Tübingen, 1928), pp. 58 ff.

whole; the frequency with which he speaks of 'the collection for the saints' does not suggest that he felt any embarrassment on this score.

27. *It hath pleased them verily; and their debtors they are.* The contribution was a voluntary gesture on the part of the Gentile churches; yet it was the recognition of a debt—a moral debt, however, not a legal one.

Their duty is also to minister unto them in carnal things. The view that this was not simply a charity collection, but a tribute which the mother-church had every right to expect from the Gentile Christians,[1] may represent well enough the attitude of the church of Jerusalem, but not Paul's attitude. This is evident from the terms in which he speaks of it to the contributing churches; it is an act of grace and not of formal obligation on their part (cf. 2 Cor. viii. 6–9). It may well be, too, that by this material token of the grace of God among the Gentiles he hoped more particularly to stimulate that salutary 'emulation' of which he speaks in xi. 14.[2] The verb 'to minister' here is *leitourgeō* (cf. the noun *leitourgos* in verse 16). In 2 Corinthians ix. 12 the collection is called a *leitourgia* (av, 'service')—the word from which English 'liturgy' is derived.

28. *And have sealed to them this fruit.* neb, 'and delivered the proceeds under my own seal'; Paul uses a formal business expression. Perhaps, however, it is not of Paul's own seal that we should think, but the seal of the Spirit; here is conclusive confirmation of His work among the Gentiles (cf. verse 16).

29. *The fulness of the blessing of the gospel of Christ.* Read, with rv, etc., 'the fulness of the blessing of Christ'.

30. *Now I beseech you, brethren.* We should probably omit 'brethren', with P46 and B.

The love of the Spirit. That is, the love which the Holy Spirit imparts and maintains (cf. v. 5).

[1] Cf. K. Holl, *op. cit.*, pp. 44-67.
[2] Cf. J. Munck, *Paul and the Salvation of Mankind*, p. 303.

33. *Now the God of peace be with you all. Amen.* The title 'the God of peace' recurs in xvi. 20. For evidence that one early edition of the Epistle came to an end with this benediction see Introduction, pp. 28 f.

b. Greetings to various friends (xvi. 1–16)

The letter, when completed, was evidently taken to its destination by Phoebe, a Christian lady who was in any case making a journey to that place. Paul takes the opportunity to commend her to the hospitality and fellowship of the Christians to whom he is writing. This word of commendation is followed by a list of personal greetings to a number of people who are mentioned by name.

It has been widely held that this final chapter was directed not to Rome but to Ephesus—that it was for Ephesus that Phoebe was bound and that the friends to whom Paul sends greetings lived in Ephesus.

That a separate letter to the church in Ephesus has somehow been tacked on to a letter addressed to Rome is highly improbable; in any case, 'a letter consisting almost entirely of greetings may be intelligible in the age of the picture-postcard; for any earlier period it is a monstrosity' (Hans Lietzmann). But this objection does not lie against the view that Paul sent a copy of this Epistle to his friends at Ephesus (as he may have done to other Christian communities),[1] and appended to it a number of personal greetings.

But 'possession is nine points of the law', and since this chapter comes at the end of a letter which was manifestly intended for the Christians of Rome, it is natural to suppose that this chapter was intended for them too, unless very weighty reasons to the contrary can be adduced.

What then are the principal arguments for postulating an Ephesian destination for chapter xvi?

1. In this chapter Paul sends personal greetings to twenty-

[1] For the evidence that copies were sent to other places than Rome see pp. 18 ff.

six individuals and five households or 'house-churches'. Is it probable that he knew so many people in a city which he had never visited? We think rather of one of the cities with which he was well acquainted. Corinth does not come into the picture, because this letter was written from Corinth; but Ephesus (where he had recently spent two and a half years) is clearly indicated, especially for the two following reasons.

2. The first persons to whom Paul sends greetings here are his friends Priscilla and Aquila. When we last heard of them, either in Acts (xviii. 26) or in Paul's correspondence (1 Cor. xvi. 19),[1] they were resident in Ephesus, where they had a church in their house, as they have here. In the absence of any hint to the contrary, we may presume they were still in Ephesus.

3. The next person to be greeted by name is Epaenetus, 'the firstfruits of Asia (not "Achaia", as in AV) unto Christ'. Paul's first convert in the province of Asia would naturally be looked for in Ephesus, not in Rome.

4. Another argument, based on the admonition in verses 17–20, is considered below (pp. 276 ff.).

What now can be said in favour of the Roman destination of this chapter, over and above the initial presumption that it was sent to the same people as the rest of the letter to which it is appended?

1. Such a list of greetings would be exceptional in a letter written to a church with which Paul was well acquainted. If this chapter was intended for Ephesus, we can envisage the occasion when it was read aloud at a meeting of the church. Those present would hear Paul's greetings read out to twenty-six of their number. But Paul certainly knew more than twenty-six members of a church in whose midst he had spent such a long time. What would the others think? Each of them would surely ask: 'Why leave *me* out?' But in a letter written to a church in which he was personally unknown Paul might

---

[1] In 2 Tim. iv. 19 they may also be in Ephesus; but this is uncertain.

well send greetings to friends whom he had met elsewhere in the course of his apostolic service, and who were now resident in Rome. If he mentioned them by name, the other members of the church would not feel aggrieved at being omitted, because they would not expect to be included. In the Epistle to the Colossians, which was also written to a church which Paul had never visited, similar greetings are sent to a few individuals—only a few, because Colossae was off the beaten track and not nearly such an important place as Rome. But Rome was the capital of the world; all roads led to Rome, and it is not surprising that many people whom Paul had come to know in other places should in the meantime have made their way to Rome. In particular, the death of the Emperor Claudius in October, AD 54, probably meant for all practical purposes the lapsing of his edict of five years earlier, expelling the Jews from Rome. If there was a general return of Jews to Rome about this time, Jewish Christians would certainly be among them. Priscilla and Aquila, who had been compelled to leave Rome because of the edict of AD 49 (Acts xviii. 2), may well have gone back in AD 54 or shortly afterwards, leaving caretakers, perhaps, in charge of the Corinthian and Ephesian branches of their tent-making business (as they may have left one in charge of their Roman branch when they had to leave the capital). Tradespeople like Priscilla and Aquila led very mobile lives in those days, and there is nothing improbable or unnatural about their moving back and forth in this way between Rome, Corinth and Ephesus.[1]

[1] Little reliance can be placed upon the argument for Rome as the place where Priscilla and Aquila spent their closing days, which is sometimes based on the Cemetery of Priscilla. This is a very early Christian burying-place in Rome, situated on the Via Salaria. It was presumably called after the lady who owned the land, but there is no evidence for her identification with the New Testament Priscilla. All that we can say is that the two ladies probably belonged to the same family (the *gens Prisca*). This cemetery contains a crypt belonging to the noble Roman family whose members bore the name Acilius Glabrio. There is, however, no good reason to associate the *nomen gentile* Acilius (Aquilius) with Aquila; our Aquila, a Pontic Jew by birth, was certainly not a member of the Roman nobility. One member of the Acilius family was among the people executed by the Emperor

2. A number of the names in verses 7–15 are better attested at Rome than at Ephesus.[1] This is due in large measure to the much larger number of inscriptions available from Rome than from Ephesus; and in any case it is, for the most part, the names and not the persons that are well attested. Details are given in the notes below, and the reader can weigh the evidence for himself. Perhaps the strongest case can be made out for the members of 'the household of Narcissus' in verse 11; we know of a 'household of Narcissus' in Rome at this very time. Rufus (verse 13) was a commoner name at Rome than at Ephesus, but if he is the Rufus of Mark xv. 21 it was probably not at Rome that he received his name. Yet the Rufus of Mark xv. 21 was evidently well known in the Roman church; we cannot say that there was not a Rufus in the church of Ephesus, but we do not know that there was. On the whole, a study of these names inclines the balance of probability in favour of Rome.

3. 'The churches of Christ' who send their greetings to the readers in verse 16 would be the Gentile churches whose delegates were joining Paul at this very time to convey their churches' contributions to Jerusalem.[2] It would be a particularly happy thought to send these churches' greetings to Rome. Of course it might be said that it was an equally happy thought to send the churches' greetings to Ephesus, but since Ephesus

Domitian in AD 95 on a charge involving a mixture of 'atheism' and addiction to Jewish ways, which has often been taken to imply Christianity (cf. Dio Cassius, *History, Epitome* lxvii. 14).

[1] The evidence is presented conveniently by J. B. Lightfoot in *The Epistle to the Philippians* (1868), pp. 171 ff., in his excursus on 'Caesar's Household'. Accepting the Roman provenience of Philippians, Bishop Lightfoot collected such evidence as he could find, from Rom. xvi. 8–15 and extra-biblical literary and epigraphic material, with a possible bearing on the identity of some of the 'saints . . . of Caesar's household' mentioned in Phil. iv. 22. This evidence, in so far as it is relevant to Rom. xvi, is summarized for what it is worth under the individual names in the following notes on verses 8–15.

[2] The churches mentioned in Acts xx. 4 are Beroea, Thessalonica, Derbe (or, according to the western text, Doberus in Macedonia), and the churches of Asia. Philippi was probably represented by Luke, and Corinth was the church with which Paul was staying at the time of writing.

was one of the churches represented—by Trophimus and possibly Tychicus (Acts xx. 4)—there would not be the same point in sending their greetings there.

1. *Phebe our sister . . . a servant of the church which is at Cenchrea.* Phoebe (RV, RSV, NEB) was evidently about to set out on a journey to the place to which Paul was sending these greetings, and may have been entrusted with the letter containing them. Cenchreae (RV, RSV, NEB) was one of the two seaports of Corinth, situated on the Saronic Gulf (cf. Acts xviii. 18). The church there may have been a daughter-church of the city-church of Corinth. The word 'servant' is *diakonos* (RVmg., RSV, 'deaconess'; NEB, 'a fellow-Christian who holds office in the congregation at Cenchreae'). That the duties of a *diakonos* could be performed by either men or women is suggested by 1 Timothy iii. 11, where 'their wives' (AV, NEB) is more probably to be rendered 'women' (RV), i.e. 'women-deacons' (cf. RSV, 'the women'; NEBmg., 'deaconesses').

2. *Receive her in the Lord,* i.e. as a fellow-Christian. Travelling Christians in the days of the primitive Church could always be sure of finding hospitality with their fellow-Christians in any place where there was a church. (Cf. xv. 7.)

A succourer of many, and of myself also. What kind of help she gave to Paul we can only surmise; probably Phoebe was in Cenchreae what Lydia was in Philippi.

3. *Greet Priscilla and Aquila.* Read 'Prisca' (RV, RSV, NEB) for 'Priscilla'. Paul calls her Prisca (cf. 1 Cor. xvi. 19, RV; 2 Tim. iv. 19), while Luke calls her by the more familiar form of her name, Priscilla (cf. Acts xviii. 2, 18, 26). 'Luke regularly uses the language of conversation, in which the diminutive forms were usual; and so he speaks of Priscilla, Sopatros and Silas always, though Paul speaks of Prisca, Sosipatros and Silvanus.'[1] Both Luke and Paul generally put Prisca (Priscilla) before

[1] W. M. Ramsay, *St. Paul the Traveller and Roman Citizen* (1942), p. 268.

Aquila, her husband; this may have been due to her having the more impressive personality of the two, although some have inferred that her social rank was superior to his. She may have belonged by birth or manumission to the *gens Prisca*, a noble Roman family, while he was a Jew from Pontus in Northern Asia Minor. See pp. 14 f., 268.

4. *Who have for my life laid down their own necks*, i.e. 'risked their own lives'. When Priscilla and Aquila did this we can only speculate; it could have been during one of the critical phases of Paul's ministry at Ephesus.

5. *The firstfruits of Achaia unto Christ*. For 'Achaia' read 'Asia', which is by far the better attested reading. The 'Received Text' has been influenced here by 1 Corinthians xvi. 15 where, however, it is 'the household of Stephanas'—a Corinthian family—that is 'the firstfruits of Achaia'.

6. *Greet Mary, who bestowed much labour on us*. The better attested reading is 'you' (RV, RSV, NEB). This has been thought to point to the Ephesian church as the recipients of these greetings; Paul would know who did outstanding service in that church, but how would he know who had 'bestowed much labour' on the Christians of the capital? He certainly had some sources of information about the Roman church (cf. i. 8 f.); if Mary's association with that church went back to its earliest days, Priscilla and Aquila would have known her. But we can only speculate; this is the only reference we have to this Mary (one of the six bearers of that name in the New Testament).

7. *Andronicus and Junia*. It is impossible to decide whether the second of these names is feminine, Junia (as in AV), or masculine, Junias (as in RV, RSV, NEB). We know nothing of these two apart from Paul's reference to them here, but this reference makes us wish we knew more. They were evidently

Jewish Christians (nothing more than this need be meant by
'my kinsmen'); they had shared one of Paul's frequent im-
prisonments (2 Cor. xi. 23)—where, we cannot say; certainly
not in Philippi, quite possibly in Ephesus. Moreover, they
were 'of note among the apostles', which probably means
that they were not merely well known to the apostles but were
apostles themselves (in a wider sense of the word), and eminent
ones at that; and they had been Christians from a very early
date, since before Paul's own conversion. In that case they
may well have been included in the Hellenists of Acts vi. 1
(their names suggest that they were Hellenists rather than
'Hebrews'); their title to apostleship may even have been
based on their having seen the risen Christ.

8. *Amplias.* An abbreviated form of Ampliatus (which
indeed is the better attested reading here; so RV, RSV, NEB).
The name is common in Roman inscriptions of the period, and
is found repeatedly as borne by members of the imperial
household. A branch of the *gens Aurelia* bore this cognomen.
Christian members of this branch of the family are buried in
one of the oldest Christian burying-places in Rome, the
Cemetery of Domitilla, the beginnings of which go back to the
end of the first century (see note on verse 15, p. 275). One
tomb in that cemetery, decorated with paintings in a very
early style, bears the inscription AMPLIAT in uncials of the first
or early second century.

9. *Urbane.* Urbanus ('belonging to the *urbs*' or 'city'—i.e.
Rome), a name by its very nature specially common in Rome.
   Stachys. This name, meaning 'ear' (of grain), is not common;
one or two of its occurrences are in association with the imperial household.

10. *Apelles.* A name sufficiently common among the Jews of
Rome to be used by Horace as a typical Jewish name—'*credat
Iudaeus Apella*' (*Satire* i. 5. 100). One notable bearer of the

name Apelles was the tragic actor from Ascalon to whom at one time the Emperor Gaius showed signal marks of favour (Philo, *Embassy to Gaius*, 203–206). It is found in Roman inscriptions, both in relation to the imperial household and otherwise.

Them which are of Aristobulus' household. Who this Aristobulus was cannot be certainly determined; Lightfoot suggests his identification with a brother of Herod Agrippa I, who lived at Rome as a private citizen and, like his brother, enjoyed the friendship of Claudius. If he bequeathed his property to the emperor, his slaves and freedmen would have been distinguished from other members of the imperial household as *Aristobuliani* (the Latin equivalent of Paul's *hoi ek tōn Aristoboulou*). In the light of this suggested identification of Aristobulus with a member of the Herod family, is it a coincidence that the next name in Paul's list is Herodion?

11. *Herodion.* Perhaps a member of the *Aristobuliani* personally known to Paul; 'my kinsman' (cf. verse 7) may simply mark him out as being of Jewish birth.

The household of Narcissus. Calvin and others have identified this Narcissus with Tiberius Claudius Narcissus, a wealthy freedman of the Emperor Tiberius, who exercised great influence under Claudius, but was executed by order of Nero's mother Agrippina soon after Nero's accession in AD 54. His goods being confiscated, his slaves would become imperial property and would be distinguished from other groups in the imperial household by the designation *Narcissiani*. If the identification is sustained, then this greeting would be addressed to Christians among those *Narcissiani*. But how Paul would know, or know of, members of the *Narcissiani* we have no means of ascertaining.

12. *Tryphena and Tryphosa.* Probably near relatives or sisters, and quite possibly twins, to whom it was not uncommon to give names derived from the same root. Of the two names

Tryphosa is the more frequently found, but both occur in Roman inscriptions in connection with the imperial household and otherwise. The names, however, have Anatolian associations; Tryphena (RV, 'Tryphaena') appears in the fictitious second-century *Acts of Paul* as the name of the queen who showed kindness to Thecla at Pisidian Antioch (this queen was a historical character, grand-niece to the Emperor Claudius).

Persis. This name (meaning 'Persian woman') appears on Greek and Latin inscriptions at Rome and elsewhere as that of a slave or freedwoman, but not in connection with the imperial household.

13. *Rufus.* This name, meaning 'red', 'red-haired' (a word of Italic rather than Latin origin), was so common in Rome and Italy that there would be little purpose in discussing it were it not for two points: first the mention of Rufus in Mark xv. 21 as one of the two sons of Simon of Cyrene, and second the intriguing reference to the mother of this Rufus as being a mother to Paul as well. Mark, writing his Gospel in the first instance (according to second-century tradition) for the Christians in Rome, identifies Simon of Cyrene for his readers thirty years after the incident in which Simon figures by saying in effect: 'You will know which Simon I mean if I tell you that he was the father of Alexander and Rufus.' There was thus a Rufus well known in Rome around AD 60, and it is tempting to identify him with Paul's *Rufus chosen in the Lord* ('an outstanding follower of the Lord', NEB). (Gk. *eklektos*, 'chosen', naturally acquires the meaning 'choice' and hence 'outstanding'.)

But if this Rufus was the son of Simon of Cyrene, when did his mother prove a mother to Paul? We cannot be sure, but one might hazard the guess that it was at the time when Barnabas fetched Paul from Tarsus to become his colleague in ministry at Syrian Antioch (Acts xi. 25 f.). Simeon surnamed Niger ('the dark-skinned'), one of the other teachers of the church there (Acts xiii. 1), has been identified with Simon of

Cyrene; if Paul lodged with him we can well envisage the wife of Simeon (or Simon) playing the part of a mother to their disinherited guest. (Would a dark-skinned father have a red-haired son? It is not impossible.)

14. *Hermas.* An abbreviation of some such name as Hermagoras, Hermogenes or Hermodorus, and a very common name. A couple of generations later it was borne by the Roman Christian (a slave) who wrote *The Shepherd*.

Patrobas. Abbreviated from Patrobius. This name was borne by a wealthy freedman of Nero; Lightfoot suggests that Paul's Patrobas 'might well have been a dependent of this powerful freedman' (*Philippians*, p. 177).

Hermes. As the name of the god of good luck this was extremely common as a slave-name.

15. *Philologus and Julia.* Perhaps husband and wife (less probably brother and sister). The name Julia suggests some kind of association with the imperial household. The name Philologus appears more than once in connection with the imperial household.

Nereus. Roman ecclesiastical tradition, as far back as the fourth century, associates Nereus (and a companion of his named Achilleus) with Flavia Domitilla, a Christian lady of the imperial house who was banished to the island of Pandateria, off the Campanian coast, by her uncle Domitian in AD 95, but was released after his death in the following year, and whose name is perpetuated in the 'Cemetery of Domitilla' (see note on verse 8, p. 272).

Olympas. An abbreviated form of Olympiodorus.

16. *Salute one another with an holy kiss.* (Cf. 1 Cor. xvi. 20; 2 Cor. xiii. 12; 1 Thes. v. 26; 1 Pet. v. 14.) The 'kiss of peace', which plays a part to this day in the liturgy of the Eastern Church, is first mentioned as a regular feature of Christian worship in Justin Martyr's *First Apology*, 65 ('when we have ceased from our prayers, we greet one another with a kiss').

The name of Peter is conspicuously absent from the list of those to whom greetings are sent. If the view be accepted that these greetings were destined for Rome, the absence of Peter's name suggests that he was not in Rome at the time.

The churches of Christ salute you. Read 'all the churches of Christ . . .' (cf. RV, RSV, NEB). This sentence, as has been said, is a strong argument for the Roman destination of these greetings. Why should Paul send greetings from *all* the churches to another church to which he was writing an ordinary letter? But at a time when one very important phase of his ministry was being concluded he might well send greetings from all the churches associated with that phase of his ministry to a church which not only occupied a unique position in the world (as the Roman church did) but also, in Paul's intention, was to play an important part at the outset of a new phase of his ministry.[1]

c. Final exhortation (xvi. 17-20)

This admonitory passage is unlike the rest of the Epistle in substance and style alike. Here Paul seems to depart from his policy of not addressing the Roman church with the note of apostolic authority which he used when writing to churches which he had founded himself. Besides, the dissensions referred to in this paragraph do not correspond to anything in the life of the Roman church which could be gathered from other places in the Epistle. Elsewhere in the Epistle the only possibility of tension within the church that is hinted at is that which might arise if the Gentile members began to adopt an air of superiority over their brethren of Jewish origin (xi. 13 ff). On the other hand, the admonition in this paragraph has points of affinity with Paul's words of exhortation and foreboding to the elders of the Ephesian church in Acts xx. 28 ff. We may compare the dissensions and false teaching at Ephesus mentioned in the two Epistles to Timothy (not to speak of the

---

[1] See K. Holl, *Gesammelte Aufsätze*, ii, p. 47, n. 2.

heresy which, according to the Epistle to the Colossians, was finding an entrance among Christians in another region of the province of Asia). This, added to the arguments based on the preceding greetings, is thought to point to Ephesus rather than Rome as the destination of this chapter.[1]

On the other hand, it would not be surprising if, after long self-restraint in addressing a church which he had not founded himself, Paul should at last break out in an urgent warning against certain trouble-makers of a class with which he was only too familiar in his own churches. From his description of them they are evidently such 'evil workers' as he denounces in Philippians iii. 18 f. Their teaching was evidently antinomian in tendency, and possibly marked by incipient gnosticism; it was as contrary to the teaching which the Roman Christians had received from their founders and leaders as it was to Paul's own teaching, and was bound to lead to division and dissension wherever it was introduced. Paul had, earlier in the Epistle, emphasized the ethical demands of the gospel in terms which might well be directed against people like these (cf. iii. 8, vi. 1 ff., viii. 5 ff., xii. 1 ff.). If he had reason to believe that the Roman church was likely to receive attentions from them, as his own churches had done, he would undoubtedly have been impelled by a sense of duty to issue a plain warning against them. The reputation of the Roman church for fidelity to the gospel, however, was such that a brief warning against such sowers of discord would be sufficient. Discord was the work of Satan, but if the Romans kept these trouble-makers and their teaching at a distance, God, who is 'the God of peace' and not of discord (cf. 1 Cor. xiv. 33), would give them the victory over Satan and all his works.

18. *Our Lord Jesus Christ.* Read 'our Lord Christ' (RV, RSV), or 'Christ our Lord' (NEB).

[1] The argument for the Ephesian destination of chapter xvi is presented most cogently by T. W. Manson (*Studies in the Gospels and Epistles*, 1962, pp. 234 ff.); that for its Roman destination by C. H. Dodd (*The Epistle to the Romans*, 1932, pp. xvii ff.).

Such serve . . . their own belly. Cf. Philippians iii. 19, where Paul warns the Philippian Christians against people 'whose God is their belly'; in both places the reference probably is to antinomians who made the gospel a pretext for indulging their own appetites (cf. vi. 1).

19. *I would have you wise unto that which is good, and simple concerning evil.* Cf. Matthew x. 16b: 'be ye therefore wise as serpents, and harmless as doves' (in Greek the same two adjectives, *sophos* and *akeraios*, are used in both places). A similar Pauline injunction is 'in malice be ye children, but in understanding be men' (1 Cor. xiv. 20).

20. *The God of peace.* This title is repeated from the benediction of xv. 33 (cf. also the benediction of Heb. xiii. 20). It is specially apposite here, since Satan is the author of discord.

Shall bruise Satan under your feet shortly. An echo of Genesis iii. 15, where God declares that the seed of the woman will bruise the serpent's head. The people of Christ receive a share in His victory.

The grace of our Lord Jesus Christ be with you. For 'our Lord Jesus Christ' read 'our Lord Jesus' (NEB), and omit the liturgical 'Amen' at the end of the benediction (RV, RSV, NEB).

d. Greetings from Paul's companions (xvi. 21–23 (24))

Paul sends greetings from various friends who are with him at the time of writing, including Timothy, his *fidus Achates*; Gaius, his host; and Tertius, his amanuensis, who writes his salutation in the first person singular.

21. *Timotheus.* Timothy (to use the more familiar Anglicized form of the name) was a native of Lystra, a convert of Paul's, whom Paul chose as an assistant and colleague in his apostolic ministry (Acts xvi. 1–3), in whom he found a peculiarly like-minded colleague, and who, he said, 'has been at my side in the service of the Gospel like a son working under his father'

(Phil. ii. 20–22, NEB). According to Acts xx. 4, he was in Paul's company along with others on the eve of his setting out for Jerusalem.

Lucius. If 'my kinsmen' refers to all three names which precede, then Lucius would be a Jewish Christian. An identification with Lucius of Cyrene (Acts xiii. 1) can hardly be made out. What then of his suggested identification with Luke the physician (maintained by A. Deissmann; denied by H. J. Cadbury)? The author of Acts (or at any rate the author of the 'we' passages[1]) was with Paul at this time (Acts xx. 5 ff.), but he mentions no Lucius in the list of Paul's fellow-travellers (Acts xx. 4). Luke was a Gentile Christian (this is indicated by Col. iv. 14 in the light of Col. iv. 10f., and is borne out by the internal evidence of his writings); but here it would be possible to punctuate after Lucius so as to leave only Jason and Sosipater to be described as Paul's 'kinsmen'. In the three places where Paul certainly refers to Luke (Col. iv. 14; Phm. 24; 2 Tim. iv. 11), he calls him Lucas (*Loukas*) but there is good evidence that Lucas was used as an equivalent of Lucius. The matter must remain undecided.

Jason. Perhaps the Jason who was Paul's host on his first visit to Thessalonica (Acts xvii. 6, 7, 9); he is not listed, however, as one of the Thessalonian delegates among Paul's companions in Acts xx. 4.

Sosipater. Probably 'Sopater of Beroea, the son of Pyrrhus' who, according to Acts xx. 4 (RV), was also in Paul's company at this time. On Paul's preference for the more formal name see note on xvi. 3 (p. 270).

22. *I Tertius, who wrote this epistle.* He is not mentioned elsewhere in the New Testament. Paul seems regularly to have employed amanuenses to write his letters, but this is the only one who is known to us by name. Whether he sent his greetings personally on his own initiative or at Paul's suggestion, Paul would certainly approve of his sending them. Perhaps he was

---

[1] One and the same person, in my firm judgment.

a professional amanuensis, since Romans is rather more formal than most of Paul's letters; but he was evidently a Christian, since he sends his greetings 'in the Lord'. On other occasions one of the apostle's companions (such as Timothy, to judge by the frequency with which his name is added to Paul's in the superscription of letters) may have acted as his amanuensis.

23. *Gaius mine host, and of the whole church.* There is much to be said for the identification of Gaius with Titius Justus of Acts xviii. 7 (so RSV, NEB, rightly), who extended the hospitality of his house to Paul and the infant church of Corinth when they were expelled from the synagogue next door. 'Gaius Titius Justus' would then be his full designation (praenomen, nomen gentile, and cognomen) as a Roman citizen (a citizen of the Roman colony of Corinth).[1]

Erastus the chamberlain of the city, i.e. the city treasurer (of Corinth). This Erastus has been identified with the civic official of that name mentioned in a Latin inscription on a marble paving-block discovered at Corinth in 1929 by members of the American School of Classical Studies at Athens: 'ERASTVS PRO: AED: S: P: STRAVIT' ('Erastus, commissioner for public works, laid this pavement at his own expense'). The pavement belongs to the first century AD, and may well have been laid by Paul's friend. The public offices, however, are not the same: in Greek the commissioner for public works, or 'aedile', is called *agoranomos,* whereas the city treasurer (as here) is *oikonomos tēs poleōs.* If we have to do with the same Erastus, he had presumably been promoted to the city treasurership from the lower office of 'aedile' by the time Paul wrote this Epistle. (If anyone prefers to suppose, on the contrary, that he had been demoted from the higher to the lower office on account of his Christian profession, there is no evidence against this supposition!) There is no good reason to identify this

[1] See W. M. Ramsay, *Pictures of the Apostolic Church* (1910), p. 205; E. J. Goodspeed, 'Gaius Titius Justus', *JBL*, LXIX (1950), pp. 382 f.

Erastus with the Erastus of Acts xix. 22 or 2 Timothy iv. 20;
the name was common enough.

Quartus a brother. Lit., 'Quartus the brother' (RV). He is
otherwise unknown. Perhaps 'brother' means 'brother in the
Lord', 'fellow-Christian'; but in that case why is he singled
out to receive a designation which was common to them all?
If the word means 'brother in the flesh', whose brother was he?
Erastus's, since his name immediately precedes? Or, since
Quartus is Latin for 'fourth', and *Tertius* for 'third', would it be
excessively far-fetched to think of him as Tertius's brother, born
next after him?

24. *The grace of our Lord Jesus Christ be with you all. Amen.*
This benediction is probably not part of the original text. The
western authorities have it here instead of in xvi. 20b; the
Byzantine text (whence the Received Text and AV) took over
the western benediction here in addition to the earlier one in
verse 20b. A few authorities have the benediction at the end of
the doxology (after verse 27).

e. Doxology (xvi. 25–27)

The varying positions of this doxology in our witnesses to the
text of Romans have been discussed in the Introduction
(pp. 26 ff.). But its original position is not the only question
which has been raised regarding it. Harnack[1] argued that, as
it now stands, it represents an orthodox expansion of a shorter
Marcionite doxology:

'Now to him that is able to stablish you according to my gospel,
according to the revelation of the mystery which hath been kept in
silence through times eternal, but now is manifested, according to
the commandment of the eternal God, unto all the nations unto
obedience of faith; to the only wise God, through Jesus Christ, to
whom be the glory for ever. Amen.'

[1] In *Sitzungsbericht der preussischen Akademie der Wissenschaften* (1919), pp.
531 ff., reprinted in *Studien zur Geschichte des Neuen Testaments und der Alten
Kirche* (Berlin and Leipzig, 1931), pp. 184 ff.

This, he supposed (and others have followed him[1]), was a paragraph added by followers of Marcion as a conclusion to the Epistle.

We have, indeed, no MS or other objective evidence for such a shorter original text of the doxology. It has been pointed out, however, that those phrases which, on Harnack's hypothesis, are orthodox additions to the original wording are awkwardly attached,[2] especially the reference to 'the scriptures of the prophets' (verse 26). This reference would certainly have to be recognized as an orthodox addition, if the doxology is originally Marcionite; 'the scriptures of the prophets' played no part in the Marcionite scheme of things. But in the absence of independent evidence for a shorter text of the doxology, the burden of proof lies upon the view that it is not part of the apostolic text. If it is Marcionite, it cannot be ascribed to Marcion himself; Origen, as we have seen (p. 27), says explicitly that Marcion's edition of the Epistle lacked the doxology (together with everything else that comes after xiv. 23).

On the other hand, there is in the doxology a recognizable echo of dominant themes in the opening salutation: in particular, the mention of 'the scriptures of the prophets' recalls 'which he had promised afore by his prophets in the holy scriptures' (i. 2), and 'made known to all nations for the obedience of faith' is practically a repetition of 'for obedience to the faith among all nations' (i. 5). This rounding off of the Epistle on the same note as was struck at its commencement suggests the author himself.[3]

25. *According to my gospel.* Cf. ii. 16 (and 2 Tim. ii. 8).

And the preaching of Jesus Christ. This phrase is synonymous with 'my gospel'; 'preaching' represents Gk. *kērugma*, the

---

[1] Cf. G. Zuntz, *The Text of the Epistles* (1954), pp. 227 f.

[2] Calvin observes that 'Paul has made a long period by introducing many ideas into a single sentence, and has complicated this period by a grammatical rearrangement.'

[3] It is worth considering whether the doxology might not have been Paul's autographic addition to the Epistle, after Tertius had read it through to him. Cf. H. C. G. Moule, *The Epistle to the Romans* (1893), pp. 435 ff.

message proclaimed (as in 1 Cor. i. 21); Jesus Christ is its subject-matter.

According to the revelation of the mystery. For 'mystery' (which in the New Testament regularly denotes a secret once kept dark but now divulged) cf. xi. 25; but here the 'mystery' is 'the mystery of Christ' of Colossians iv. 3, where Paul speaks of himself as being 'in bonds' on account of it.

25, 26. *Which was kept secret since the world began, but now is made manifest, and . . . made known to all nations.* Cf. Colossians i. 26 f.; Ephesians iii. 3 ff., where the mystery has special reference to Paul's apostleship to the Gentiles, through which Gentile believers (as joint-heirs with Jewish believers) were incorporated into Christ—an outpouring of divine blessing on a scale not contemplated in the Old Testament.

26. *By the scriptures of the prophets.* Harnack regarded this phrase as an orthodox addition to a Marcionite doxology— and an inept one at that, for if the mystery was 'kept in silence through times eternal' (verse 25, RV) and only manifested now, how could it be made known through the writings of the prophets? Harnack was not the only one to recognize this difficulty; but his solution is not the only possible one. 'Although the prophets had formerly taught all that Christ and the apostles have explained, yet they taught with so much obscurity, when compared with the shining clarity of the light of the Gospel, that we need not be surprised if these things which are now revealed are said to have been hidden' (Calvin). Paul and his fellow-apostles used 'the scriptures of the prophets' copiously in their gospel preaching; but it was only in the light of the new revelation in Christ that they were able to under- stand and expound these scriptures (cf. 1 Pet. i. 10–12).

27. *To God only wise, be glory through Jesus Christ for ever. Amen.* The best attested reading is that followed in RV: 'to the only wise God, through Jesus Christ, to whom be the glory for ever. Amen.' This reading involves an anacoluthon, which may well serve as Paul's own sign-manual. Paul's common practice of authenticating his letters by signing his name at the end (cf. 2 Thes. iii. 17; 1 Cor. xvi. 21, etc.) is not followed here; but the authorship of the Epistle to the Romans is not in doubt.

The appended note in AV ('Written to the Romans from Corinthus . . .') is not part of the original text.

William Tyndale's prologue to the Epistle to the Romans ends with the following admonition:

'Now go to, reader, and according to the order of Paul's writing, even so do thou. First behold thyself diligently in the law of God, and see there thy just damnation. Secondarily turn thine eyes to Christ, and see there the exceeding mercy of thy most kind and loving Father. Thirdly remember that Christ made not this atonement that thou shouldest anger God again: neither died he for thy sins, that thou shouldest live still in them: neither cleansed he thee, that thou shouldest return (as a swine) unto thine old puddle again: but that thou shouldest be a new creature and live a new life after the will of God and not of the flesh. And be diligent lest through thine own negligence and unthankfulness thou lose this favour and mercy again.'

SELECT BIBLIOGRAPHY

I. ON THE EPISTLE TO THE ROMANS

This list is confined to works available in English. When a commentary is based on the Greek text, that fact is indicated; all others are based on the English text.

*Barclay, W., *The Epistle to the Romans* (Daily Study Bible, 1957).

Barrett, C. K., *The Epistle to the Romans* (Black's New Testament Commentaries, 1957).

Barth, K., *The Epistle to the Romans* (E.T. from the sixth German edition, 1933).

Barth, K., *A Shorter Commentary on Romans* (E.T., 1959).

Beet, J. A., *The Epistle to the Romans*[10] (1902).

Brunner, E., *The Letter to the Romans: A Commentary* (E.T., 1959).

Calvin, J., *The Epistles of Paul the Apostle to the Romans and to the Thessalonians* (First Latin edition, Strasbourg, 1540; E.T. by Ross Mackenzie, 1961).

Denney, J., *St. Paul's Epistle to the Romans* (The Expositor's Greek Testament, Vol. II, 1900, pp. 555–725). On the Greek text.

*Dodd, C. H., *The Epistle of Paul to the Romans* (Moffatt New Testament Commentary, 1932; reprinted in Fontana Books, 1959).

*Evans, E., *To the Romans* (1948).

*Garvie, A. E., *Romans* (Century Bible, 1902).

Gifford, E. H., *The Epistle to the Romans* (Speaker's Commentary, 1886).

Godet, F., *The Epistle to the Romans* (E.T., 1880; reprinted, Grand Rapids, 1956).

Gore, C., *The Epistle to the Romans* (1907).

* In both parts of the bibliography an asterisk indicates books which are designed mainly for the non-specialist.

Haldane, R., *Exposition of the Epistle to the Romans* (1835–39; reprinted, 1959).

Hodge, C., *Commentary on the Epistle to the Romans* (Philadelphia, 1835; reprinted, Grand Rapids, 1951).

Hort, F. J. A., *Prolegomena to St. Paul's Epistles to the Romans and the Ephesians* (1895).

*Hunter, A. M., *The Epistle to the Romans* (Torch Bible Commentaries, 1955).

Kelly, W., *Notes on the Epistle to the Romans* (1873).

*Kirk, K. E., *The Epistle to the Romans* (Clarendon Bible, 1937).

Knox, J., 'The Epistle to the Romans', *Interpreter's Bible*, IX (New York, 1954), pp. 355 ff.

Lee, E. K., *A Study in Romans* (1962).

Leenhardt, F. J., *The Epistle to the Romans* (E.T., 1961).

Liddon, H. P., *Explanatory Analysis of St. Paul's Epistle to the Romans* (1893).

Lightfoot, J. B., *Biblical Essays* (1893), pp. 285–374, 'The Structure and Destination of the Epistle to the Romans.'[1]

Lightfoot, J. B., *Notes on the Epistles of St. Paul* (1895), pp. 237–305, 'The Epistle to the Romans: Analysis and Commentary (Chapters i–vii).' On the Greek text.

Luther, M., *Lectures on Romans* (translated and edited by Wilhelm Pauck, Library of Christian Classics, 1961, from the Weimar edition of 1908, which was based on Luther's autograph of 1515–16).

*Luther, M., *Commentary on the Epistle to the Romans* (abridged and translated from the Weimar edition of 1908 by J. T. Mueller, Grand Rapids, 1954).

*Lüthi, W., *The Letter to the Romans* (E.T., 1961).

Manson, T. W., *Studies in the Gospels and Epistles* (1962), pp. 225–241, 'St. Paul's Letter to the Romans—and others' (first published 1948).

*Manson, T. W., *Romans* (Peake's Commentary on the Bible, 1962, pp. 940–953).

[1] Including a critique of Lightfoot by Hort, and Lightfoot's reply.

Moule, H. C. G., *The Epistle of Paul the Apostle to the Romans* (Cambridge Bible, 1879).

*Moule, H. C. G., *The Epistle of St. Paul to the Romans* (Expositor's Bible, 1893).

Murray, J., *The Epistle to the Romans* (New International Commentary on the New Testament, Grand Rapids, Vol. I, 1959; Vol. II, forthcoming).

Nygren, A., *Commentary on Romans* (E.T., 1952).

Parry, R. St. J., *The Epistle of Paul the Apostle to the Romans* (Cambridge Greek Testament, 1912). On the Greek text.

Sanday, W., and Headlam, A. C., *A Critical and Exegetical Commentary on the Epistle to the Romans*[5] (International Critical Commentary, 1902). On the Greek text.

*Scott, E. F., *Paul's Epistle to the Romans* (1947).

*Taylor, V., *The Epistle to the Romans* (Epworth Preacher's Commentaries, 1956).

Vaughan, C. J., *St. Paul's Epistle to the Romans*[4] (1874). On the Greek text.

*Vine, W. E., *The Epistle to the Romans* (Bangalore, 1935; reprinted, London, 1948 and 1957).

II. ON PAUL

The literature on Paul is immense; only a brief and reasonably representative selection of works available in English can be listed here.

*Barclay, W., *The Mind of Paul* (1958).

Davies, W. D., *Paul and Rabbinic Judaism* (1948).

Deissmann, A., *Paul*[2] (E.T., 1926).

*Dibelius, M., and Kümmel, W. G., *Paul* (E.T., 1953).

*Dodd, C. H., *The Meaning of Paul for Today* (1920; reprinted in Fontana Books, 1958).

Dodd, C. H., *New Testament Studies* (1953), pp. 67–128, 'The Mind of Paul' (first published 1933–34).

Ellis, E. E., *Paul's Use of the Old Testament* (1957).

Ellis, E. E., *Paul and his Recent Interpreters* (Grand Rapids, 1961).

*Guthrie, D., *New Testament Introduction: The Pauline Epistles* (1961).

*Hunter, A. M., *Interpreting Paul's Gospel* (1954).

Hunter, A. M., *Paul and his Predecessors*[2] (1961).

Knox, J., *Chapters in a Life of Paul* (New York, 1950).

Knox, W. L., *St. Paul and the Church of Jerusalem* (1925).

Knox, W. L., *St. Paul and the Church of the Gentiles* (1939).

Lake, K., *The Earlier Epistles of St. Paul*[2] (1914).

*Loewenich, W. von, *Paul: his Life and Work* (E.T., 1960).

Machen, J. G., *The Origin of Paul's Religion* (New York, 1921; reprinted, Grand Rapids, 1947).

Munck, J., *Paul and the Salvation of Mankind* (E.T., 1959).

*Nock, A. D., *St. Paul* (1938).

Ramsay, W. M., *St. Paul the Traveller and the Roman Citizen*[19] (1942).

Ramsay, W. M., *The Teaching of Paul in Terms of the Present Day* (1913).

Ridderbos, H. N., *Paul and Jesus* (E.T., Grand Rapids, 1957).

Schoeps, H. J., *Paul* (E.T., 1961).

Schweitzer, A., *Paul and his Interpreters* (E.T., 1912).

Schweitzer, A., *The Mysticism of Paul the Apostle* (E.T., 1931).

Scott, C. A. A., *Christianity according to St. Paul* (1927).

Vos, G., *The Pauline Eschatology* (Grand Rapids, 1952).

*White, E., *St. Paul: the Man and his Mind* (1958).